Journal of Semitic Studies Supplement 20

A MEDIEVAL ADMINISTRATIVE AND FISCAL TREATISE FROM THE YEMEN:

THE RASULID *MULAKHKHAṢ AL-FIṬAN* BY AL-ḤASAN B. ʿALĪ AL-ḤUSAYNĪ

A facsimile edition of the Arabic text together with an introduction and annotated translation

by
G. Rex Smith
with additional material from the unpublished research of the late Claude Cahen and R.B. Serjeant

Published by Oxford University Press
on behalf of the University of Manchester
2006

OXFORD JOURNALS
OXFORD UNIVERSITY PRESS

Great Clarendon Street, Oxford OX2 6DP

Oxford University Press is a department of the University of Oxford.
It furthers the University's objective of excellence in research, scholarship,
and education by publishing worldwide in

Oxford New York

Athens Auckland Bangkok Bogotá Buenos Aires Cape Town
Chennai Dar es Salaam Delhi Florence Hong Kong Istanbul Karachi
Kolkata Kuala Lumpur Madrid Melbourne Mexico City Mumbai Nairobi
Paris São Paulo Shanghai Singapore Taipei Tokyo Toronto Warsaw

with associated companies in Berlin Ibadan

Oxford is a registered trade mark of Oxford University Press
in the UK and in certain other countries

Published in the United Kingdom
by Oxford University Press, Oxford

First published 2006

A catalogue for this book is available from the British Library

Library of Congress Cataloguing in Publication Data
(Data available)

ISSN 0022-4480
ISBN 0-19-921948-6
ISBN 978-0-19-921948-3

Subscription information for the *Journal of Semitic Studies* is available at the journal website:
jss.oupjournals.org

Printed in Great Britain by Bell & Bain Ltd, Glasgow

This book is dedicated to
MAGGIE
with all my love and gratitude

CONTENTS

Preface and acknowledgements vii

Introduction 1

The Rasulids 1
al-Malik al-Nāṣir Aḥmad 2
Rasulid Trade 3
Rasulid Administration 5
The Author 8
The Text of the Mulakhkhaṣ
The Language 9
Orthography 9
Morphology 9
Syntax 10
The Lists 11
The Numerals 11
The Manuscript 12
The Translation 13
The Notes 13

Abbreviations Used in the Notes of the Translation 15

The Translation of the *Mulakhkhaṣ* 17

Notes 73

References 103

Indices 107
1 Commodities in the translation 107
2 Commodities in the text 110
3 Weights, measures and units of currency 113
4 Place and tribal names 113
5 Government officials in the translation 118
6 Government officials in the text 119
7 Government departments 119

The Facsimile Text of the *Mulakhkhaṣ*

Preface and Acknowledgements

> And one might therefore say of me that in this book I have only made up a bunch of other people's flowers, and that of my own I have only provided the string that ties them together.
>
> *Montaigne* (d. 1592)

My first knowledge of the existence of the *Mulakhkhaṣ* came in conversations with the late R.B. Serjeant when he was supervising my PhD thesis in Cambridge in the 1960s–1970s. I recall vividly on one occasion that he suggested I should look carefully at the photocopy of the MS and, in his usual generous way, he lent it to me. I found it a daunting document in those days and confess that I probably got little from it which was of relevance to my work at that time on the primarily political and military history of the Ayyubids and early Rasulids in the Yemen. Throughout many years of contact with Serjeant until his death in 1993, the subject of this fascinating Rasulid treatise returned constantly to our conversations and I revisited the copy of the MS on several occasions. The potential loss to the scholarly world of the fruits of Claude Cahen's and Serjeant's labours on the *Mulakhkhaṣ* came home to me after the latter's death. Cahen had died in 1991 and now there seemed no hope that all their immense hard work would ever be made available in any form to the scholarly world. I was busy with other work, notably with my annotated translation of Ibn al-Mujāwir's *Tārīkh al-Mustabṣir* for the Hakluyt Society. It was only in the summer of 2003 that I was able to think seriously about what might be done to rescue the *Mulakhkhaṣ* from oblivion.

We know that Cahen began work on the *Mulakhkhaṣ* in the spring of 1956.[1] He says he had been attracted to the Biblioteca Ambrosiana MS after reading Griffini's note on it,[2] as indeed we can assume Serjeant had in 1953 when he first saw it.[3] Both recognized the importance of the text for the economic history of the Islamic world in general and for that of the Yemen in particular. It was their mutual friend and colleague, the late S.D. Goitein, who informed each of the interest of the other and their agreement to collaborate followed. Cahen and Serjeant, hoping to proceed with their publication without delay, though fully recognizing all the difficulties to be

1 CSFS, 28.

2 See 'Sammlung'.

3 CSFS, 28.

faced in the text, decided to inform the scholarly world of their intentions and published a preliminary joint article on it in 1957.[4]

When my late wife and I were asked by Serjeant's widow, Marion Serjeant, to assist her in sorting out his books and papers immediately after his death in 1993 and prior to their despatch to the University Library in Edinburgh, we readily agreed and stayed with her in their cottage near St Andrews for several days to carry out the task. By an immense stroke of good fortune, a package was delivered to the cottage while we were there. Under cover of a letter to Marion Serjeant written by Cahen's son, all his notes on the *Mulakhkhaṣ* and copies of correspondence between him and Serjeant on the work were included. We were thus able to unite all these with Serjeant's own notes and copies of his letters addressed to Cahen. This material now rests in the University Library in Edinburgh.

It is no exaggeration to state that this work has been both a struggle against a medieval Arabic text with all its complexities and difficulties and also the challenge of a modern Anglo-French archive, itself no easy task of interpretation. I hasten to add, however, that the archival effort involved has heightened the pleasure of the labour as a whole. It is most interesting to note the clearly developing relationship between the two scholarly giants, not only from the highly formal 'Dear/Cher Colleague/Collègue' in the beginning to the later 'Dear Serjeant'/'Cher Cahen', but also from the initial total lack of 'small talk' to later personal comments, culminating in the details of arrangements for family holiday exchanges.

I cannot be sure that I have remained within the general remit of Cahen and Serjeant as proposed in their papers and that I have prepared this book — I am thinking in particular of the introductory material here — as closely as possible to what they had in mind. That this publication falls short of what they would have produced together, had Fate allowed them to complete their labours, is clear for all to see. I have in less optimistic moments been tempted to abandon the enterprise altogether, arguing that no one could possibly move in the same circles as two such consummate scholars with countless years of experience in the field between them. But this would deny to scholars all their efforts spent on the *Mulakhkhaṣ* over a period of nearly forty years and I fervently hope that the following pages, inadequate as they are, in some way preserve at least some of the unique scholarship which both Cahen and Serjeant brought to all their academic writings. I am comforted by the fact that the text in its original form is here published in facsimile for all to see. My errors of

4 CSFS.

commission and omission are there for readers to observe; they are my responsibility and mine alone. It is my further fervent hope that some readers at least will be able to correct and add to what they find below, once they can study the original text for themselves.

It is my great pleasure to acknowledge with gratitude the help of the following. Enormous thanks go to Professors Daniel Varisco and Dionisius Agius who took time to read the whole of the draft before it was submitted and offered between them many suggestions and corrections. In the summer of 2003, I visited Edinburgh and am grateful to the University Library, in particular the staff of Special Collections, for allowing me access to the Serjeant papers. My old friend Yasir Suleiman received me there with overwhelming kindness and generosity and gave me enormous assistance in my work. I mention too with thanks the kind help of Dr Marina Smyth and Professor Li Guo of the University of Notre Dame, US, the staff of the Branford Millar Price Library of Portland State University, Oregon, US, and that of the John Rylands University Library Manchester. I acknowledge with much gratitude the decision of the Biblioteca Ambrosiana in Milan to allow me to publish their MS in facsimile. The editors of the *JSS* responded very quickly and positively to my request to publish this in the supplement series and I thank them most sincerely, in particular John Healey, who gave me great encouragement and practical help from the start. Bronwen Campbell rescued me from many a computer disaster and has worked on this book with a cheerful diligence which goes way beyond the call of the duty of the *JSS* editorial assistant. Her husband, Stuart, too has been ever ready to help. I offer my thanks to them both. Finally, I dedicate the book to my wife, Maggie, who recognized immediately with little or no prompting just how important my academic work is to me and who has encouraged and inspired me ever since.

G. Rex Smith
Llansadwrn, Ynys Môn, Wales, UK
August 2006

INTRODUCTION

1 The Rasulids

It is no longer necessary to introduce the Rasulid dynasty of the Yemen at great length.[1] They ruled over the southern highlands and Tihāmah between the years *c.* 626–845/1228–1441. In brief, it can be said that they were of Menjik Turkomen origin and that they moved firstly into Egypt and later into the Yemen, amirs in the train of the Ayyubids. The Ayyubids were present in the Yemen for about fifty-six years (569–626/1173–1228) during which time they fought hard to bring under the control of the house the Red Sea coastal plain, Tihāmah, and the southern highlands of the Yemen, ridding the country of the several local dynasties they found in their way. Theirs was a time of military activity; they had little opportunity to build lasting monuments and a sound administration, though they certainly began to organize the latter, depending at times on what previous dynasties had put in place.[2] The Rasulids took control from them by default from about 626/1230; no Ayyubid arrived in the Yemen after the departure of the last monarch, al-Masʿūd Yūsuf, for Egypt, and their hold over the south of the country and Tihāmah became official and even sanctioned by the Abbasid caliph in Baghdad.

The Rasulids thus inherited a region thoroughly subdued by the huge Ayyubid armies from Egypt with their large numbers of horse. They were blessed too with a number of strong and efficient rulers, in particular the second, al-Muẓaffar Yūsuf (reg. 647–94/1249–95), who, from the capital Taʿizz, presided over the area

---

1 See in particular the following on their politico-military history: S*A*, 83–90; my 'The Ayyubids and Rasulids — the Transfer of Power in 7th/13th Century Yemen', *Islamic Culture* 43 (1969), 1–13; 'The Rasulids in Dhofar in the VIIth-VIIIth/XIIIth-XIVth Centuries', *Journal of the Royal Asiatic Society* (1988), 26–44; 'The Political History of the Islamic Yemen down to the First Turkish Invasion (1–945/622–1538) in Werner Daum (ed.), *Yemen: 3000 Years of Art and Civilisation in Arabia Felix*, Innsbruck and Frankfurt-am-Main, 1988, 136–7, 139; *EI* 'Rasūlids'; Daniel Martin Varisco and G. Rex Smith, *The Manuscript of al-Malik al-Afḍal ... a Medieval Arabic Anthology from the Yemen*, Gibb Memorial Trust, 1988, 6–8. For their art and architecture, see Finster's, Porter's and Lewcock's chapters in Daum, *Yemen*; for their literature, see El Shami and R.B. Serjeant, 'Regional Literature: the Yemen' in Julia Ashtiany et al. (eds), *The Cambridge History of Arabic Literature 'Abbasid Belles-Lettres*, Cambridge, 1990, 460–8.

2 I am thinking in particular of the case of Aden where they undoubtedly began to organize port practices and a regular system of taxation, both by innovation (or the practices brought from Egypt) and by borrowing from their predecessors there, the Zurayʿids. See IM*TM*, 140 ff.; SMT, 128–34; SPP, 208–9. See more below under the Rasulid Administration.

controlled by the dynasty with great skill. This period of brilliance saw the flowering of the arts and literature and — very importantly in the context of this study — the steady and efficient organization of a civil service and a state administration which was undoubtedly one of the major success stories of the medieval Islamic world. It was too the period of the greatest expanse of Rasulid territory: land as far north as Ṣanʿāʾ was in their hands, as well as Ḥaḍramawt and southern Arabia as far east as the maritime settlement of Ẓafār. This zenith of Rasulid political and military power can be associated in particular with an amir named ʿAlam al-Dīn al-Shaʿbī who was appointed over Ṣanʿāʾ in 658/1260 and who managed a highly effective team of Rasulid troubleshooters. Al-Shaʿbī died in 682/1283 and it is noteworthy that after his death Ṣanʿāʾ was rarely in Rasulid hands. After al-Muẓaffar Yūsuf's death in 694/1295, the dynasty was led by a number of his descendants of high calibre, excellent guardians of the house. They suffered much, however, at the hands of fickle and rebellious Yemeni tribes and equally of envious and mutinous slaves and mamluks.

2 al-Malik al-Nāṣir Aḥmad

The *Mulakhkhaṣ* was composed during the reign of the eighth Rasulid sultan, al-Nāṣir Aḥmad (reg. 803–27/1401–24).[3] His early years were spent establishing his authority throughout traditional Rasulid lands, particularly in the southern highlands, Tihāmah and the coastal areas of Jīzān and Ḥaly.

At this time too we hear first of the Tahirids who were eventually to succed the Rasulids from about 858/1454. The Zaydī imams from their northern strongholds attacked the Tahirid towns of Juban and al-Miqrānah and clashes between the Zaydīs and the Tahirids in this area are reported.

We read during this period of the constant tribal and other insurrections, of sieges and fortresses captured and won back by the Rasulids, and of battles against Zaydīs and Tahirids. Despite the up-beat reporting of the pro-Rasulid sources in which all these events are portrayed as wondrous successes for the monarch, his amirs and his armies, nothing can disguise the plain fact that they were all serious challenges to the Rasulid house.

---

3 Most useful are the following sources: *Tārīkh al-Yaman fī al-dawlah al-Rasūliyyah. A Chronicle of the Rasūlid Dynasty of Yemen*, ed. Hiloichi Yajima, Tokyo, 1974, 67–118 (a passionately pro-Rasulid anonymous text); ʿAbd al-Raḥmān b. ʿAlī Ibn al-Daybaʿ, *Qurrat al-ʿuyūn bi-akhbār al-Yaman al-maymūn*, ed. Muḥammad b. ʿAlī al-Akwaʿ, 2 vols, Cairo, 1977, II, 119–26 (a later Tahirid source); Yaḥyā b. al-Ḥusayn, *Ghāyat al-amānī fī akhbār al-quṭr al-Yamānī*, ed. Saʿīd ʿAbd al-Fattāḥ, 2 vols, Cairo, 1968, II, 557–66 (a rather brief, though interesting Zaydī view of events).

In 822/1419, family squabbles came to a head and erupted into violent civil war when al-Nāṣir's brother, Ḥusayn, took Zabīd, proclaimed himself sultan and gave himself the honorific title of al-Ẓāhir. The rebellion was quelled by al-Nāṣir and Ḥusayn's eyes were put out. Al-Nāṣir died in 827/1424.

His reign is generally looked upon as a success, but the seeds of the Rasulids' downfall were sown. His military campaigns kept most of traditional Rasulid territories under control despite the recalcitrant tribes, troublesome slaves and mamluks and antagonistic rival dynasties, the Zaydīs and the Tahirids. Evidence certainly exists that the maritime trade on which the Rasulids depended so heavily still flourished and al-Nāṣir was careful to promote all trading interests. His successors fared less well, however; in less than twenty years, southern Yemen and Tihāmah fell into the hands of their Tahirid rivals.

3 Rasulid Trade

My feeling in the current early stage of the study of Rasulid economic history is that we should regard the late seventh/thirteenth century, as al-Muẓaffar Yūsuf's long reign drew to a close, as the dynasty's political, military, administrative and economic zenith.[4] Although he was succeeded as monarch by five competent members of the house, we can begin to see during the time of al-Nāṣir Aḥmad (803–27/1401–24) that the decline was already underway.[5] Al-Muẓaffar was not only an exceeding adept all round military leader, politician, administrator and financial wizard, but also a monarch of considerable negotiating skills who knew well how to woo the merchant classes and the wealth creators, as well as foreign leaders and dignitaries. His fiscal policies in particular were aimed at creating and maintaining the ideal circumstances in which international trade and internal Yemeni agriculture and industry could flourish. Part of that policy must have been his successful attempt at changing the dynasty from one of foreign intruders, protégés of the Ayyubids, to one fully recognized as a 'Yemeni' state with a centralized and efficient administration.[6]

---

4 I agree entirely with Daniel Varisco who makes a similar point in his 'Texts and Pretexts: the Unity of the Rasulid State under al-Malik al-Muẓaffar', *Revue du Monde Musulman et de la Méditerranée*, 67 (1993), 13. Varisco makes a number of highly important and extremely perceptive observations concerning al-Muẓaffar and the dynasty in this article which are entirely relevant to the subject under discussion.

5 I deal with this very subject in an article to be published in the forthcoming Festschrft of Qadi Ismāʿīl al-Akwaʿ entitled 'Some Preliminary Thoughts on the Decline and Fall of the Rasulid Dynasty of the Yemen'. I take some comments from this article and use them here.

6 See Varisco, 'Texts and Pretexts', 15–16.

Moreover, taxes could be seen to be fair and efficiently and firmly enforced by a trained, rigidly regulated civil service, in which, one can imagine from the pages of the *Mulakhkhaṣ*, there could be no place for corruption or fiscal imprudence.

The internal agricultural and industrial picture looks rosey.[7] Shamrookh highlights the cultivation of the date palm, a variety of cereals and fruits and livestock as the principal agricultural successes of the period. Textiles, semi-precious stones, leather and metals were in particular the products of local industry, providing both income for the state in the form of taxation and also in some cases earning wealth as exports.

The *Mulakhkhaṣ* provides us with a wonderfully comprehensive picture of the vast international trade of the period, with the Yemen and her primary port, Aden, sitting at the geographic centre of the trade which encompassed the Mediterranean basin in the west and India, South-East Asia and China in the east. The range of imports and exports listed is nothing short of amazing; and the state was in a situation to promote, and benefit from, this commerce to the full. Political and military stability fuelled the commercial fires which in turn provided the wherewithall to maintain the physical power of the state.

What began to go wrong? In the absence of detailed research, it is impossible at present to answer the question. It has been suggested that[8] '… al-Nāṣir Aḥmad … abandoned the sound policy of his predecessors, and drove the merchants away with his arbitrary exactions.' Be that as it may, we certainly know that Jeddah was beginning to take the place of Aden as the major Arabian port from the early ninth/fifteenth century.[9]

Shamrookh has managed to reveal some interesting statistics concerning the port revenues of the Rasulids in Aden.[10] They are as follows:

718/1318	300,000 dinars
796/1393	500,000
796/1393	1,000,000[11]
801/1398	1,700,000

7 See Shamrookh's helpful study, *SCT*, particularly 99–129, 133–52.

8 By P.M. Holt, *The Age of the Crusades: the Near East from the Eleventh Century to 1517*, London and New York, 1986, 187.

9 See Serjeant, 'Fifteenth Century "Interlopers" on the Coast of Rasulid Yemen', *Itinéraires d'Orient: Homage à Claude Cahen.Res Orientales*, 6 (1994), 83. The technical term to avoid Aden and put in at Jeddah was *jawwara ilā Jiddah*. The *mujawwirīn* become more and more numerous in that century.

10 *SCT*, 275.

11 Shamrookh does not explain the two readings for this year, taken as they are from two sources.

813/1410	1,000,000
814/1411	1,470,000
817/1414	1,000,000
834/1430	500,000
835/1431	300,000
836/1432	400,000
840/1436	100,000

The figures speak for themselves, but perhaps we should note the considerable drop from 817/1414 (under al-Nāṣir) of 1,000,000 to 500,000 in 834/1430 (under al-Ẓāhir) and this suggests we should look very carefully at the 820s/1420s in order to discover what precisely was going on in the field of maritime trade. Some twenty years later, the Tahirids, local Yemeni *mashāyikh*, wrested control of the southern highlands and Tihāmah from the grasp of the by now seriously bickering Rasulids and the brilliant dynasty, brought to such great heights by al-Muẓaffar, was no more.

4 The Rasulid Administration

Having looked briefly at the flourishing trade under the Rasulids, let us now turn our attention to their administration. Trade and commerce in particular on such a scale needed to be well administered and we learn much from the *Mulakhkhaṣ* about how that was accomplished.

Our knowledge of any form of state administration prior to the establishment of the Rasulid government in the Yemen is tantalizingly scant. The administrative history of the Yemen before the Ayyubids is to all intents and purposes a closed book. It is only when the Zurayʿids, the Ismāʿīlī family who controlled Aden between the years approximately 473–561/1080–1166 before the Ayyubid conquest, appear on the scene that we find a few crumbs of information. The indications are[12] that their control of the port of Aden forced them into taking one or two tentative steps towards regularizing a government administration.

We know a little more of the Ayyubids. Although for the most part during their period in the southern highlands and Tihāmah (569–ca. 626/1173–1228) they were compelled to throw most of their efforts into the military subjugation of this difficult

12 The only source which is readily available to us at present is IM*TM* (see in particular 140) which includes references to administrative practises which were introduced by the Zurayʿids and it must be hoped that other sources will become readily available. I refer to these references in my 'Ibn al-Mujāwir's 7th/13th Century Guide to Arabia: the Eastern Connection', *Occasional Papers of the School of Abbasid Studies*, 3 (1990), 75; SMT, 129; SRA, 224.

terrain, there are some detailed remarks in IM*TM* (especially under his description of Aden, 138 ff.) which point clearly to the beginnings of an organization of the port for the smooth processing of incoming merchant ships and of the establishment of an official customs regime.

What of the Rasulids?[13] They would surely have been able to take over whatever they found useful in the Yemen of the administrative efforts of the Ayyubids, their predecessors. Their early amirs had spent much time with the Ayyubid administration, both in Egypt prior to their accompanying the Ayyubids into the Yemen at some stage during the later decades of the sixth/twelfth century, and with them during their rule of the country. The Ayyubids in their turn had undoubtedly been influenced by their original masters, the Zengids, and of course by their predecessors in power in Egypt, the Fatimids. The Rasulids, too, had reasonably close official ties with their contemporaries in Egypt, the Mamluks, themselves subject to ideas from the Mongols and Ilkhanids.[14]

A reading of the *Nūr*, the archive produced during the long reign of al-Muẓaffar Yūsuf (647–94/1249–95), confirms the long-held view that this was the political and administrative zenith of the dynasty. We know that this was a period of military strength and stability, of a flourishing commercial activity, both by land and sea, and of the formation of an elaborate governmental system, along side a flowering of the arts, architecture and literature, the latter in the widest sense of the word. We know too that such was the strength in these fields that they were able to continue and develop under the able successors of al-Muẓaffar Yūsuf.[15]

We now have available two major texts which throw light on the administrative and fiscal policies and organization of the Rasulids in the Yemen: the *Nūr* from the seventh/thirteenth century and the *Mulakhkhaṣ* from the early ninth/fifteenth. It must be made clear, however, that the two are vastly different in content and aim. The *Nūr* is a collection of official commercial and administrative papers and archives and what we learn of the Rasulid government organization is in a sense incidental; the *Mulakhkhaṣ* is a treatise written by a senior civil servant, listing and describing the various government bureaux and their officials and also providing detailed lists of taxes paid, state revenues and expenditure.

---

13 See also my SRA, 228–9.

14 See R*S*, in particular in the context of the system of fiefs, 30–1. See also above note 2.

15 The MS of al-Afḍal al-ʿAbbās (764–78/1363–77) is indicative of the literary achievements of the early Rasuids. See Varisco and Smith, *Manuscript*.

Turning firstly to the *Nūr*, it can be noted that few bureaux are mentioned; only the special bureau (*al-dīwān al-khāṣṣ*) appears together with various euphemisms for the government administration as a whole (*al-dīwān, al-dīwān al-sa'īd*) and for a royal bureau (*al-dīwān al-sultānī, … al-malakī al-Muẓaffarī*).[16] This may of course indicate as yet a paucity of government bureaux under al-Muẓaffar, but it is much more likely to reflect the difference in the content and aim of the *Nūr* when we compare it to the *Mulakhkhaṣ*. A good sprinkling of government officials can be found in its pages, terms all well known from the later *Mulakhkhaṣ*. What is entirely clear from the *Nūr* is that there existed during this period a highly sophisticated and regulated Rasulid civil service which was entirely necessary in view of the vast Indian Ocean trade which flourished already at this time and in view of the taxes due within the Yemen itself which had to be administered by the state.

The *Mulakhkhaṣ* deals in detail with the following departments: the royal court (*al-bāb al-sharīf [al-sulṭānī]*),[17] the grand bureau (*al-dīwān al-kabīr*), the royal crop tax bureau (*dīwān al-kharāj al-sulṭānī*), the special bureau (*al-dīwān al-khāṣṣ*), the movable property bureau (*dīwān al-ḥalāl*), the army bureau (*dīwān al-jaysh*), the port customs house (*al-furḍah*) in Aden, pious emdowments bureau (*dīwān al-wuqūfāt*), administration of the fortresses (*ḥusūn*), the stables (*al-iṣṭablāt al-sa'īdah*), the treasury (*al-khizānah*), the trading establishment (*al-matjar*), the provision store (*al-ḥawā'ij-khānāh*) and the secretariat (*al-inshā' al-sa'īd*). Other departments are mentioned incidentally: the mint (*dār al-ḍarb*) and immovable property (*al-amlāk*). In addition, Ḥusaynī provides detailed information on the government officials who run and manage these departments and we can get from this a fairly clear picture of the role of each and of a rigid system of rank within the Rasulid administration. I do not intend to go further here; I have already published on the subject of the different departments and their officials and of course the reader is directed to the relevant sections of the text and translation below.[18] All that remains here now is to discuss briefly to which period what we read in the *Mulakhkhaṣ* refers.

The date of the *Mulakhkhaṣ* appears clearly in the text: Jumādā II 815, September–October 1412.[19] Serjeant writes,[20] '… though from the internal evidence

16 *Nūr*, I, 622; II, 248.

17 Incidentally, branches of the royal court existed in various places in the Yemen, all with their own administrations, ready to administer the visits of the monarch whenever he thought it necessary to visit his provinces outside Ta'izz and in the winter especially outside Zabīd. See SRA, 229–30.

18 My SRA, passim, represents an introduction to the subject of Rasulid government departments and their officials as described in the *Mulakhkhaṣ*.

19 MS f. 5a.

of the text itself his treatise covers existing practice for some considerable time anterior to the author's composition of the *Mulaḫḫaṣ*.' My own hunch is that this is about right. There is now ample evidence that the political, administrative and commercial high watermark of the dynasty was contemporary with the reign of al-Muẓaffar Yūsuf (647–94/1249–95). In all probability, under the following five Rasulid monarchs, this situation changed very gradually for the worse and the rule of al-Nāṣir Aḥmad (803–27/1401–24) does seem to mark the beginning of a more rapid decline in the circumstances of the house.[21] Ḥusaynī mentions a previous fiscal work which he composed under the father of al-Nāṣir, al-Ashraf Ismāʿīl, presumably at some time during the late decades of the eighth/fourteenth century, and this points to a man of long and distinguished service in the Rasulid administration. At the time of composition of the *Mulakhkhaṣ*, Ḥusaynī must have been aware that he was witnessing a decline in the importance of the Rasulid ports and indeed in the general prosperity of the state. The *Mulakhkhaṣ* may well represent a wistful looking back at better times, rather than an exact indication of the administrative and fiscal situation of the early ninth/fifteenth century.

5 The Author of the **Mulakhkhaṣ**

We know little of the author and what we do know comes from the text itself. He must have been a Ḥusaynī sharif[22] and what is clear also is that he was a senior civil servant in what was a staunchly Sunnī Rasulid administration. We might also hazard the guess, from the plethora of material concerning the chief port of Aden, that he was employed there in his official capacity. He informs us[23] that he wishes 'to compile a book containing information about the regulations of the royal crop tax bureaux …' and that he has done something similar before, when, under al-Ashraf Ismāʿīl,[24] al-Nāṣir's father, he compiled *al-Dīwān al-jāmi' li-l-taysīr fī ma'rifat al-taghliyah wa-al-tas'īr*, a work not to my knowledge extant.

The employment of this Shīʿī Ḥusaynī official in the Sunnī Rasulid administration is an interesting, though not surprising, one within such a sophisticated government. It reminds me of that of Ibn Ḥātim, an Yāmī Ismāʿīlī, who held a high politico-military position under the second monarch, al-Muẓaffar Yūsuf.[25] Ibn Ḥātim

---

20 CSFS, 23.

21 See above, Rasulid Trade.

22 See f. 5b of the Arabic text.

23 See f. 5b of the Arabic text.

24 Reg. 778-803/1377–1401.

25 *SA*, 1–3.

was, as far as we can ascertain, during the years 647-702/1249-1302 a member of a small cadre of amirs under the leadership of ʿAlam al-Dīn al-Shaʿbī who were employed throughout Rasulid lands to represent the monarch at an extremely senior level in the different political and military affairs of the régime.

6 The Language of the **Mulakhkhaṣ**

The language I discovered in the continuous prose of the text was something of a surprise. One might expect a senior civil servant writing to instruct his subordinates to compose in the elevated classical language. Far from it. Our author is clearly not an employee of the secretariat, for there is little here of 'correct grammatical wording, masterly and precise' and 'sweet, connected diction'![26] Rather, as will be briefly illustrated below, we have here a presentation on the part of the author which is the written record of his oral directions and which therefore manifests itself as Middle Arabic (MA).[27] I discuss below the orthography, morphology and syntax of Ḥusaynī's continuous prose with some examples from the text, and there follow some short comments on the language of the lists.

Orthography

There is little to note in this category and the examples below highlight only the use of *alif mamdūdah* where one would expect *alif maqṣūrah*:
f. 10a - *yudʿā.*
f. 10b - *al-majrā.*

Morphology

f. 7b - *wa-aṣḥāb dīwān al-khāṣṣ nafarayn.* 'The staff of the special bureau is [made up of] two persons,' where *nafarān* would have been expected.
f. 8a - *wa-amwāl hādhih al-dawawīn mutaʿayyin li-l-maṣrūf.* 'The revenues of these bureaux are earmarked for expenditure,' where *mutaʿayyinah* would have been expected.
f. 8a - *fa-hāʾulā al-thalāthah al-dawāwīn* ... 'These three bureaux ...,' where fem. sg. *hādhih* would have been expected.

---

26 See f. 9a of the Arabic text.

27 By MA I mean 'that literary form of the Arabic language which is a mixture of non-classical Arabic elements and pure classical Arabic (CA) elements'; see my 'The Language of Ibn al-Mujāwir's 7th/13th Century Guide to Arabia' in J.R. Smart (ed.), *Tradition and Modernity in the Arabic Language and Literature*, Richmond, 1996, 328–9, where the subject is dealt with at some length and other relevant publications, particularly those of Joshua Blau, are listed.

f. 8a - *wa-lā yarfaʿū illā ilā al-malik*. 'They submit [accounts] only to the monarch,' where *yarfaʿūna* would have been expected.
f. 8a - *wa-al-ʿummāl wa-al-mubāshirūn fī hādhih al-thalāthah al-dawāwīn yakūnū bi-darajah wāḥidah*. 'The comptrollers and stewards in these three bureaux are of one rank,' where *yakūnūna*, or indeed no verb at all, would have been expected.
f. 9a - *wa-lam yastafīd*. 'Without his deriving any benefit', where *yastafid* would have been expected.
f. 9a - *wa-ammā al-mudarrisīn* … 'As for the teachers, …', where a nom. *mudarrisūna* would have been expected after *ammā*.
f. 9a - *thumma kuttāb al-bāb al-sharīf al-sulṭānī kātiban wāḥidan lā ghayr*. 'Then come the secretaries of the noble royal court, one single secretary, no more', where a nom. *kātib wāḥid* would have been expected.

Syntax

f. 8a - *wa-bāqī al-amwāl ... lā yukhlaṭu maʿa māl al-kharāj*. 'The remainder of the revenues … is not mixed together with the revenue of the crop tax', where the preposition *bi-* would have been expected.
f. 11a - wa-qad yuradd ʿalay-h al-amr bi-an yushīr ilā mushiddīn al-jihāt yastakhrijū wa-yursilū al-ḥawāṣil. 'The command may come back to him to direct the district inspectors to collect and despatch the returns', where … ilā mushiddī al-jihāt an yastakhrijū … would have been expected.
f. 26b - *fa-ammā mafātīḥ al-abwāb fa-yaṣilū al-bawwābīn wa-aṣḥāb al-dawl yaqbiḍū fī kull ṣabāḥ*. 'As for the gate keys, the gate-keepers and those on duty come and take them every morning'. NB the pl. verb in front of the pl. expressed subject (in the accusative!) and the asyndetic second verb.
f. 26b - *fa-idhā kān ṣalāt al-ʿaṣr fa-yaṣilū ilā ʿind al-wālī*. 'After late afternoon prayer, they come to the governor's residence.' NB after the *idhā* clause, we have the main clause introduced by *fa-*, followed by the imperfect. It might perhaps be noted further that the conditionals of the text are for the most part orthodox CA.
f. 27a - *wa-yakūn al-taʿshīr yaḥḍur al-jamīʿ*. 'Everyone is present at the calculating of the taxes.' An extremely interesting sentence which defies precise analysis. One might have expected something like *ʿind al-taʿshīr yaḥḍur al-jamīʿ* or (*fī*) *waqt al-taʿshīr* etc.

To sum up, we observe here a number of linguistic features which point clearly to MA. Nominative case endings for accusatives, and *vice versa*, accusatives for nominatives; masculine gender for feminine; masculine plurals for feminine singulars;

apocopated imperfect indicative endings; accusatives after *ammā*; verbal asyndeton etc. etc.

7 The Lists in the text

Away from the passages of continuous prose, whose language is discussed above, the text appears in columns of figures (ff. 13a, 15a, 15b, 16a, 16b and 17a) which naturally resist any attempt to analyse the language of the contents. The list of fortresses (ff. 13b, 14a and 14b) and those of commodities and government officials take up the rest of the work and a few brief comments on the language of the latter are offered here. Certainly within these folios most grammatical rules have been thrown out of the window. Remarkably, concord counts for nothing and it will suffice to give a few examples to illustrate the point as follow: *al-naṣāfī al-baghdādī al-rifā'* (f. 18b) (on the same folio we have correctly *al-naṣāfī al-baghdādiyyah*); *wa-al-maḥārim al-ḥarīr* (18b); *al-maḥābis al-ḥumr al-fiḍḍī* (19a); *al-thiyāb al-maqṣūr* (19a); *al-kubābah al-ṣīnī* (21b).[28] Whenever continuous prose is encountered, it can be said that it is MA and that it fits in well with the analysis given above under the heading of the language.

8 The Numerals

Cahen, who had taken sole responsibility for the numerical signs in the MS in his joint venture with Serjeant, was true to his word: '... j'ai donc pu transcrire en notation moderne tout le tarif douanier d'Aden'.[29] My one huge fear as I began my work proved groundless. In the initial stages, I wondered if it would be necessary to involve myself deeply in the numerical signs, neither figures nor the numbers spelt out in words, but seemingly secret code signs used only by civil servants. By dint of his knowledge of what he calls '*dīwānī* classique'[30] for the whole numbers and by reference to Artin Pacha[31] and Hinz[32] for the fractions, Cahen had indeed cracked the code. I have had to do no more than check carefully the text with Cahen's table.[33] He

---

28 It should be noted that the *Nūr*, the archive produced during the reign of al-Muẓaffar Yūsuf, a century and a half before, reads much the same. We are in all probability dealing in both cases with a fixed-style grammatical structure used throughout the civil service in medieval times for all fiscal lists.

29 CSFS, 33.

30 CSFS, 30.

31 CSFS, 32, referring to 'Signes employés dans la comptabilité copte pour la transcription des fractions', *Bulletin de l'Institut d'Egypte* (1889, 285 ff.).

32 W. Hinz, 'Das Rechnungswesen orientalischer Reichsfinanzämter im Mittelalter', *Islam* 29 (1950), fig. 28–9.

33 CSFS, 31.

would surely have been intrigued to learn of Little's late 1990s discoveries in what he calls 'Mamluk *siyāqah*'[34] and would have rejoiced at the publication of the *Nūr*, II, which contains a whole section entitled *Ma'rifat a'dād al-ḥisāb min al-āḥād ilā al-a'shār ilā al-mi'ayn* (*sic* read *al-mi'āt*) (p. 59). Over pages 59–67, we find a comprehensive description of the numerical signs.[35] This has come to me late, but clearly where I have been able to relate it to the *Mulakhkhaṣ* MS text it is of great relevance.

9 The Manuscript

I much regret that I have been unable to handle the MS of the *Mulakhkhaṣ* for myself and I have used a good photocopy throughout my work. The MS figures in Griffini's 1915 article[36] and in Brockelmann's *GAL*.[37] Serjeant describes[38] the binding as 'interesting, but damaged, and the back is older than the front.' The MS text is incomplete, though comparing it with the list of contents[39] little appears missing. The text proper begins on f. 5a and finishes abruptly at the end of f. 27b.[40] Ff. 4a–4b, however, are clearly part of the text and I am very confident that the catchword at the bottom of f. 24b reads '*al-mā'i'ah*' and thus that ff. 4a and 4b fit in after f. 24b. Nevertheless, it is impossible to tell whether f. 4b leads directly to f. 25a and certainly a thorough reading of the text at this point indicates that it probably does not.

Griffini expresses the opinion that the MS is the author's autograph and Serjeant supports this view with the comment,[41] '... and draft corrections in the margin or between the lines seem to support this view'. I cannot however concur. Firstly, there are at least two hands, possible even more, involved in the copying of the text. Even if the author began the work in a neat, formal, fairly large *naskhī* hand, complete with elaborate title panel (f. 5a), dots and even a good supply of vowels, fully intending it to provide the final draft of the text, primarily a treatise for junior civil servants, from f. 5b onwards, as long as the continuous prose goes on (until f. 13a), a second hand settles down into a less formal, smaller *naskhī* script, fifteen lines

34 See e.g. Donald P. Little, 'Documents Related to the Estates of a Merchant and his Wife in Late Fourteenth Century Jerusalem', *Mamluk Studies Review* 2 (1998), 93–193, 178 ff.

35 See also *Nūr*, II, 223-26 which contain the editor's numerical tables.

36 See E. Griffini, 'Die jüngste ambrosianische Sammlung arabischer Handschriften', *Zeitschrift der Deutschen morgenländischen Gesellschaft* 69 (1915), 78–9.

37 See *Geschichte der Arabischen Litteratur*, Supplementband II, Leiden, 1938, 253.

38 See CSFS, 21.

39 Ff. 6a–6b.

40 F. 28a begins equally abruptly in the middle of a chapter of Ghazālī's *Ihyā' 'ulūm al-dīn*.

41 See CSFS, 21.

to the page. F. 13a comprises in the main a revenue table and forces the scribe into a more hurried, less legible script. F. 13b begins the typical list format, the hand small and less neat, introducing of course the difficult numerical notations (see above, The Numerals) and this might well be a third hand. More tables take up ff. 15a, 15b, 16a, 16b and 17a and part of f. 17b (this time the headings are more formally written) and from 18a onwards, until we return to continuous prose on f. 26b, we find nothing but lists of commodities etc. with fewer dots and vowels, where legibility is much more difficult. I am of the opinion that the scribes have eventually abandoned the idea of a final text for a draft, as they add more and more interlinear and marginal insertions. It seems to me that they meant the whole thing to be recopied before it was bound for posterity.

10 The Translation

I have attempted a complete translation of the text with annotations numbering 872. There is little need to stress the difficulties involved in interpreting this ninth/fifteen century MS text, as they must be obvious for all to see. There are lacunae in my translation, words or phrases which I am totally unable to read and these are clearly indicated by dots in the translation and there is a comment in the appropriate note. Where I fail, I come clean and hand over to others who, I hope, will use this volume to good effect in the future, both in the context of Rasulid and wider Arabian, even Middle Eastern, economic history. Where I am in doubt, I make this clear in the relevant note and make every attempt to provide a possible alternative interpretation. During the translation process, I have trawled the unpublished notes of both Serjeant and Cahen and have for the most part used the contents to assist me, even when I find no secondary evidence to support their ideas. My guiding principle has been to be fully transparent and to say exactly what I am doing in any given circumstance. I have anglicized where possible non-Yemeni place names, both in the translation and in the end notes. Finally, I must return to the somewhat vexed question of the translation of words such as *iqṭā'* and *muqṭa'*. I come back in this regard to a note in my recent article on the Rasulid adminstration:[42] with little hesitation I translate here and elsewhere the former 'fief' and the latter 'fief-holder'.

11 The Notes

Having fought for years against what is known as the 'dustbin' method of annotation, I now find myself, *faute de mieux*, following that very path. In other words, I see no

42 SRA, 228, note 20.

alternative to including all necessary observations on the text in one set of notes. All my ideas to proceed otherwise eventually came to naught and multiple sets of notes would have ended up, I am sure, a nightmare of confusion.

My first concern is to provide what I can by way of an *apparatus criticus* to be used in conjunction with the facsimile text provided. In this context, it should be noted that the word 'reading' in the note gives the precise meaning of 'this is how I would suggest my reader reads the word or phrase.' Either I am suggesting there is a scribal error, or there is an extremely difficult reading which I consider I have worked out. The word 'text' in a note merely draws the attention of the reader to an interesting word or a technical term which then figures in the indices.

In addition, I have been at pains to help with the interpretation of the word or phrase which is annotated. I have also provided some help with place and tribal names and here and there there are relevant comparisons with other sources. All these observations have been supported by reference to useful sources available to me which are listed under 'References'. This latter list pertains to my textual annotations and to my introductory notes. On occasions in these latter, I refer to works not in the list of text references, in which case I give full bibliographical references at the first mention and follow up with an abbreviated one if necessary.

Of course, it has been necessary to keep the notes to an absolute minimum and to assist in this I have assigned to every source quoted in the notes an abbreviated form. A list of these abbreviations appears immediately before the translation and is entitled 'Abbreviations'. Readers will also find there an explanation of the two types of bracket used in the translation, viz. [ ] and { }, the former indicating an editorial addition and the latter used for insertions, interlinear and marginal, in the original MS text. Where I am annotating continuous prose passages, I provide a folio and line reference in the note.

ANNOTATED TRANSLATION OF THE MULAKHKHAṢ

[ ]	addition of the editor/translator
{ }	interlinear/marginal insertion in the MS

ABBREVIATIONS USED IN THE NOTES

A*LW*	Agius, *Arabic Literary Works.*
A*ME*	Allouche, *Mamluk Economics.*
A*W*	Agius, *In the Wake of the Dhow.*
B*A*	Government of Bombay, *Account.*
CC	Claude Cahen's unpublished notes.
CCE	Cahen, 'Contribution à l'étude'.
C*D*	Cahen, *Douanes.*
CSFS	Cahen and Serjeant, 'Fiscal Survey'.
D	Dozy, *Supplément.*
D*M*	Dimyāṭī, *Mu'jam.*
D*V*	Dozy, *Vêtements.*
EI	*Encyclopaedia of Islam*, 2nd edition.
E*T*	Ehrenkreutz, '*Taṣrīf*'.
FN	Forand, 'Notes'.
G-G*G*	Grosset-Grange, *Glossaire.*
G*MT*	Gacek, *Arabic Manuscript Tradition.*
GNL	Goitein, 'New Light'.
G*Q*	Garcin, *Qūṣ.*
G*S*	Goitein, *Society.*
H*D*	Hava, *Dictionary.*
H*I*	Hajji, *Internal Affairs.*
Ḥ*M*	Ḥajarī, *Majmū'.*
H*MG*	Hinz, *Masse und Gewichte.*
H*Ṣ*	Hamdānī, *Ṣifah.*
IB*T*	Ibn Baṭṭūṭah, *Travels.*
IM*L*	Ibn Manẓūr, *Lisān.*
IM*Q*	Ibn Mammātī, *Qawānīn.*
IM*TM*	Ibn al-Mujāwir, *Tārīkh al-Mustabṣir.*
K	Kazimirski, *Dictionnaire.*
K*S*	Kahl, *Sābūr ibn Sahl.*
K*SA*	Kindermann, *Schiff im Arabischen.*

K*Y*	Kay, *Yaman*.
L	Lane, *Lexicon*.
L*AT*	Löfgren, *Arabische Texte*.
L*E*	Landberg, *Etudes*.
L*G*	Landberg, *Glossaire daṯînois*.
L*L*	Le Strange, *Lands*.
L*T*	Løkkegaard, *Taxation*.
M*M*	Maqḥafī, *Mu'jam*.
M*WR*	Maktari, *Water Rights*.
N*S*	Nashwān, *Shams*.
Nūr	*Nūr al-ma'ārif*.
P*D*	Piamenta, *Dictionary*.
Q*Ṣ*	Qalqashandī, *Ṣubḥ*.
RBS	R.B. Serjeant's unpublished notes.
R*S*	Rabie, *System*.
S*A*	Smith, *Ayyubids*, II.
SCC	Serjeant, 'Cultivation of Cereals'.
S*CT*	Shamrookh, *Commerce and Trade*.
SH*T*	Sharjī, *Ṭabaqāt*.
SL*Ṣ*	Serjeant and Lewcock, *Ṣan'ā'*.
SMT	Smith, 'Maritime Trade'.
SP	Serjeant, 'Ports'.
S*P*	Serjeant, *Portuguese*.
S*PD*	Steingass, *Persian Dictionary*.
SPP	Smith, 'Port Practices'.
SRA	Smith, 'Rasulid Administration'.
S*T*	Serjeant, *Textiles*.
T*AN*	Tibbetts, *Arab Navigation*.
V*MA*	Varisco, *Medieval Agriculture*.
VMS	Varisco, 'Magical Significance'.
W*D*	Wehr, *Dictionary*.
W*G*	Wilson, *Gazetteer*.
W*GC*	Werdecker, *Geography and Cartography*.
YB*HJ*	Yule and Burnell, *Hobson-Jobson*.
Y*M*	Yāqūt, *Mu'jam*.
ZT	Zabīdī, *Tāj*.

[5a] *SHORT TREATISE [FOR THOSE WITH] NATURAL INTELLIGENCES AND MINDS AND THE LAMP OF GUIDANCE FOR OFFICIALS*

concerning the knowledge of the rules of the revenues of the sultanic, royal, Nasirid,[1] Salahid[2] tax bureaux in the districts of the Yemen — God render the authority of her master everlasting and him victorious. [This is] the composition of the servant in need of the forgiveness and approval of God — He is ever almighty — al-Ḥasan b. ʿAlī al-Sharīf al-Ḥusaynī, going back in lineage to the Chosen One — God bless him and his family and grant them peace. I have rendered service in this [composition] to the auspicious state, seeking the very core of its loving care, pure with the favours and charitable gifts it granted and the generous good fortune of its presents, praying long for it — God (praise to Him) prolong its existence and provide success all around it, front and back. This was begun and finished in the month of Jumādā II, AH 815.[3] The best blessings and peace be upon its lord. Praise be to God, him alone. God bless our lord, Muḥammad, the Prophet of the nation [of the Arabs], his family and Companions and grant them peace.

> She is the Yemen, to the right of all regions;
> her location has come in the sound tradition.
> There there are souls which yearn for mercy;
> for us there the Prophet, her intercessor, has spoken of our pride in her.

[5b] In the name of God, the compassionate, the merciful. God bless our lord, Muḥammad and his family and grant them peace. Praise to God whose attributes are munificence and generosity, unique in His oneness and His timelessness, who created everything from nothing. 'He taught Adam the names'[4] [of all things] before he knew [them]. By means of His power He drew attention to the knowledge of the obliquely cut nib[5] in the reed-pen. I bear witness that there is no god but God alone, having no partner, a testimony with which I shall seal the writing of [this] work when it is finished. I bear witness that Muḥammad, His servant and messenger, is the best of those who move on foot, sent to all nations. God bless him and his family, sources of knowledge and generosity, his companions and caliphs, as long as light and darkness follow one after the other.

To continue. [I am] the servant in need of the forgiveness and approval of God — He is ever almighty — al-Ḥasan b. ʿAlī, the Ḥusaynī, sharif by descent — God treat them kindly and the Muslims. I wanted to compile a book containing information about the rules of the royal tax bureaux in the Yemeni districts, just as I rendered a service to the felicitous Ashrafī state[6] {— God requite it with mercy —}[7]

with a book which I called 'The Comprehensive Register of the Ready Knowledge of Price Raising and Crop Apprizing'.[8] I shall render service to the felicitous Nāṣirī government with this book. I have called it 'Short Treatise [for Those with] Natural Intelligences and Minds and the Lamp of Guidance for Officials'. I have arranged it in districts and chapters so that the knowledge [contained in] it may be easily be accessed.[9] Many people are prevented from gaining access,[10] simply because they neglect to acquaint themselves with the fundamentals. It has been said, 'Whoever seeks knowledge of the end after the beginning succeeds; whoever seeks knowledge of the end before the beginning has been seeking the impossible.' I have arranged it in four chapters like the characters of man which are all combined in him.

Someone has said:

[6a] The craft of penmanship in its execution is [made up of different] disciplines
and those who practice it [regard it as having different] divisions,
Like the characters in man, [which are] four:
hand, ink, paper and pen.

Another has said:

Penmanship [consists of] four things: the colour [of the ink]
[should be] night on the paper of clear daylight,
[The pen should be] nibbed obliquely, running on its point [as if] with finger-tips,
those of the script, not showing defects.

Another has said:

A quarter of writing is in the blackness of its ink,
a quarter of it is in the hand of the scribes;
A quarter is in a fine pen with its owner,[11]
and the fine quality of the paper is the fourth of the means [of achieving good penmanship].[12]

The first chapter — the virtue of the pen and those who use it.

The second chapter — the knowledge of the rules of the royal bureau{x}[13] of crop taxes, that to which the name of the bureau applies, what is due to it and what its duties are and those of the financial officers and stewards on the question of taxes [in which] the office [of the bureau] acts with the authority of the ruler over them and what is due to them and what their duties are.

The third chapter — knowledge of the rules of the tax revenues of the districts of the Yemen in their entirety. This section comprises three statements: *the first* on the rules of the revenues of the mountains, this comprising two districts: the first the highlands called al-Bilād al-ʿUlyā. Longtitudinally, [it lies] from the eastern part of Ḥaḍramawt to Bilād al-Tawīlah and Sharaf Qilḥāḥ in the west;[14] latitudinally, [it lies] from Ḥaql Qatāb {in the south} to the village of Bīshah [in the direction of the] *qiblah* and north,[15] with the amount of its crop tax. The second district, known as al-Yaman al-Akhḍar, is circular in shape, longtitudinally and latitudinally, south and north. The first part of it is from the Yaḥṣubī provinces of Raymān B. Sayf to Ẓafār al-Wādiyayn **[6b]** to Bilād B. Sarḥah to Bilād B. Nājī to al-Mushayriq with its fortresses and districts to Balad B. ʿAlī and B. Murghim, to Balad B. Wuḥāḍah and it wadis, Dhū Saydam, Balad al-Aḥmūd to Balad Wuṣāb. It returns to Mikhlāf al-Shawāfī, al-Khaḍrā', al-Naʿmān, Jabal al-Taʿkar, Jabal Baʿdān with what it contains and what adjoins it, Balad Ṣuhbān, Mikhlāf Jaʿfar, Mikhlāf Raymah, al-Jabalayn, ʿUnnah, al-Qufāʿah, Sharʿab, Jabal al-Ṭawr, i.e. Ṣabir,[16] and the fortresses, towns, {wadis}[17] and rivers lying between them, the fortress of Taʿizz, the noble,[18] the preserved, seat of the Yemen, and its districts, Jabal Dhakhir, Mikhlāf al-Maʿāfir, Jabal Dhubḥān, the fortress of al-Dumluwah and its tenth,[19] Balad al-Rakb, Khadīrayn, al-Janad, al-Salif, Jibāl al-ʿArsayn[20] and Zabīd and their environs.[21]

The second statement is on the knowledge of the rules of the revenues of the regions of Tihāmah, such districts as are similar to them and the fief districts.

The third statement is on the rules of the revenues of the ports and places of entry, those concerned with them [22] and their taxes.

The fourth chapter — on the knowledge of the business and accounts[23] which must be submitted to the felicitous bureau in accordance with the ordinance of what will be mentioned below. Then [come] the rules whereby the revenues are safe-guarded and which have a hand in growth and increase. Then [come] pleasant anecdotes which need to be read; I have concluded the book by mentioning the pen. However, mention of God is the loftiest of aims.

The first chapter

On the virtue of the pen and those who use it who are responsible for the regulations of state. God — He is ever almighty — has said, 'Recite in the name of your Lord who created, created man from clotted blood. Recite and your Lord is the most beneficent who taught [the use of] the pen. He taught man what he did not know.'[24] He also said, what a noble sayer He is, 'Nūn. By the pen and what they write.'[25]

A certain one of them recited **[7a]** in praise of the pen and those who use it the following two lines by al-Bustī — to God is attributed his eloquence.[26]

When the brave in battle glory in their sword
and they reckon it to be what earns [them] honour and nobility,
[Yet] in the pen of secretaries resides their glory and eminence
for all time [in that] God swore an oath by the pen.
{By the same poet at the end of the chapter is [the following]:
If he unsheathes his pens one day [of battle] to bring them into action,[27]
he will make you forget any brave in full armour who draws his slender spear-shafts.[28]
If he allows his finger-tips to rest on a sheet of paper,[29]
all the secretaries of man[30] will acknowledge servitude to him.[31]
He has lines of writing concerning his affair
…}[32]

Another said:

They brandish thin yellow [pens];[33] 'tis as if they are
the finger-tips of the buxom girls of the chambers.
Whenever they make [the pens'] nose bleed, adorned by their nose-bleeds
are papers which resemble girls with pinkish throats.[34]

Another said:

Occupying oneself with account-books, ink pots and studying
is the basis of devotion, asceticism, leadership and good management.

A certain sage has said: Writing is a spiritual craft; the reed pen is the interpreter of minds and the substance of speech. The scratching of pens is more eloquent than the clash[35] of sharp swords. The pen equips the armies of the will and puts what one says in order, not wearying of seeking pasture.[36] It is as if it kisses a sultan's carpet or opens up the blossoms[37] of a garden.

Buzurgmihr[38] the sage has said: The world is a garden the fence of which is the state. The state is an authority through which the Sunnah is kept alive. The Sunnah is policy which the monarch controls. The monarch is a shepherd supported by the army. The army is [made up of] aides provided for[39] by wealth. Wealth is income collected from subjects. Subjects are servants preserved from rapacity[40] by justice. Justice is often resorted to; in it is the support of the world.

A certain sage has said: The pen is the magnet of wealth, attracting it as iron is attracted. He has also said: There can be no royal authority except through men; and no men without wealth; no wealth except from subjects; and no subjects without justice. Justice is the support of what is right, **[7b]** the vizier of the intellect, the keeper of the house whose keeper and confidant is the pen. He is trusted by the monarch and his aide is he whom his right hand grasps. The pen collects wealth and establishes [a sound] state of affairs.

Someone has recited:

When I noticed that my tongue was not eloquent [enough],
I made my explanation to you when I needed to with my pen;
In awe and shyness of you [my tongue] holds me back,
O best of men, Arabs and non-Arabs!

A certain sage has recited:

The pen is the commander of wealth and the sword its helper.

He also recited as follows, describing the pen and the secretary:

We have never seen a blow from a brave hero
with a sharp sword cut through a thousand pens;
But we have seen an article[41] [written with] {a pen}[42] in ink
which has turned upside down a thousand chiefs.[43]

Another has recited, describing a secretary:

'Tis as if the pen, the reed, in his hand
were a spear by which foes were habitually driven off;
And 'tis as if there were in his hand a sea giving
generously of its waves; its giving is plentiful, praise-worthy.[44]

The second chapter

On the knowledge of the rules of the bureau{x}[45] of the royal crop taxes, that one to which the name of bureau applies, what is due to it and what its duty is, the duties of the financial officers and stewards in the districts in which the pen serves with the authority of the monarch over them and what is due to them and what their duties are.

As for the rules of the bureau{x},[46] they are [made up of] those who wield the pen directly, the officials; their highest-ranking are the officials of the royal court. They have [different] grades, {their highest-ranking}[47] being the *mashāyikh*, the accountants, {the highest-ranking}[48] of them being the staff of the grand bureau: a comptroller, a supervisor and below these a bookkeeper. It is experience which promotes them. The staff **[8a]** of the special bureau is [made up of] two persons: a comptroller and a supervisor.{The special bureau [deals with] taxes that have the specialized function of registering totals[49] and there is nothing laid as a charge upon the two of them[50] except their dealing directly[51] [with it] and the office [itself].}[52] The comptroller and the supervisor in the grand bureau and in the special bureau are the most experienced and knowledgeable of officials[53] who have already been directly involved with their knowledge and experience in [the administration of] bureaux and who know how to elaborate on what is precise and to give detailed interpretation[54] and [who are knowledgeable of] port activities.

No consideration is given to the official who is quick at adding up, [but] who does not have the knowledge of basic rules, for he will not bring a laudable result and errors and mistakes may well befall him. It has been said, 'Take it slowly and don't make a mistake!'

The officials of the bureau of movable property[55] are two, a comptroller and a supervisor, having the greatness of properties because they are the property, honour and esteem of the monarch.

The salary is the same in all three bureaux, i.e. whatever the comptroller receives, the supervisor receives the same.

The revenues of these bureaux {i.e. the bureaux of crop taxes}[56] are earmarked for expenditure, except for the revenue of the bureau of movable property, none of which is expended apart from the salaries of the movable property kitchen. The remainder of the revenues are referred for future eventualities {to the treasury of the movable property [bureau and] not mixed together[57] with the revenue of the crop tax. The [revenue of the] movable property bureau works well with a serious, honest inspector who adds it up and takes responsibility for it.[58]}[59]

These three bureaux require that the accounts be submitted [to them] from those officials, deputies[60] and tax farmers[61] who deal directly with their districts. They submit [them] only to the monarch or someone the monarch designates. The comptrollers and supervisors in these three bureaux are on the same level of experience, rank and salary, for the supervisors have most responsibility,[62] it being their duty to collate well. They are experienced in drawing up abstracts and detailed accounting. Otherwise there is no part for them in the office of accounting.

Now the officials of flourishing treasury are two: a comptroller and a supervisor who are highly experienced. Treasury copies[63] may be issued to them, a special item from one[64] of the budgets.[65] The monarch asks them to provide details of this account and they are requested to act in secret so that no one knows what they are doing and the monarch does not learn of the actions of these persons. When the detailed accounting falls short in one as opposed to another — I mean the employees of the bureaux who carry out detailed accounting **[8b]** — the ruler is made aware of this; it will either be through [the official's] lack of experience or as a result of accusations.[66]

Now the officials of the army granted victory [by God][67] are three: a comptroller, a supervisor and a bookkeeper. The bookkeeper is inferior to the financial officers in salary and rank. They have the right to review the garrison troops in the districts. They are due from [the troops] at the two great feasts monetary gifts,[68] each soldier must pay [them] ten dinars at the two feasts. A {single}[69] infantryman must pay two dinars, this every year in all districts. When they discover substitutes[70] among them at the review, they fine them[71] their salary and cut them off from [military] service. But in the fief districts they do not speak out against substitutes, but they have the right to review and perquisite. It is their duty to write down the brevets[72] which are made to include the troops of the royal court each month and the officials of the felicitous treasury take [the brevets] from them and present them to the noble gaze so that he might set his noble mark on them. The only testimonies of the staff[73] of the felicitous treasury are the [said] brevets, as was the custom from the beginning of the felicitous dynasty.[74] {The brevets are originated in the thriving treasury[75] and they are often required.}[76] [It is also their duty] to write on the feudal titles[77] [giving details of] the fiefs with the obligation [to provide] soldiers, revenue and shared contribution[78] and also the detailed reckoning they make[79] concerning the fief of the fiefholders, such as landed properties,[80] estates without heirs, common lands[81] and also camel tithes and crimes of murder. They should also write on square sheets the person exempt {in the crop tax districts},[82] they and all the officials of the office of accountant.

Then comes the secretary of pious endowments. He, like the accountant, calls each deputy of a *madrasah* endowment to account for what accrues from its endowment, pays the maintenance money and writes down[83] [what] building [is to be done], what he judges to be in accordance with [the amount of] the income. If there is a surplus above that in any way, he calculates it[84] in his register. {The endowment has an inspector like the overseer.}[85] It is the duty of the inspector of the endowment to be involved personally in the building, if it is new, or he delegates a person whose probity and faith are sound. He has notables and trusty persons who are present when subsistence {is paid out},[86] {or he attends himself}[87] and puts his voice and mind with the teachers and orphans as far as the payment of their subsistence is concerned. **[9a]**{He follows the stipulations of the founder of the endowment without deviating from them.}[88] When an orphan reaches puberty, he will appoint another in his place. He appoints instead of any student who completes three years {without his deriving any benefit}[89] the most select of the students and orphans. Teachers who are recognized for learning, experience and perseverance in teaching [for whom] there is evidence of benefit [from their teaching] are not replaced by him. {If he is clearly of benefit [in his teaching], he promotes him to a higher position and keeps him in post until he advances to the place of [his highest] attainment(?).[90]}[91] The deputy will not lease out the endowment for more than three years, nor to anyone of rank.[92]

Then come the officials of the felicitous stables, two officials in each stable: a comptroller and a supervisor. {They receive the perquisites of the animals belonging to the amirs and the victorious army, ...,[93] ten dinars a head, except fief-holders. When a fief-holder is given a fief and animals, many or few, are granted to him from the stable, he has to pay the staff of the stable one hundred dinars [payable to] the head of stable,[94] the secretaries, the steward and the grooms.[95] It is the responsibility of the officials to submit the finances[96] to the department of accounts each month.}[97] They will have an official of steward rank[98] with them called a veterinary surgeon[99] who will be accomplished and knowledgeable in the ailments of animals and what benefits and harms them. He will study the book of farriery and cures for animals. {He is}[100] the subordinate of the head {of stables}.[101]

Then come the officials of the felicitous secretariat, they being the officials of the noble scroll[102] for the writing of titles,[103] written orders,[104] tax exemptions[105] and enrolments[106] to all districts where the monarch's order reaches. [They also write] feudal titles, [official] correspondence in correct grammatical wording, masterly and precise,[107] sweet commended verse in keeping with the topic in question. All this is [as if it were] on the ruler's [own] tongue with fresh, sweet and connected diction.

Then come the officials of the noble[108] provision store.[109] They write down what the provisions officer[110] spends in respect of fixed and extraordinary allowances on each current day. He submits it to the department, [i.e.] the accountant, thereby writing out a requisition. From the noble bureau of movable property[111] is expended whatever the allowance of the monarch alone is in accordance with current custom. Whatever the allowance of the great kitchen and the great and noble provision store, this allowance is assigned to the account of one of the bureaux of Tihāmah in accordance with current custom.

Then comes the secretary of the noble royal court, one single secretary, no more. He registers information of all those {notable}[112] sharifs, Arab tribesmen and *mashāyikh* of the districts who come to the noble court. Whatever the head[113] of the noble court wishes to take **[9b]** to the sovereign[114] the secretary writes down and the head marks [it] with a sign of his approval.[115] Then comes the dispensing of the salaries of the amirs, the servants [of the ruler], to which he applies himself, deputizing for the secretaries of the flourishing treasury. If they wish to attend, they do so, he being of their number. It is his responsibility to attend to their fixed salary throughout the year. He will be keeping an eye on what comes in to the head so that they receive the allowance in full. The unexpected may happen with which only the secretary of the noble court deals. The criteria of his appointment[116] are {that he should be}[117] of adult age, mature, upright, honest in money matters and [in his dealings with other] persons, guarding his reputation, responsible, cultivated, sensible, active, proficient in penmanship, perfectly endowed with good traits and agreeable qualities, God — He is ever almighty — willing.

Then comes the official of the preserved fortresses, called supervisor of the fortresses, he being the senior supervisor, with many supervisors under him. The junior supervisors have salaries only in some fortresses and not others. There is in the fortress of Taʿizz the preserved, a supervisor; in the fortress of Ṣabir called al-ʿArūs there is a supervisor; in the fortress of al-Taʿkar there is a supervisor; in the fortress of al-Dumluwah the preserved are two secretaries; in the Ṣabāḥī fortresses, {the fortresses of al-Mahjam}[118] and the fortress of Qāf, known as the fortress of Manābir, there is a supervisor. The remaining supervisors are confirmed in office by his pen[119] and they have a salary of the highest of those assigned [a salary]. They [are drawn] from trusty officials, their sons and relatives and incumbent upon them are contractual obligations and [other] responsibilities.[120] These are [namely] that the chief supervisor reviews all the fortresses at the beginning of the year. If anyone of the garrison dies, or withdraws,[121] he takes on another in his place. Such as has accumulated of the salary of those absentees he instructs the tax-collectors to retain, writing copies of the requests at the end of this.[122] He remembers what accumulates from the absentees and writes a copy of it to the accountant, the inspector and the staff of all the bureaux who attend the grand allotment of salaries.[123] The junior supervisors supervise the fortresses **[10a]** for the rest of the months of the year, each month by month, and they write down in their registers the descriptions of the garrison soldiers with them so that no deceptions escape their notice as follows: 'so-and-so, son of so-and-so — his description is {thus and thus,' describing his [own particular] qualities.[124]}[125] This is [because] one may present himself in the name of another {who is absent.}[126] This is what dishonest officers do. Then the chief supervisor, after {completion}[127] of the review {at the beginning of}[128] the year, writes the castle reports,[129] then the minister consults them and they are set before the noble scrutiny [of the monarch] for [his] mark of authorization and publication. When the reports are issued to the minister, he summons the fortresses supervisor and hands over the reports to him. He takes them and proceeds to his house, calling for those [he wishes] to address and makes his proclamation to all those in charge of the fortresses, each one according to the distance of the stages [they will have to cover]. He equips the supervisors and they range from the lowest to the highest ranks,[130] as the custom goes. The head supervisor is called the overseer[131] of the fortresses. He had great importance during the period of al-Mu'ayyad[132] and earlier until some years of the period of al-Mujāhid,[133] when it was curtailed. His mount[134] was a mule with a girth[135] made up of hair plaits[136] and a blazon of fans,[137] like the inspector of accounts and the overseer of the sultan's special bureau.[138] The minister has sole authority for the fortresses and no one can speak on their subject but he. It is not good that the command of the fortresses should be in the hands of anyone but the most loyal, for fortresses are like birds: it is feared that they might fly away. Moreover, no governor, nor officer, was confirmed in charge of fortresses or anything else except by a title crowned with the noble signature.[139] The minister only writes a paper when contractual obligations or the like {are handed over}.[140] There is no harm if fortresses are kept under surveillance with guardianship and vigilance, for the sultanate[141] remains noble as long as watching over [its affairs] renders it support.

Then come the calculators of astronomic observations, experts, philosophers who have read instructive books who {have a reputation}[142] for sound favourable astrological judgements[143] and whose selections [of favourable times to undertake some action] conform with the auspicious movements [of the heavenly bodies]. What they have laid down, old and new, has [proved to] have been sound. **[10b]** They do not leave the noble court because of the sovereign's needs, because of [their] astrological observations on newly-born children and because of [their] selections[144] of the [favourable] movements [of the heavenly bodies]. Even if they were two, three or four, they are [all] indispensable.

Now the bureau[145] is the accountant, the senior comptroller of the accounts [bureau], {also called 'lord of the bureau'}.[146] If he is absent for some good reason, either ill or because of some accident, the supervisor takes his place, taking the leading role [in dealing] with anything new in the way of taxes[147] and any important matters.[148] The accountant is the one upon whom matters turn and [who is] responsible for acting, for raising revenue, for knowing what cultivable lands are irrigated in every district in the various tax categories[149] which are computed, from the date-palm assessment to that of *sābi'ī*.[150] For the accountant is the monarch's deputy, honest [in his dealings] with the treasuries, tight-fisted in apportioning [monies] when salaries[151] are allocated. Correspondence from the governors in all the districts are never cut off from him, nor are the share-cropping agreements[152] of the financial officers[153] and those responsible[154] for district[155] affairs. Any news that comes to him he passes on immediately to his sovereign. The appointment[156] of the district officials is his prerogative so that he can place the accomplished official where he knows he will be employed to best advantage. In every district he appoints an inspector,[157] an overseer, a superintendent, a supervisor, a bookkeeper[158] and an official for what has been paid as salary[159] and deficiencies.[160] [He also appoints] a property official and two [other] officials according to the extent of the [workload] of the district. If there are there common lands[161] and estates of deceased without heirs,[162] he appoints two officials for each task. The inspectors, those involved in finance,[163] may be of the ordinary folk or one of the soldiers assigned for this purpose. His only responsibility is [to carry out the duties of] the office of the inspector[164] in what the secretaries have specified. But the responsibility is on the officials to work on[165] papers, papers concerning dates and the specification of revenue. There must be in each district someone responsible[166] and we shall mention what is his due and his duty.

We begin with the office of the senior inspector, the felicitous office of the inspector of accounts. **[11a]** It is his responsibility to collect[167] what the accountant[168] has specified to him. If the command of the monarch to proceed with the collection of the revenues comes to him, he applies[169] to one of the accountants to proceed with him. The monarch's command may come that he proceed accompanied by two persons, one from each bureau, or the command may come for one specific person, and he will collect what the accountants have specified to him. It is their responsibility and he is ordered to see to[170] the revenues and come up {with the money-bags one by one}.[171] The command may come to him to direct the district inspectors to collect and despatch the returns[172] in one instalment or in several. The assayers[173] go up along with the returns to assay a bag or two of the returns from each district, as is current practice, and return to their own districts. One of the duties of the district inspectors is to undertake the maintenance of the wadi, both land irrigated by running water[174] and that watered by rain,[175] repair of the heads, deflector-bunds,[176] fields,[177] observation posts[178] and water channels[179] and to exert themselves in collecting all revenues, leaving no arrears, but extracting them from the [district] chiefs. He hastens to the districts which require his personal attention to be dealt with quickly or their revenues collected. What is collected is only in the bureau agreed upon {and this is wherever the inspector sees fit.}[180] Not a single dirham is collected without all the stewards[181] being present. If any one of them excuses himself from attending with a clear and evident excuse such as illness or accident, the inspector will oblige him to send his deputy to attend at the collection place. Anyone of them who is tardy he hurries up and makes a note[182] against him because of his being prevented [thus from carrying out his work]. He is responsible for controlling the frontiers and suppressing the error of dissidence in his district. The district chief[183] is subordinate to him and[184] his is the ordering of the appointment of a chief, just as the command of the troops and the garrison are his. He assists the overseer to [promote] what is advantageous for the felicitous bureau and to collect revenues, the crop tax, the monthly tax,[185] the estimated tax[186] and the [tax on the] produce of the granaries.[187] He treats unjustly neither a peasant **[11b]** nor a tax-farmer [paying] monthly and he protects them against all acts of injustice. When the overseer asks for a peasant of the royal crop tax, he does not prevent him [from seeing him], except if [the matter] is unfounded, then he will prevent him. He submits the accounts of the district from the stewards and the land-surveyors[188] on the [agreed] dates, each week[189] according to its date. He sends them to the royal court to the inspector of the felicitous accounts bureau, each month by month, [consisting] of the transactions of what has been paid out and those of the treasury and the closed monthly accounts.[190] [There is] a detailed account by heads of revenue,[191] the basic under the [heading] of the basic, the surplus[192] [of revenue over expenditure] under the [heading] of the surplus and the estimated [revenue] detailed according to its districts. [There is the same procedure for] the finances[193] of the granaries which he carries to the inspector of the felicitous accounts bureau and the inspector hands them over to the accountant. At that time, he gives to each one of the stewards his copy; he gives the inspector his copy and the latter gives it to his deputy to use, whether the inspector is an official or an ordinary person. However, the responsibility remains with the accountants. The treasury copy[194] is submitted to the noble royal court. The supervisor of the accounts bureau is like the superintendent in this part in affairs, experience and trustworthiness in guarding against accidents of fate and the afflictions of tribulation. So when an accident happens to one of the two, the administration of finance[195] will be defined with the other and with the bookkeeper.[196] Payment by instalments[197] is the responsibility of the chief revenue collector,[198] each day by day. When revenue is collected, {the stewards}[199] do not disperse until the inspector has hold of a paper with the total quotient completely ratified by signatures. The quotient is audited. If it is correct as mentioned on the sheet, [all well and good]. If not, the auditor[200] immediately imposes the deficiency [on the person responsible]. The estimated revenue and that of what has been sold are [dealt with] only when the coin[201] and granary officials are present so that the conduct [of business] might be co-ordinated one part with the other, so that none of the stewards might think it a good idea to take money from the bureau revenue without all the stewards being aware. When knowledge of this becomes evident to three persons, the secret becomes public and the [culprits] are disgraced. The inspector attends what is received in the granaries, so that the peasants are not unjustly treated and the act of receiving [taxes] is carried out **[12a]** with the iron on the measure showing. The inspector only leaves when he has in his possession a paper confirmed by signatures concerning what has been received. He treats the peasants in accordance with what the royal rescript[202] written for them each year attests so that their minds might be at rest. He it is who details the land-surveyors. When the accountant's letter on the subject of the detail reaches him, he details anyone indicated by the accountant (the person present being an inspector), adding and reducing, acting as he considers to be in the best interest. He submits invoices,[203] each one properly dated, every week. He gives the district officials their originals to use and sends the accountant copies, as is customary, every eight days. On the completion of the dates of the arrival of the abstracts[204] and the scrutinies of the collation {of the finances[205]},[206] the accountant submits them to the noble court, {they being sent}[207] in a bag by themselves, until such time as it is required to study them. When the surveyors and stewards complete their task and write an abstract in each district of what is in being and what has been removed, the name of a peasant is not written along with the name of a holder of an exemption,[208] nor a man of some eminence,[209] by a soldier, official, shaykh or deputy. He obliges the land-surveyors and measurers[210] when they are carrying out their duties to take only from the peasants the customary fee.[211] If it becomes known that someone has taken more than what is customary, he will be reprimanded, punished[212] and required to return to the peasant what is due to him. Whenever any of the arrears in the district is deducted at the end of the account,[213] the inspector in the district must collect it.[214]

The overseers in the districts and their responsibilities, especially in the crop tax districts

It is the responsibility of the overseer to designate the revenues which are for maintenance expenses, while the collector is present. The distribution is done by the collector in the felicitous bureau. However, not a dirham will be expended except as the overseer designates. The maintenance expenses and [the expenses for] supplies[215] are not paid out without [the authority of] chits ratified by the signatures of the overseer and officials, with the endorsement **[12b]** of the inspector at the top in his own hand. Whatever the overseer requires of the employees of the chest and the granaries, like day-book sheets recording all transactions[216] and invoices[217] each day by day and the account each month by month in accordance with what the memorandum for the inspector testifies, the latter will oblige them to write for him. The inspector does not prevent him from spending in the interests of the bureau and his assigning the maintenance expenses to its proper place in accordance with the authority conferred upon him by his responsibility. What the overseer is unable to collect he transfers[218] to the inspector to collect. When either of them is remiss in collecting it, he must be fined once that [duty] is transferred to him. The principal tax-farmers[219] of the lunar-monthly taxes[220] are his responsibility; the appointment of the witnesses of the land-surveyors are [also] his responsibility. When the accountant indicates to him that he should appoint the land-surveyors and others, he does so, appointing a reliable, honest and experienced person. Whatever order reaches him demanding supplies or [anything from] the provision store, he hastens to issue what is required, calculate[221] it and total[222] it up in as short a time as possible. Whoever writes out an account will be obliged to verify it with all the stewards. {When the accountant of the annual budget[223] draws up the consultation budget[224] at the beginning of the year, he must begin by deducting the revenue of any district. [If][225] there is a deficit in the revenue of this district which has fallen below the basic, be it crop tax or lunar-monthly tax, he does not subtract it, but rather he deducts the revenue, even if he assign it as money retained, though still owed, to make improvements.[226]}[227]

The district tax-farmers[228] and their duties

The tax-farmer must lead the water to its main channels[229] from the heads[230] of the peasants into the terraces[231] and the wadi. No one nearer to the main-stream[232] is irrigated without those further up[233] having enough [water] and he irrigates each plot of land[234] with its share.[235] Whenever he does not follow the regulations, he is reprimanded, fined and dismissed, another being appointed in his place. It is his duty [to acquire] the experience of the peasants with regard to who is trustworthy and who at variance. He informs the inspector in the district the irrigation of which is complete. When the first crop comes, he informs the inspector in the marginal lands,[236] the squatter-cultivators[237] and those who cultivate for a single yearly harvest,[238] so that collection can be made from them before they move off and disperse.[239] If the tax-farmer is able [to ensure] that these people and those like them do not sow and do not come near to the wadi from the start of the [season's] work, he should do so. There is no harm in their sowing on rain-irrigated land[240] and he will not prevent them from tilling entirely.

The third chapter

[13a] On the knowledge of the rules of the tax revenues of the districts of the Yemen in their entirety. This chapter comprises three statements: *the first* on the rules of the revenues of the mountains, this comprising two districts, one called the Uplands. This is, longtitudinally, from east of Ḥaḍramawt to Bilād al-Ṭawīlah and Sharaf Qilḥāḥ in the west, overlooking Tihāmah and al-Maḥālib; latitudinally, from Ḥaql Qatāb in the south, to Bīshah in the north-west[241] and north. [This also includes] the total amount of the tax-farming of its districts with what they contain at present.

List[242] *of the revenue in the first district of the first statement, the Uplands and the total amount of what is in them*

Items Districts	Coin 1,220,000 dinars	Yield of wheat and barley 200,000 dinars	Raisons 5,000 dinars	Cavalry 950 horsemen	Infantry bowmen[243] and swordsmen[244] 7,000
Ṣanʿāʾ region, al-Sirr, al-Raḥabah, Hamdān region, Janb region, Dhayfān region, al-Bawnayn	150,000 dinars	nil	3,000	nil	nil
Radāʿ al-ʿArsh region, Dhamār Asʿad, ʿAns region, B. Ṣirār[245] region, Thawbān, Qāʿifah, al-Ḥadd, Ḥaṣy[246]	3,000,000 dinars	nil	nil	300 horsemen	nil
al-Maghrib al-Ashyam region,[247] Thulā region, ʿAbīdah region	90,000	nil	nil	nil	nil
al-Maghrib al-Ayman region, Kubbah, al-Maʿsaj, Sumāʾah[248]	100,000	nil	nil	nil	nil
al-Ḥizyaz region,[249] B. Sahl, al-Sifl, Wādī al-Ḥār of al-Ḥuqūl	90,000	nil	2,000	nil	nil
Sinḥān region,[250] al-Aʿrūsh region, Ṭiwāl B. Juban, Jabal al-Lawz	60,000	nil	nil	200	1,000
Jabal B. Shihāb, Khawlān region, Ḥaḍūr region[251]	100,000	nil	nil	nil	1000
Jabal Ḥajjah and its territories, al-Sharafayn, Maytak, Ḥimlān, al-ʿAẓīmah, al-Mīqāʿ[252]	80,000	nil	nil	nil	nil
Madhḥij region,[253] Ḥabbān, the tribal regions and adjacent lands	nil	200,000	nil	nil	2,000
Upper and lower al-Jawf	nil	nil	nil	200 horsemen	1,000

Ṣaʿdah region and adjacent lands as far as Bīshah, Najrān and Mārib	250,000	nil	nil	200 horsemen	2,000
What is governed by the fief of the regions of al-Ḥujariyyah and adjacent lands, that being Dānah, Maqmaʿ and al-Ḥāḍinah	nil	nil	nil	150 horsemen	2,000

al-Nijād, Mikhlāf Yafāʿ, al-Maḥraqah, al-Ṣayrāt, Yaʿḥuj, Jushmān, the region of al-Amlūk, the region of Ahl Anʿam, Malaḥ, al-Miqrān[ah], Juban the region of Mufaḍḍal b. Abī Rawāḥ, region and forts, Khallah, Saba' al-Ṣuhayb,[254] Jabal Juḥāf, Jabal Ḥarīr, the region of al-Bawn, al-Jaʿdiyyah region, Mudal, the region of ʿAbdallāh b. Saʿīd al-Kurdī, al-Tanāʿim region, Dathīnah and its territories, al-Tawāliq, al-Ṣīf, al-Hajarayn, Ḥaḍramawt, Khulfāt, Qishn, the highlands of the region of al-Mashāqiṣah on this side of the districts of Ẓafār al-Habūẓī.

[13b] To this I have added the royal fortresses and the total amount of their budget[255] with the revenue of their districts, separately from the revenue mentioned first, while the felicitous immovable properties have an additional budget over and above that of their districts.

The basic revenue in coin[256]	Yield of the felicitous immovable properties
119,279	750
Revenue of the fortresses	Yield of the immovable properties in Ṣanʿā' and Dhamār[257]
coin 11,000	yield 750

Income[258] of the territory of the fortresses

Coin 52,079
The details of this:
Dhamarmar region
21,200
al-Jawf
19,135
Regulation for Darwān[259] and ʿArās region[260]
2,300

Ḥaḍūr al-Shihābiyyah region[261]
3,500
The region of the fortress of Ẓufur al-Jawf
4,944
al-Khārid region
1,000 dinars

Expenditure of the governors, officers[262] and supervisors

7,500 dinars
Expenditure of the governors and officers
4,500
The details of this:

lord of al-Rabʿah	150
lord of Dhahbān[263]	150
lord of al-Kumaym[264]	400
lord of al-Rikz	100
lord of Ḥiṣār	200
lord of Hilāl al-Kumaym	200
officer of Barāqish and al-Zāhir	400
officer of the fortress of Taʿizz Ṣaʿdah	250
officer of the fortress of Birāsh Ṣanʿāʾ	200
lord of the fortress of Taʿizz and Birāsh Ṣaʿdah	1,000 dinars
officer of the fortress of Ẓufur[265]	150
shaykh[266] of al-Bawn	1,000
lord of Darb al-Ḥazm[267]	200

Expenditure of the supervisors
3,000 dinars

supervisor of the fortresses of Darwān, al-Rabʿah, Birāsh[268] and Haddād	200
supervisor of the fortress of al-Kumaym	350
supervisor of the fortress of Dhamarmar	350
supervisor of the fortress of Birāsh Ṣanʿāʾ	150
supervisor of the fortress of Ḥaḍūr and al-Shihābiyyah	250
supervisor of the fortress of Barāqish and al-Zāhir	300
supervisor of the fortress of al-ʿAẓīmah and al-Mīqāʿ	100
supervisor of the fortress of Birāsh and Taʿizz Ṣaʿdah	450
supervisor of al-Manṣūrah	150
supervisor of the fortress of Ẓufur	150

supervisor of the fortresses of Kawkabān, Madaʿ,

Shurayb and al-Qurāniʿ	500	
supervisor of the fortress of Ḥaqīl	50	
in addition	48,800	
Districts		
Ṣaʿdah territories	43,000 dinars	
Revenue collector[269] from the servants of the overseer's office[270] in the fortresses	2,000	
Revenue collector from the districts of the province[271] (the overseer takes it up each year)	4,800	
[14a] The budget assigned to this	114,381	
Expenditure on hostages, servants,[272] construction and billeting[273]	17,624	
What is especially allocated for the stipend of hostages	10,080	
hostage[274] of the lord of Bukur[275]	1,800	
hostage of the lord of Sanad	1,800	
hostage of the lord of al-Ṭawīlah	1,200	
hostage of the lord of al-Kh.ṣ.rī	1,200	
hostage of the lord of Ẓafār	1,200	
hostage of the lord of Thulā	1,800	
hostage of the lord of Shuqāq[276]	360	
hostage of the *mashāyikh* B. Shihāb	360	
hostage of the *mashāyikh* Sinḥān	360	
Stipends of the servants of the felicitous immovable properties	1,344	
the deputy	50 per mensem	
caretaker[277]	10 per mensem	120
the bureau, six men	24 per mensem	288
porter	9 per mensem	108
blacksmith	180 per annum	
irrigation official[278] at Ghayl al-A.l.f	48	

What is expended for billeting for the victorious troops when they go out to collect the revenue of the fortresses etc., by the hand of one of the chiefs

chief's personal stipend[279]	2,000
stipend of the supervisor accompanying him	1,200
building of enclosures[280]	2000
Expenditure of the stipend of the fortresses	96,757 dinars

The details of this:

Dhamarmar fortress and what pertains to it

ten months

per mensem	2,329½
per annum	23,295

addition for the chiefs per mensem	280	
total	23,575	
special stipend of Dhamarmar fortress		
per mensem	1509½	15,095[281]
al-Faṣṣ al-Kabīr fortress[282]		
per mensem	141	1,410
al-Faṣṣ al-Ṣaghīr fortress		
per mensem	50	500
Maṣnaʿat al-Maḥājir fortress		
per mensem	60	600
Riqbān fortress and Bayt Riqbān		
per mensem	188½	1,885
Wadd fortress		
per mensem	215	2,150
Dhahbān fortress		
per mensem	170	1,700
addition for the chiefs in Dhamarmar fortress		
per mensem	...[283]	
governor	150	
officer of the soldiers	40	
officers of the infantry[284]	60	
supervisor	30 [**14b**]	
Barāqish and al-Zāhir fortresses		
per mensem	1,613½	16,135
The details of this:		
Barāqish fortress		
per mensem	888½	8,885
al-Zāhir fortress		
per mensem	725	7,250
Shurayb and al-Qurāniʿ fortresses		
per mensem	600	6,000
Ẓufur fortress		
per mensem	1.236	
eleven months	13,596	
Mudaʿ fortress		
inducement money[285] [allotted] to the region	728	
Ḥaqīl fortress		
per mensem	500	
ten months	5,000	
Kawkabān fortress		
inducement money to the region (when [taxes] are collected		

[from] Jabal Tays and al-Bawāqir, there is a supplement to it)[286]	2,863
Hirrān fortress (it has no region)	
per mensem	160
ten months	1,600
Ashyaḥ fortress[287]	1,500
Ḥaḍūr al-Maṣāniʿ fortress	
additional payment to its region	20,000
al-ʿAẓīmah and al-Mīqāʿ fortresses	
inducement money, additional payment to their region	800
Birāsh and Taʿizz Ṣaʿdah fortresses	20,960 dinars
The details of this:	
Birāsh Ṣaʿdah fortress	11,670
Taʿizz Ṣaʿdah fortress	9,290
Costs from the blessed crop	
total 750 *zakāh* a tenth 75 remainder	675
expended for the chief in accordance with custom	30
specified for lodging[288] - number of men 21 [at] 19	399
income … preserved in one of the fortresses[289]	
coin	359
crop	246

The total sum of its tax-farming of the second district of the first statement of the mountains known as al-Yaman al-Akhḍar may **[15a]** increase and decrease in accordance with the discretion and forbearance [exercised]. It does not occur in anything without embellishing it; good deeds are its brethren, upright dealings its intimate friends, the good angels its supporters and the fortunate its neighbours.

List of the revenue in the second district of the first statement, it being al-Yaman al-Akhḍar

Items / Districts	Coin 948838	Yield 628,800 *bahār*	Honey 500,000 *raṭl*	Red Sugar 120,000 *raṭl*	Male goats 2,000 head
Yaḥṣib territories, B. Sayf region and adjacent areas	15,850	25,000	nil	nil	nil
Tax-farming of Wuṣāb, after sum sufficient for the maintenance[290] of the fortresses	150,000	150,000	40,000 *raṭl*	nil	nil
Uḥāẓah region and adjacent areas and al-Aḥmūd region	28,000	200,000	nil	nil	nil
B. Sarḥah region, B. Nājī region and al-Saḥūl	28,210	20,000	nil	nil	nil

al-Mushayriq region and adjacent areas	25,000	nil	nil	nil	nil
Jabal al-Shawāfī and what pertains to it	25,000	nil	nil	nil	nil
Mikhlāf territories, bureau of Jiblah and ʿAnnah	89,490	nil	nil	70,000	nil
Jabal Baʿdān, al-Shaʿir, Jabal Tabālah and what pertains to it and the districts by it	48,340	85,500	nil	nil	nil
Ṣuhbān region, al-ʿArūsayn region and Zabīd	30,000	nil	nil	nil	250
al-Janad and al-Salif territories	23,100	35,000	nil	nil	400
Mikhlāf Raymah	47,500	nil	nil	nil	nil

[15b] *Continuation of the list of the second district of the first statement. known as al-Yaman al-Akhḍar*

Items Districts	Coin	Yield	Honey	Red Sugar	Male goats
Region of al-ʿAnsiyyīn[291] of Miʿshār al-Taʿkar the protected	2,550	nil	nil	nil	nil
al-Qufāʿah and Sharʿab[292]	26,070	nil	nil	nil	nil
Mikhlāf Baḥrānah,[293] al-Thawābī[294] and al-Z.r.tayn[?] up to Miʿshār al-Taʿkar the protected	19,300	nil	nil	nil	nil
Mikhlāf Shayyibah	8,500	nil	nil	nil	nil
Taʿizz territories and Dhakhir	85,750	20,200	nil	nil	nil
Region of Khawlān B. al-Biʿm[295]	4,500	20,200	nil	nil	nil
Jaba', Ḥaṣab and Sawā territories[296]	71,837	20,200	nil	nil	250
al-Samadān territories[297]	21,740	nil	nil	nil	nil
al-Mafālīs territories	14,615	2,800	500 *raṭl*	nil	200
Jabal al-Rakb	14,272	nil	nil	nil	150
al-Dumluwah territories and Sāmiʿ	24,500	nil	nil	nil	nil
Dhubḥān territories	27,800	nil	nil	nil	nil

[16a] *Completion of the list of the second district of the first statement in al-Yaman al-Akhḍar*

al-Ḥawjiyyah territories	20,000	nil	nil	nil	200
al-Burqah territories	8,800	nil	nil	nil	200
al-Sārah territories and Nakhlah	25,000	nil	nil	50,000	nil
B.ṭ.ḥ.wāt territories	7,000	nil	nil	nil	150
Khadīrayn territories[298]	25,000	nil	5,000	nil	500
Jabal al- Ṭawr, i.e. Ṣabir the protected	22,000	nil	nil	nil	nil

The second statement on the knowledge of the rules of the revenues of the Tihāmahs and those districts and fief districts which resemble and are similar to them. This is in the form of a table on the next page.[299] According to the [state of] cultivation,[300] they may increase or decease.[301] In God lies success.

[16b] *List of the second statement on the rules of the revenues of the Tihāmahs*

Items Districts	Coin 3,290,000	Lunar-monthly 393,200	Crop tax 2,650,40 0	Date palms 20,000
Lahej territories	220,000	10,000	190,000	20,000
Abyan territories	100,000	5,000	95,000	nil
Mawzaʿ territories	125,000	12,000	32,600	80,4000
Ḥays territories to which are joined al-ʿAbsiyyatayn and al-Ṣulayy	120,000	30,000	83,000	7,000
Ḥuṣayb territories, Zabīd the protected and al-Ḥāzzatayn	940,000	122,000	700,000	11,800
Rimaʿ territories	100,000	15,000	125,000	nil
Dhu'āl territories, in accordance with the rule by fief, al-Mudabbī, not held as a fief,[302] being joined to them	135,000	5,000	125,000	Nakhl al-Mudabbī to the flourishing treasury 15,000 dinars
Sihām territories to which is adjoined al-Ghānimiyyah	350,000	23,000	327,000	nil
Qaḥrah territories in accordance with the fief rule	100,000	6,200	93,800	nil
Surdud and al- Muqaṣṣiriyyah territories	325,000	85,000	240,000	nil
Mawr and al-Qahabah territories	575,000	65,000	510,000	nil
Raḥbān territories in accordance with the fief rule	200.000	15,000	185,000	nil

[17a] al-Mikhlāf al-Sulaymānī, Jāzān, al-Nujaymiyyah, al-Ḥubb, al-Rāḥah, al-Habīrah, al-Lu'lu'ah with the Ḥasanī sharifs in accordance with the rule of exemption from taxes[303] and fief. They are due to pay each year a contribution of horses, 50 head, and coats of mail, thirty Ḥasanī coats of mail. When they are required for service, they come at once to where they are asked [to go].

The third statement on knowledge of the rules of the revenues of the ports and places of entry and those who are concerned with them and their taxes. The first of the ports is that of Ẓafār al-Ḥabūḍī and the last that of Jeddah on the coast of Mecca the honoured, as in the following table:

List of the third statement on the rules of the port revenues

Items Districts	Coin 2,360,500	Kinds of gifts
Port of Ẓafār al-Ḥabūḍī	420,000	mantles,[304] veils,[305] silk waist-wrappers,[306] anklets, bracelets and gold rings set with gems,[307] musk, ambergris, perfume[308] and Indian singing girls[309]
Port of al-Shiḥr the protected	200,000	ambergris, camphor, pearls, Indian dancing girls,[310] wild civet cats
Port of Sunbulah of the place of entry Aden the protected	1,470,000	aloes, ambergris, camphor, musk, civet; from all the other choice rarities of India and Iraq; servants and the pearl-fishery
Port of al-Buqʿah, belonging to Zabīd the protected	50,000	slaves, slave girls, Abyssinian black slaves,[311] and of all that comes from the sea in the way of choice rarities and the pearl-fishery
Northern ports	50,000	the pearl-fishery at Qunfidah on a two-year basis,[312] of the choice rarities which the pilgrims bring and the tax[313] of Mecca the honoured, Almighty God honour her.
Port of Dahlak	20,000	thoroughbred or mediocre quality horses,[314] all choice rarities, wild animals and Nubian slaves.
ʿĀzib,[315] the port of Ḥaly	12,500	of half-breed female slaves, Masʿūdī and Ḥaly camels and Masʿūdī honey
Jeddah, the port of Mecca the honoured	100,000 after the sum for the maintenance of the sharifs and commanders	thoroughbred mares and riding she-camels

[17b] *Account of the agreed taxes*[316] *of the felicitous Yemeni ports, God perpetuate the rule of their ruler*

The blessed tithes[317] in the customs house[318] of al-Shiḥr the preserved, God perpetuate the rule of its ruler.

Cloth[319] on everything valued at 100 dinars is charged 72/3.

A corge[320] of baskets 3/4.

Lighterage[321] 1/2.

Per cloth,[322] on every three corges cloth according to the value 5/12.[323]

Assaying on every 100 1 dinar.

Pepper is [taxed] by the price; what is valued at 100 dinars 1 dinar; the cost of weighing a *bahār*[324] 3 1/4;[325] assaying [each] 100 a dinar and on each person a *raṭl* [in kind of pepper].[326]

Indigo is [taxed] by the price; also what is valued at 100 72/3; the cost of weighing a bottle[327] 3 1/4 and on each bottle a *raṭl* [in kind]; assaying each 100 a dinar.

The remaining commodities such as turmeric[328] and coir,[329] the weighing of a *bahār* 2 1/4 dinars; the *bahār* 3 3/4.[330]

The rest of the districts — the eastern ports:[331] Ẓafār, Hurmūz and Qalhāt, Aden, Aḥwar, al-ʿAyn al-Ghurābī[332] — in the case of everything valued at 100 dinars 72/3.

Costus,[333] the piece 4.

Civet, on the ounce[334] 1/12 + 1/3.

Slaves from Aden and its environs, per head two and a half dinars.

Merchant ships[335] of Mogadishu — slaves per head 2 1/2.

Ghee and oil, a *bahār* 3 1/4 1/8.

The remainder the wares[336] are like the first.

Arriving by land, according to what the loads[337] bring:

dates in bulk,[338] 1/3 + 1/4.[339]

Bukr sorghum,[340] 1/2.

If [a commodity] belongs to the poor and those exempted from [certain] taxes,[341] it is weighed and the individual has to pay:

a dirham on dates;

a dinar on a load of grain;[342]

two dinars on a load of wheat;

4 on a sack of wheat;[343]

two dinars on a load of raisins;

six *raṭl* of iron on a *bahār* of iron;[344]

a fifth on henna;[345]
two dinars and a skin[346] of aloe[347] on a load of aloe;
a fifth on the doum palm;[348]
a fifth on St John's wort;[349]
a fifth on grapes;
a dirham on every three goat-wool strips;[350]
two dinars and two *zubdī*[351] [in kind] on a load of fenugreek;[352]
two dinars on a load of garlic;[353]
two dinars and two *zubdī* [in kind] on dates in fruit form;[354]
two dinars on a load of Shiḥrī[355] olibanum;[356]
1/2 on a load of fish[357] when the fish[358] arrives by land;
a dirham on shark;[359]
two dinars on a load of cloth when it comes via al-Raydah and Ẓafār;
when it comes from Ḥaḍramawt and Dawʿān the same;
a dinar on a load of *busr* dates, i.e. ripe dates.[360]

[18a] The Tax[361] of the blessed tithes at the customs house of the place of entry, Aden the protected - God prolong the rule of her ruler. On all the commodities arriving from India, Iraq, Syria, Egypt, the West and other provinces, Abyssinia and all the land of the Blacks.

Cathay[362] cloths, woven fabric,[363] *d.w.n.j*[364] and cloth interwoven with gold:[365]
a single cloth, 12 cubits[366] in length is charged 7 1/4 1/48; ten 72 1/3 1/4 1/3; hundred 726 1/24.
A woven fabric which contains much gold is tithed [as if it were] plain[367] and the *d.w. n.j* is the same.
Brocade[368] and Turkish cloths: a single cloth, 12 cubits in length, 3 1/3 1/12 1/48; ten 31 1/24; hundred 310 1/4 1/6.
Silk and cotton[369] cloth: a single cloth 1/3 1/4 1/96; ten 5 1/8 1/48; hundred 59 1/4 1/8.
Tabby,[370] *mashāyikhī*, single colour[371] and pearl-coloured[372] cloths, the length of the cloth being 12 cubits: one 1 1/4 1/8; ten 12 3/4 1/8; hundred 128 3/4.
Aden silk cloths,[373] the length of a single cloth being 16 cubits in length: one 2 1/3 1/4 1/8; ten 12 1/3 [?] 1/4; hundred 128 3/4 [?].
Chinese silk cloths, the length of the cloth being 20 cubits: one 1 1/3 1/8; ten 12 1/3 1/8; hundred 125 1/2 1/3.
When the examiner[374] notes down[375] [what] pieces are left over,[376] of a cubit, two and

three, each cubit is a *qīrāṭ*[377] of cloth, i.e. he reckons[378] it to be at a twenty-fourth up to three pieces of cloth and more than that he reckons at ten [*qīrāṭ*].[379]

Satin[380] cloths, the length of the cloth being 18 cubits: one 2 1/2 1/3 1/8 1/96; ten 29 2/3 1/48; hundred 296 3/4 1/8.

Goan[381] cloths, the length of cloth being twenty cubits: one 1 1/8 1/12; ten 12 1/14; hundred 120 1/2 1/3.

Chinese linen[382] cloths, the length of the cloth being 24 cubits: ten 7 1/4 3/96; hundred 72 2/3 1/8 1/48.

Shirazi cloths (it is said that they are muslins[383]), the length of the cloth being 36 cubits: one 1/4 1/6 1/8 3/96; ten 5 1/3 1/4 1/8 1/48; hundred 57 1/6 1/8.

Yazdi cloths: one 1/2 1/8 1/96; ten 6 1/3 1/48; hundred 63 1/4 1/6 1/8.

Tawrizi[384] cloths: one 1/3 1/48; ten 3 1/3 1/48[?]; hundred 35 1/4 1/6.

Silk mantles, silk nut-coloured cloths,[385] silk *subā'iyyah*s,[386] silk cloaks,[387] silk pieces,[388] they being halves, and silk striped cloths:[389] one is charged a dinar 1/4 1/8 3/96; ten 14 1/24 1/48; hundred 140 1/2 1/8.

Mantles of mixed stuff, *subā'iyyah*s of mixed stuff with a selvage:[390] one 1 1/8 1/48; ten 11 1/3 1/8; hundred 114 1/3 1/4.

Cotton mantles and cotton *subā'iyyah*s: one 1/4 1/12 1/96; ten 3 1/4 1/6 1/48; hundred 34 1/4 1/8.

Pieces of mixed stuff: one is charged 1/3 1/4 1/8; ten 7 1/16; hundred 70 1/4 1/3.

Silk head-coverings[391] and linen with a selvage: one is charged 1/6 1/8 3/96; ten 3 1/8 1/12 1/48; hundred 32 1/6 1/8.

[18b] Silk headdresses,[392] those with a selvage and plain and the borders:[393] ten 1 1/2 1/3; hundred 1 1/3; *bahār* 55.

[Cloth] interwoven with gold and embroidered are double: ten 2 2/3; cotton is at half: ten 7/8.

High-quality Baghdadi white silk stuff:[394] ten 7 3/4 1/8; hundred 78 3/4; *bahār* 236 1/4.

Mosul white silk robes: ten 5 1/2 1/8 1/48; hundred 56 1/3 1/8; *bahār* 169 1/4 1/8.

Muslin material,[395] muslin cloths and Nahrawali material: ten 7 3/4; hundred 77 1/2; *bahār* 232 1/2. The length of [this] material is twenty-four cubits; the length of the cloth is thirty and forty cubits.

Muslin cloths, muslin napkins and Gogalah stuff,[396] the length of the turban-sash[397] being 16 and 18 [cubits]: ten 2 1/48; hundred 20 1/8 1/12.

Artī cloths,[398] white cloths,[399] muslin, red cotton cloths,[400] half- and all-silk turbans[401] with a selvage, cotton half- and all-silk turbans and Gogalah stuff: ten 6 1/3 1/8; hundred 62 1/24; *bahār* 18 1/4; ten *bahār* 1862[?] 1/2.

All-silk turbans are double and the cotton cloths with a selvage: ten 12 1/2 1/6.
Cotton cloths interwoven with gold and white cloths, the length of the cloth being 22 cubits and the half 11, half- and all-silk turbans with a selvage: ten 2 11/12; hundred 29 1/6; *bahār* 87 1/2.
Cotton turbans:[402] ten 1 1/3 1/8; hundred 14 1/3 1/4; *bahār* 43 3/4.
Shīl cotton cloths,[403] the red variety, the bleached and the unbleached:[404] ten 3 1/12 1/48; hundred 31 1/24; *bahār* 93; thousand 310 1/4 1/6.
Silk, [stuff] interwoven with gold and with a selvage are double, the length being 12 cubits.
Nut-coloured pieces, which are cotton *subā'iyyah*s: one 1/4 1/6; ten 4 1/4; hundred 41 2/3; *bahār* 125.
Towels,[405] the cotton variety with a selvage and the unbleached cotton: ten 4 1/8; hundred 41 1/4; *bahār* 123 3/4.
Silk towels are double: ten 8 1/4.
Short garments,[406] i.e woollen cloths: one 1/4 1/6; ten 4 1/6; hundred 41 2/3; *bahār* 125.
High quality pieces of cloth:[407] ten 3 1/2 1/48; hundred 31 1/6 1/8.
Red velvets:[408] ten 7 1/2 1/8 1/48; hundred 76 1/4 1/6 1/8 1/48; *bahār* 229 2/3 1/8.
White velvets: ten 6 3/4; hundred 67 1/2; *bahār* 22 1/2.
Coloured robes: one 2/3 1/8 1/96; ten 8 1/48; hundred 8 1/8 1/12; *bahār* 24 1/2 1/8.
[19a] Covers,[409] i.e. red woollen strips[410] etc.: ten 3 3/96; hundred 30 1/6 1/8 1/48; *bahār* 90 7/8 1/48.
Red carpets,[411] resembling cloaks: ten 1 1/3 1/4 1/8 1/48; hundred 17 1/6 1/8. Silk is double.
Carpets from Tabaristan: ten 1 1/6 1/8 1/48; hundred 13 1/8; *bahār* 39 1/4 1/8; corge 2 1/2 1/8.
Red pillows from India and the eastern ports: ten 1/2 1/8 1/48; hundred 6 1/3 1/8; *bahār* 19 1/4 1/8.
Veils,[412] coloured and silk and with a selvage: ten 5 1/3 1/4 [?]; hundred 57 1/12; *bahār* 171 1/4; corge 11 1/4 1/6.
Veils woven with gold: one, when it is by itself, a dinar; when there is a number together, [but dealt with] as a single, 1/2 1/48; ten 11 1/24.[413]
White linen veils: ten 4 2/3 3/96; hundred 46 1/2 1/3 1/8 1/48.
Head ropes, coloured and white: ten 1 1/4 1/6 1/48; hundred 14 1/4 1/8; silk is double.
Red and silver bed covers,[414] *maṣāḥifī*, from Broach and Bengal:[415] ten 2 1/3 1/4 1/48; hundred 36 1/24; *bahār* 108 1/8; corge 7 1/8 1/12.
Bed covers of indigo dyed cloth:[416] corge 4 1/96; hundred 20 1/24 1/96; *bahār* 60 1/8

3/96.

Bleached cloth: ten 2 3/96; hundred 20 1/6 1/8 1/48; *bahār* 60 7/8 1/48.

Unbleached cloth of indigo dye: ten 1 1/4 1/6 1/8 3/96; hundred 15 1/8 1/48; *bahār* 47 1/6 1/48.

'Ushārī cloth:[417] one 1/6 1/96; ten 1 3/4 1/48; hundred 17 1/3 1/4 1/8; *bahār* 53 1/8; Batuli,[418] three corges 10 1/6 1/8.

Striped cotton cloaks,[419] unbleached and bleached: ten 3 1/4 1/96; hundred 32 1/3 1/4 1/48; corge 6 1/2 1/48; silk is double.

Shāwirī[420] striped cloaks: one 1 1/6 1/8 3/96; ten 13 1/8 1/12 1/48; hundred 132 1/6 1/8; *bahār* 396 3/4 1/8; corge 26 1/6 1/8.

Cotton turbans:[421] ten 1 1/8 1/12 1/48; hundred 12 1/6 1/8; *bahār* 3 3/4 1/8; corge 2 1/3 1/8; the length of the turban is 14 cubits and it is not very wide.

Linen turbans from India: ten 3 1/4; hundred 32 1/2; {and with a selvage and the cotton turban up to four turbans, no more}.[422]

[19b] Cotton napkins;[423] a single napkin when it is by itself, up to five napkins, 1/24 1/48; ten 1/3 1/4 3/96; hundred 6 1/8 1/48; *bahār* [?] 1/48 1/6; corge 1/8 1/12 1/48 [?];[424] the linen variety and that with a selvage are double.

Silk waistwrappers[425] and silk strips, with a selvage and plain: ten 5 1/2 1/3 1/96; hundred 58 1/4 1/6 1/48; *bahār* 175 1/6 1/8 1/48; that interwoven with gold and embroidered is double; cotton and strips are half.

Waistwrappers, of mixed stuff and with a selvage, and linen with a selvage: ten 3 1/2 1/8; hundred 36 1/4; *bahār* 108 3/4; corge 7 1/4.

Linen waistwrappers: ten 2 1/4 1/6 1/8 1/48; hundred 25 1/2 1/8; *bahār* 76 3/4 1/8; corge 5 1/8.

Linen Quilon[426] waistwrappers and Maʿbarī,[427] a corge, which is sixty waistwrappers, is charged 8 2/3 1/8; *bahār* 43 1/4 1/6 1/8; waistwrappers up to 13, no more: one 1/6 1/8 1/48 1/96.

High quality *subā'ī* waistwrappers, the silver variety and the Broach: corge (being forty waistwrappers) 4 3/4 1/8 1/96; one, when it is by itself, and the work [required] on it,[428] is charged 1/8.

Medium quality *subā'ī* waistwrappers and the work on them: corge (being forty waistwrappers) 40.

Waistwrappers with borders[429] and the work on them: corge (being forty waistwrappers) 3 1/8.

Red waistwrappers of high quality and the work on them: corge (being sixty waistwrappers) 5 1/6 1/96; *bahār* 25 3/4 1/8 1/60.[430]

Small red waistwrappers and the work on them: corge (being a hundred waistwrappers) 3 3/4 1/8 1/96; *bahār* 11 1/2 1/8 3/96.[431]
Small silver waistwrappers with borders: corge (being sixty waistwrappers) 3 1/4 1/6 1/8 1/96; hundred 5 3/4 1/8 1/96; *bihār* 17 1/2 1/8 3/96 and the work on them.
Medium quality waistwrappers: corge (being sixty waistwrappers) 4 1/8; ten 2/3 1/48; hundred 6 3/4 1/8.
Broach waistwrappers with borders: corge (being sixty waistwrappers) 3 1/4 1/6 1/8 1/96; hundred 5 7/8 1/96; *bahār* 17 3/4 1/96.
Silver waistwrappers with borders: corge (being sixty waistwrappers) 3 7/8 1/96; *bahār* 19 1/2 1/8 1/96 and the work on them.
Iraqi and Baghdadi paper:[432] bundle[433] (being twenty quires[434]) 1 2/3 1/8 1/48; hundred 9 1/24 1/48; *bahār* 27 1/6 1/48.
Kutch,[435] Chinese and Bangali paper (coming entirely from India): bundle (being twenty quires) 1 1/6 1/96; hundred 5 3/4 1/96; *bahār* 17 1/2 1/6 3/96.
Aloe,[436]…[437] and excellent quality: ten *mann*[438] 29 1/2 1/8 (?) 1/48; hundred 296 1/3 1/8; *bahār* 889 1/4 1/8.
Agalloch:[439] in respect of all odoriferous woods, in respect of a *mann* four dirhams, the *mann* in the case of all odoriferous woods being 26 dirhams; a *mann* of agalloch is 30. An example of this is when the examiner at the customs house notes down excellent quality odoriferous woods, …[440] five *mann* is multiplied by four dirhams [and] the tax taken[441] is 20 dirhams. **[20a]** 5 *mann* of agalloch 4 1/2 1/3 1/48; 10 *mann* of agalloch 33 2/3 1/8;[442] 15 *mann* agalloch 43 3/4 1/96.[443] The *qīrāṭ*[444] of a *mann* is 260 dirhams. The multiples of the *mann*: *qīrāṭ* 10 1/2 1/3; half *qīrāṭ* 5 1/4 1/6; quarter *qīrāṭ* 2 1/3 1/8. When it is a single *mann*,[445] no more, its tithes are 3 1/2 3/96.
Qaqula aloe[446] of excellent quality: ten *mann* 37 1/2 3/96; of excellent quality and middle grade: ten *mann* 25 1/2 1/8 1/96.
Conclusion of the aloe *mann* and the *mann* with its aloe: 25; any aloeswood in excess of a *mann*: 2 1/2 1/3 1/8 3/96; aloe of medium quality: ten *mann* 21 1/3 1/4 3/96. Conclusion of the aloe *mann*, the *mann* with its aloe and the work on it: 2 1/4 1/6 1/8.
Solid,[447] strung pearls, from all districts, charged at an eighth of the price.
Ambergris: every eight *mithqāl*[448] 1/4 1/6 1/8 1/96; *bahār* (i.e. 300 *mithqāl*) 20 1/6 1/4 1/8; it does not change,[449] but on each *mithqāl* 1/24 3/96. If it arrives by sea from the eastern ports, the weight of the *raṭl* in the tithes at the customs house is 91 *mithqāl* and the weight of the *raṭl* in any purchase at the customs house is 88 1/6 3/96 *mithqāl*. [In any] sale it is ten *mithqāl* and …[450] The weight of the *raṭl* in trading at the [present] time is 84 *mithqāl*.

Musk: in its vesicles; there is a reduction in it of a third, [i.e. the] vesicles, two thirds remaining [to be charged]. The [full] tithe is taken on musk which is not in a vesicle.[451] Empty vesicles are part of the reduction of the musk [when it is] in its vesicles and of its tithe is the *mann* (it being 182 *qaflah*[452]), 2 3/4 1/8 1/96 dinars. The *qīrāṭ* in what is taxed is 7 1/3 1/4 1/4 1/2[453] 5 2/3 1/48 1/2[454] 3 2/3 1/8 1/4[455] 1 3/4 1/8 1/48. Musk not in a vesicle: one *mithqāl* 1/8 1/12 1/48; ten 2 1/6 1/8; hundred 22 11/12; *bahār* 98 3/4; thousand *mithqāl* 229 1/6.

Agalloch: on every hundred *mithqāl* two *mithqāl*. Agalloch in cash 5 dinars. The ten *mithqāl* in agalloch, if they are not bagged 3 1/4. This is the practice up to four *mithqāl* and above that figure, agalloch is taken on it [in kind].

[20b] Pure camphor: one *mann* (it being 182 *mithqāl*, 260 *qaflah*) 16 2/3 1/8. *Mann* of liquid [camphor][456] 193; with the liquid in it, when it is by itself 18 1/4 1/48; *mithqāl* 1/2 1/48; two *mithqāl* 1/8 1/12; three *mithqāl* 1/6 1/8 1/96. Anything less than a *mann* is only subject to the tithe because of this established practice. Qaysuri[457] camphor: one *mann* 11 1/2 1/3; liquid among all the camphors, on the *mann* two dirhams. Anything less than a *mann* is subject to the tithe. *Mann* of liquid 20 1/48; *mann* with the liquid it contains 12 1/24 1/48. Chinese camphor: one *mann* 2 1/2 1/8; ten 26 1/4; *mann* of liquid 12; *mann* with the liquid it contains 2 1/8 1/48. Camphor water: ten *mann* 2 1/24 1/48.

Silk:[458] ten *mann* 14 3/96; hundred 140 1/6 1/8 1/48; *bahār* 420 11/12 1/48.

Cleaned cloves:[459] ten *mann* 14 1/2 1/8; hundred 145 1/8 1/12.

Nutmeg:[460] ten *mann* 8 1/4 1/8 1/48. Nowadays a third is taken in tax on it.

Mace:[461] ten *mann* 10 1/6 1/8 1/96.

Saffron:[462] one *mann* 2 1/24 1/48.

Greater celandine:[463] ten *mann* 4 1/8.

Chinese rhubarb:[464] ten *mann* 10 1/2 1/96; hundred 105 1/12 1/48. Different proportions[465] are taken on it [in kind] in accordance with the instruction[466] of the late sultan, al-Malik al-Mu'ayyad Dā'ud,[467] when ʿIzz al-Dīn al-Ḥalabī arrived from Quilon in the year 701/1301–2.

Macassar sandal wood:[468] ten *mann* 3 1/4 1/6 1/8 1/48.

Galingale:[469] ten *mann* 3 1/4 1/8.

High quality rosewater:[470] ten *mann* 1 1/4 1/8 1/96.

Good quality nacre:[471] ten *mann* 3 1/4 1/48.

Medium quality nacre: ten *mann* 2 1/4 1/6 1/8.

Poor quality[472] nacre, it being light: ten *mann* 2 1/2 1/3 1/48.

Nacre, the best of medium quality: 2 3/4 1/8 3/96.

Chinese bamboo:[473] thousand canes 3 1/3 1/4 1/48. The large ones are not charged tithes.

Spear shafts:[474] thousand 13 1/3 1/8.

Coconuts:[475] thousand 13/4 1/8.

Areca nut,[476] dry with no husk: hundred [to] a thousand[477] 12 1/4 1/6 1/96; a thousand to fourteen thousand …[478]

Red and multi-coloured carnelian:[479] *bahār* 36 1/3 1/4.

[21a] Aleppan glass: charged on a hundred 5 1/6 1/8.

Small beads:[480] ten thousand 4 1/8 1/12 3/96; *bahār* when they are single[481] 5 1/2. Large beads, those with red in them, up to a thousand 3 1/8; ten thousand 4 1/4 1/6 1/8 1/48.

Myrobalan-coloured[482] and brownish-black beads:[483] thousand 1/3 1/8 1/96; ten thousand 1/2[484] 1/8. Large beads: large chest,[485] the type with engraving: ten thousand 1/4 1/6 1/8 1/96. [Coming] from the eastern ports, they are tithed thus. They were tithed in the name of Faqīh ʿAlam [al-Dīn] F.n.d Maʿāzib[ī] with a number[486] [of others] arriving [487] from Zaylaʿ in the month of Jumādā I[488] year 752:[489] chest 1/4 1/6 1/8 1/96. But when it is in large quantities, it is tithed on the basis of a half.[490] An additional tithe is made on it and this practice is followed with it in both small and large quantities.

Iron: the tax taken on it is the fifth of the price, except for mace pins,[491] stirrups[492] and anchors[493] on which there are no tithes.

Steel,[494] of the M.h.r.m.lī,[495] Sirūhī,[496] Ṣaʿdī and Chinese varieties: all iron has a fifth charged on it. Tithes are shared [by farming][497] from all districts.

Timber, raw teak[498] like planks, steel-coloured,[499] …,[500] …[501] teak: …[502] is …[503] on which tithes are paid, a quarter of the price from all districts. Stones, all timbers except teak and … are released with no tithes on them.

Leopard skins: ten 4 1/2 3/96.

Cambay sandals[504] (when they are without the strap) from India: corge (being ten) 1/12 1/96 dinar.

Wheat, rice, sesame and chick peas: *mudd*[505] (being sixty measures[506]) 2 3/4.

Rice from Mangalore, Faknur, Hili and the Malabar area is not charged tithes.[507] When Bakār[508] rice arrives from the [tax] districts, it is tithed. This was charged tithe in the year 736[509] in the sailing vessel[510] of Nākhudhā Ḥasan al-Hūrī from Mangalore, when Bakār [rice] arrived among what the stewards found at the customs house at the afore-mentioned date. [This was] in the tax [imposed] by Qāḍī Badr al-Dīn Ḥasan Saʿīd b. Ḥasan when he was overseer. Rice weighed in stones[511] was tithed in the year 727[512] in the vessel of Amir Sharaf al-Dīn Qāsim al-Daybūlī in full and completely. This was also tithed in the year 736[513] {in the vessel of Amir}[514] Nāṣir al-Dīn Sharīf Mūsā b. Ḥusayn {arriving}[515] from Kilwa in the stewardship of Qāḍī Badr al-Dīn

Ḥasan Saʿīd b. Ḥasan, the district overseer.

Sorghum (measured in *mudd*,[516] it being sixty measures): charged 1 1/2 1/8 2/60.[517] When it is pounded,[518] it is charged at 1 1/2 dinars a *mudd*.**[21b]** An additional tax on it is the commission[519] and the galley tax.[520]

The tithe on grain coming from India consisting of sorghum - and what comes from Barwah,[521] Diu, Furmiyan, …, …, Dunbas, al-ʿ.r.sh, Daybul, Chitor, Kathiwa, Chaul, Mahwah, Mangalore, Surat, …, al-Sūqiyān, Sāmḥūḥ,[522] and all the districts of Gujerat — the tithes of all specified commodities, *'ushārī*, calico cloth,[523] cloaks, are charged according to custom. Calico cloth is what follows:

'Ushārī cloth: one cloth 1/8 1/12 1/96; corge 4 1/3 1/8; hundred …[524]

Butali[525] calico cloth: corge 3 1/3 1/48; hundred 30 1/4 1/6 1/8.

Cotton cloaks: ten 3 1/3 1/8 3/96 and the work on it. Silk [cloaks] from these districts are double: 6 1/2 1/3 1/8 1/48.

Delhi calico: corge 3 1/3 1/48. Dunbasi calico: corge 3 3/4 1/48.

Chinaware,[526] Cantonese[527] and Bakār:

Cantonese platters,[528] large drinking bowls[529] and plates:[530] one 1/4 1/12 3/96; ten 2 1/6 1/8; hundred …[531] 1/2 1/4 1/8;[532]

Cantonese half-size vessels[533] and full-size[534] plates: 1.

Cantonese third-size vessels:[535] ten 1/4 1/6 1/8 1/48.

Cantonese quarter-size vessels[536] and full-size drinking bowls: ten 1/2.

Cantonese bowls[537] and small drinking bowls: ten 1/6 3/96.

Bakār platters: ten 1 1/4 1/6 1/48.[538]

Bakār half-size vessels and plates: ten 1/2 1/8 1/48.

Bakār bowls, large and small drinking bowls: ten 1/2 1/3 1/48.[539]

What commodities are found in *bahār* from India and elsewhere are as follows (the commission and galley tax are added on certain designated [items]):

Chinese cubeb:[540] *bahār* 17[541] 1/8 1/12.

Indigo:[542] *bahār* 18 1/4 1/8 1/96.[543]

Crude borax:[544] *bahār* 16 1/8 3/96.

Sugar of bamboo:[545] *bahār* 14 1/3 1/4 1/8 3/96.

Chebulic myrobalan:[546] *bahār* 13 1/4 1/6 1/8.

Spikenard:[547] *bahār* 11 1/4 1/6 1/48.

Asafoetida resin:[548] *bahār* 10 1/8 1/12 3/96.

Pepper: *bahār* 9 1/8 1/12.

[22a] Long pepper:[549] *bahār* 8 1/4 1/48.

Lycium,[550] also called *khawlān*:[551] *farāsilah*[552] 4 1/4 1/8 1/96.

Bakār cubeb: *bahār* 3 7/8.

Ginger:[553] *bahār* 6 1/24 1/48.

Ginger from the [various] districts of the Yemen: *bahār* 5 1/4 1/6 1/8.

Cultivated[554] ginger: *bahār* 5 1/6 1/8.

Perfume:[555] *bahār* 5 1/8 1/48.

Oil-coloured[556] asafoetida: *bahār* 7 3/4.

Yellow and white[557] asafoetida and beleric myrobalan:[558] *bahār* 5 1/4 1/12 1/96.

Orache:[559] *bahār* 5 1/4 1/48.

Turmeric: *bahār* 2 2/3 1/8 1/48.

Khuri sandalwood, Zanji and Khuri: 1/3 1/4 1/48.

Malabar Bakār canella:[560] *bahār* 3 1/3 1/4 3/96.

Sili canella: *bahār* 2 1/2 1/3 1/8.[561]

Liquorice:[562] *bahār* 1 7/8.

Tamarind:[563] *bahār* 1 1/12 1/48.[564]

Purging cassia:[565] 1 1/2 1/8 1/48.

Hypericum:[566] *bahār* 2 1/4 1/6 1/8.

In the time of our lord, al-Malik al-Mu'ayyad[567] — Almighty God's mercy be upon him — there was a [system of] sharing [by farming] by half.[568] His instruction was issued to the [government] bureau for anyone taxed on the *bahār* 40 dinars, if he did not share. This practice pertained to all districts.

Sinbād:[569] every two thirds/thirty *raṭl* 1/6 2/60; *bahār* 1 1/2 1/3 1/8 1/48.

Indian cumin:[570] *bahār* 2 3/4 1/48.

Qaqula cardamom:[571] *bahār* 8 1/4 1/6 1/48.

Mildewy[572] cardamom from the Coromandel coast:[573] *bahār* 5 1/4 1/6.

East African[574] sandarac:[575] *bahār* 5 2/3.

Ceylonese[576] sandarac: *bahār* 1 1/3 1/4 1/8 3/96.

Cowries[577] (i.e. seashells[578]): *bahār* 6 1/48.[579]

Coconut fibres: *bahār* 2 1/4 1/6 1/96.

Sacks:[580] *bahār* 1 1/2.

Cyperus:[581] *bahār* 1 1/2 1/3 1/8 1/48.

Isfahan antimony:[582] *bahār* 8 1/3 1/8 1/48.

Antimony:[583] *bahār* 3 2/3 1/8 3/96.

Red yarn[584] and [from] Coromandel: *bahār* 33 1/6 1/96.

White yarn: *bahār* 8 1/6.

Costus: *bahār* 6 1/2 1/8.

Tutty:[585] *bahār* 5 1/3 1/4 1/8.

Ammoniacum:[586] *bahār* 2 2/3 1/8 1/48.

Turpeth:[587] *bahār* 6 1/2.

Juice:[588] *bahār* 1 1/24.

Oil[589] and ghee:[590] *bahār* 3 1/2 1/8.

Pewter:[591] *bahār* 1/4 1/48.

Black lead:[592] *bahār* 2 1/4 1/6 1/8 1/48.

Honey:[593] *bahār* 3 1/2 1/3 1/48.

…[594] brass: *bahār* 5 1/6.

Wax:[595] *bahār* 7 1/3 1/4.

Bark of the mahaleb cherry:[596] *bahār* 3 3/4.

Cleaned[597] mahaleb cherry: *bahār* 9 1/24 1/96.

Tamarind:[598] *bahār* 8 1/3 1/8 1/48.

Squeezed fruit:[599] *bahār* 6 1/2.

Sarcocolla:[600] *bahār* 5 1/6.

Sulphur:[601] *bahār* 1 2/3 1/48.

Hemp:[602] *bahār* …[603]

Round (sard)onyx:[604] *bahār* 4.

Oak gall:[605] *bahār* 2 1/4 1/6 1/8 1/96.

Alum:[606] *bahār* 1 1/4 1/12 3/96.

Arsenic:[607] *bahār* 2 1/2 1/8 3/96.

[22b] Farsi myrtle:[608] *bahār* 1 1/2 1/3 1/8 1/48.

Vitriol[609] from India: *bahār* 2/3.

Ebony:[610] *bahār* 1/3 1/4 1/8 3/96.

Malindi sandalwood:[611] *bahār* 1 1/8 1/48.

Cyclamen:[612] *bahār* 11 3/4 1/8.

Mahaleb cherry with its bark: *bahār* 6 1/96.

Storax bark:[613] *bahār* 2 1/2 1/8 1/48.

Litharge[614] (which is lead oxide[615]): *bahār* 3 1/2 1/8 3/96.

Iraq usnea:[616] *bahār* 2 1/3 1/8 1/48.

Poor quality[617] beads: *bahār* 19 1/2.

Farḍ dates:[618] *bahār* 1 1/2.

Low-quality[619] dates: *bahār* 1 1/4 1/96.

Dragon's blood:[620] *bahār* 22 2/3 1/48.

Socotran aloe:[621] *bahār* 5 1/3[622] 1/8 1/48.

Myrrh[623] and …[624] olibanum: *bahār* 1 3/4 1/48.

Waxy … purslane:[625] *bahār* 5 1/2 1/3 1/8 1/48.

…[626] purslane: *bahār* 5 1/4 3/96.
Ivory:[627] *bahār* 6 1/6 1/8 1/48.
Fleminin[628] from India: *bahār* 10.
Raisins:[629] *bahār* 3/4 1/8 3/96.
Ginned and yellow cotton:[630] *bahār* 16 2/3.
Mūrī cotton (i.e. which is in bud):[631] *bahār* 1 1/3 1/4 3/96.
Linen: *bahār* 2 1/4 1/6 1/8 1/96.
Lac:[632] its tithe is a quarter when shared.
But anyone tithed extra in the division of the *bahār* has five dinars [to pay]. Both a commission and galley tax are taken[633] from him, 4 1/8 dinars in every hundred. Anything over and above the quarter is [taken] from the value of the *bahār*. The extra is only five dinars when [the commodity] is called out as being for sale at the gate of the customs house. Its price is determined and five dinars added on to it. If there is no public sale and notification comes without it, there is no extra five [to pay] on it. Similarly, if the [price of] the *bahār* is 200, a quarter of it is 75, the extra 1 1/4, commission and galley tax 12 1/4 1/8 / 88 1/2 1/8.[634]
Brazil-wood:[635] its tithe is a quarter and the extra the price of the *bahār* five dinars. The extra in addition to the quarter is a dinar and a quarter and commission and galley tax for every *bahār* are 3 2/3 in the case of all Quilon and *amrī* brazil-wood etc.

The Practice of taking lighterage [fees] in the case of Indian vessels

In the case of every ship, 8 dinars, if the ship is [coming] from India. But if it comes from the eastern ports, there is no fee on it, but a 'gift'[636] is taken. Everyday practice has made it into an established one, according to what the lighterage officials testify in writing. Commodities arriving from India (and they are [the same as] those from the eastern ports), a commission and galley tax are added to it, i.e. the tithe. Indian myrobolan is tithed and the practice[637] is thus, for they…[638]

[The Taxes placed] upon commodities coming from Egypt, Sinai, Quseir, ʿAydhāb, Suakin and Dahlak are as follows:

Silk[639] from Egypt and Mecca the ennobled: ten *mann* 9 1/8 1/12.
From the distinguished Bāb, anything Indian[640] is tithed at 14 3/96.
Slit garments,[641] underpants,[642] skin garments,[643] *subāʿiyyah*s, **[23a]** striped turbans[644]

and pillow cases[645] (every pair together with a camel-hair coat[646]): one 3/4 3/96; ten 7 2/3 1/8 1/48; hundred 78 1/8; *bahār* 234 1/4 1/8. That guilded is double.[647]

Linen turbans, coloured, plain white and with a selvage: one 1/6 1/8 1/96; ten 2 1/2 1/8 1/48; hundred 29 2/3 1/8; *bahār* 89 1/4 1/8.

Qusi turbans: ten 7/8.

Without gold, embroided:[648] ten 1/24 1/48.

Bleached[649] cloths and napkins: ten 1 1/3 1/8 1/48.

Unbleached cloths and linen napkins: ten 1 1/8.

Guilded veils, coloured worked with gold and worked with gold Iraqi:[650] one 1.

Coloured veils, Iraqi, those with selvage and white ones: ten 2 1/3 1/4 1/8 1/48; one 1/4 3/96.

Coloured fabrics,[651] Iraqi, white and silk: ten 3/4 1/96.

Those worked with gold are double.

Scarlet pieces[652] (they are cloths;[653] the length of a cloth is 40[654] 'hand'[655] cubits; an 'iron' *qaṣabah*[656] is 4 cubits; a cloth is [therefore] ten 'iron' *qaṣabah* =40 cubits): ten 16 2/3; one 1 2/3. From India: one 1 1/8 1/12.

Linen[657] head-coverings[658] worked with gold and hoods[659] worked with gold: one 1/4 1/6 1/8.

Silk head-coverings, plain linen, silk,[660] polished[661] with a selvage, striped: one 1/6 1/8.

Linen head-coverings and linen headcloths[662] of medium quality: one 1/8 1/48 and the work [required] on it.

Muslin pieces[663] worked with gold, napkins worked with gold and silk: one 1/4 1/6 1/8.

Muslin pieces, striped and embroided, embroided napkins and embroided cloths: ten 3 1/2 1/3;[664] one 1/8 1/12 3/96.

Venetian cloths of high-quality:[665] one 1/2 1/3 1/8 1/48; ten 9 2/3 1/8 (the length of a cloth is twenty *qaṣabah* ...,[666] [using] the 'hand' cubit, the *qaṣabah* being 5 cubits [using] the 'hand' [cubit] and an 'iron' [*qaṣabah*] is 4 cubits); if it arrives via India, one is: 1 2/3.

Venetian cloths of medium quality: one 2/3 1/8.

Venetian cloths of mediocre[667] quality: one 1/3 1/4.

Turbans[668] worked with gold, ...,[669] collers,[670] piping,[671] horse-hair veils[672] worked with gold and the work [required] on it: one 1/3 1/12.[673]

Plain silk turbans, ...,[674] collers, horse-hair veils and plain piping: one 1/6. Pure linen is half.

[23b] Fine garments[675] worked in gold (they being two pieces): one 1 1/2[676] 1/8.

Fine silk garments (they being two pieces): ten 7 1/2 1/3.

Garments of medium quality:[677] ten 6 1/2.

Garments of mediocre quality: ten 4 1/3 1/4.

Embroided garments of high-quality: one 5 1/2 1/3 1/8 1/48.

Garments of mediocre quality: one 1/2 1/8 3/96.

Fabrics and skull caps …:[678] ten 3/4 1/96.[679]

Qusi napkins: ten 1/3 1/4 1/8 1/96.

Subā'ī napkins: ten 2.

Napkins, tabby and white:[680] ten 1 1/2 1/8 1/48.

Antali cloths: one 1 1/8; ten 11 3/4.

Antali cloths of medium quality: one 11/12 3/96; ten 9 1/3 1/8 1/48.

Yazdi and Isfahani cloths: one 1/4 1/6 1/8 3/96; ten 5 1/3 1/4 1/8 1/48.

Marwazi, Khwarazmi and Sarqasi cloths: one 1/4 1/8 3/96; ten 4 1/24 1/48.

Among [different] pieces of stuff[681] the Marwazi is the piece [quoted] in cloths.[682]

Cathay cloths, woven fabric and *d.w.n.j*[683] one 3 3/4 1/8 3/96; ten 39 1/24 1/48.

Brocade and Sarqasi cloths: one 1[684] 1/2 1/4 1/8 1/96; ten 15 7/8 1/48.

Genoan[685] and Venetian cloths (they are ornamental edging): 5 1/2 3/96.

Satin cloths (the length of one 18 cubits): one 1/3 1/4 1/8 1/96; ten 27 1/6 1/48.

Silk and cotton cloths: one 1/4 1/6 1/8; ten 5 1/4 1/6 (the length of one 6, 7, 8 and 9 cubits).

Silk[686] cloths: ten 2 1/2 1/8 (length of one 11 cubits); cubit 1/24 148.

Maltese cloths, silk[687] garments and …[688] cloths: one 1/4 1/8; ten 3 3/4.

…[689] cloths: one 3/4 1/48; ten 7 1/3 1/4 1/8.

Maʿarri silk cloths: one 1 1/6 1/8; ten 12 11/12.

Isfahani silk cloths: one 1/4 1/6 1/8 3/96; ten 5 1/3 1/4 1/8 1/48.

Good quality Damascene cloths: one 2/3 1/8; ten 7 11/12.

Shirazi cotton cloths: ten 2

Tabby, Iraqi and *mashāyikhī* cloths: one 3/4 1/48; ten 7 1/3 1/4 1/8.

Cloths covered in shells:[690] one 1 (the length of one 12 cubits).

Egyptian bleached cotton cloths: ten 1 3/4.[691]

Large woollen raincoats:[692] one 1 1/3 1/8 1/96; ten 14 2/3 1/48.

Whole woollen raincoats: one 1/4 1/8; ten 3 3/4.

Woollen, *'ushārī* and similarly Maltese silk garments (the length of one 12 cubits).[693]

Coloured and red apparel: one 1/2 1/4 1/8 1/48; ten 7 1/6 1/8.

Those worked with gold are double.

[24a] White Iraqi apparel: one 1/4 1/6 1/48; ten 4 1/6 1/8 1/48.

Woollen mantles:[694] one 1/3 3/96; ten 3 1/2[695] 1/8 1/48.

From India, Ẓafār, al-Shiḥr etc.: ten 4 1/96.

Those worked with gold and silk ones are double.

Those of silk and worked with gold from India: ten 8 1/48.

Unbleached silk Susi cloths:[696] ten 13 1/4 1/6 1/8 1/48.

Bleached Susi silk cloths: ten 19 1/2 1/3.

Bleached Susi silk cloths: ten 6 1/24.[697]

High-quality[698] white Susi cloths: ten 7 1/2 1/4 1/8.

[Those] from India: ten 8 1/3 1/4 1/8 (length 36 cubits).

Susi bed clothes[699] of medium quality: ten 6 1/24.

Unbleached Qusi Susi cloths: ten 3 1/24 1/48.

Iraqi cloaks of poor quality: ten 2 1/2 1/3 1/96.

Shādirī cloaks: ten 2/3.

Iraqi cloaks: ten 2 1/2 1/3 1/48; hundred 28 1/4 1/6 1/8; thousand 285 1/4 1/6.

Linen towels, linen waistwrappers and those with a selvage: ten 4.

From the great Bāb [al-Mandab] also the same; and from al-Shiḥr the commission and galley taxes are added to it.

Cotton towels and cotton borders: one 1/4 1/8.

Linen mantles with a selvage and whole linen ones: one 1/3 1/8 1/96; ten 4 2/3.

Mantles of mixed material: one 1 1/24 1/96.

Silk mantles and silk waistwrappers: one 1 1/2 1/8; ten 12[700] 11/12.

Homsi and Kafuri mantles:[701] ten 2 1/4 1/6 1/8 1/96.

Kanabi[702] Qannaji[703] mantles: ten 2 1/4 1/6.

Qusi mantles: ten 2 1/3 1/4 1/8.

Sharb[704] silk mantles worked with gold: one 2 3/4 1/48.

Silver mantles: ten 1 1/2 1/3 1/8 1/48.

Cotton mantles: one 1/6 1/8 1/48.

As far as the embroidered [sort] with the Awsi sulphur-coloured refurbishment[705] is concerned, in Jumādā I 750 [it was]:[706] one 1/2 1/96.

Silk waistwrappers, simple cloaks and those with a selvage and cotton with a selvage: ten 5 1/4 1/8.

Silk and embroidered cloaks and those worked with gold are double.

Linen waistwrappers and those with a selvage: ten 2.

Qannuji[707] waistwrappers: one 1/6 3/96; ten 1 1/2 1/3 1/8 1/48.

Coloured waistwrappers: one waistwrapper 1 1/8 3/96.

Large Qusi waistwrappers: ten 3/4.

Small Qusi waistwrappers: ten 1/4 1/6 1/48 1/96.

Egyptian paper (i.e. white sheets): bundle 1 3/4 on it; quire …; twenty quires …[708]

High-quality, silk pieces of cloth and hoods:[709] ten 3 1/6 3/96.

Bed clothes of medium quality: ten 2 1/6 1/48.

[24b] Qusi pieces of cloth: ten 1 1/2.

Damietta pieces of cloth worked with gold: ten 2 1/2.

Damascene pieces of cloth: ten 5.

Damietta linen pieces: ten 1 1/4 1/8 1/48.

Damietta white pieces of cloth: ten 2 1/4 1/8.

Mantles worked with gold, plain and silk: one (four pieces) 2 1/2 1/8.

High-quality Baghdadi white stuff: one 1/4 1/8 1/48; ten 3 1/2 1/3 1/8.

Baghdadi white stuff of medium quality: ten 2 3/4 1/8 1/48.

Mosul white stuff: ten 2 1/4 1/8 1/48.

White stuff worked with gold: one 1/2 1/8.

… cloths:[710] ten 1/2 1/3 1/48.

Aswan velvet pieces:[711] ten 14.

Red velvet pieces: 7.

Cushions,[712] silk … cuts,[713] one *dast* being sixty: 1/4 1/6 1/8 1/96.

Cushions, silk …cuts, plain: 1/4 1/8.

Linen pieces: ten 3/4 1/48.

Large *khalanj*-wood[714] trays[715] from Qayṣ:[716] ten 3 2/3 1/48.

From Mecca the ennobled: ten 1/2 1/8.

From Qaysh[717] and its environs: ten 1 1/3 1/4 1/8.

Plain, small *khalanj*-wood trays: ten 1/4 1/6 1/8 1/96.

Small …[718] trays:[719] ten 1/6.

Silk headdress:[720] one 1/4 3/96.

Cotton loincloths,[721] Baalbakki cloths and loincloths with a selvage: ten 1 1/12 3/96. (The length of a cotton loincloth is 7 or 8 cubits.[722])

Good-quality pearls:[723] hundred *raṭl* 84 1/3 1/4 1/8 1/96.

Egyptian and Indian pearls, including galley tax: *bahār* 150 1/4 1/6 1/8.

Pearls of medium quality: hundred *raṭl* 45 1/8 3/96.

Pearls of inferior quality: hundred *raṭl* 35 1/3 1/4.

Good-quality and pearls of medium quality [mixed together]: hundred *raṭl* 49 11/12 1/48.

Pearls of medium and inferior quality: hundred *raṭl* 40 1/4 1/8.

Saffron: *mann* 1 1/4 1/8; ten 13 3/4.

Aloes[724] wood: ten *mann* 1/3 1/4 1/8.

Sal-ammoniac:[725] ten *mann* 1/3 1/4 1/8 1/96.

Antimony:[726] ten *mann* 1/3 1/4 1/8 1/96.

Cinnabar:[727] ten *mann* 3 1/2 .

Calomel:[728] ten *mann* 2 1/3 1/8.

Commodities in bahār *from Egypt*

Sweet bismuth,[729] the rods and the sheets: *bahār* 10 1/2 1/3.

Bitter bismuth (that which is dry): *bahār* 1 2/3.

Batruh bismuth: *bahār* 3 1/6 1/8 1/48.

Rich quality[730] bismuth (i.e. whole Cypriot): *bahār* 5 1/4 1/6 1/8.

Pewter:[731] *bahār* 4 3/4 1/48.

Lead[732] (black lead): *bahār* 1 1/2 1/48.

Mastic:[733] *bahār* 11 2/3 1/8.

From India and Ẓafār: *bahār* 12 1/2 1/3 1/8 1/48.[734]

[4a] Storax, liquid and moist:[735] *bahār* 3 1/48.

Antimony: *bahār* 2 1/6.

Linen: *bahār* 2 1/3 3/96.

Tamarind: *bahār* 5 1/24.

Pressed tamarind: *bahār* 3 1/2 1/8.

Arsenic: *bahār* 2 1/4 1/6 1/48.

Cleaned mahaleb cherry: *bahār* 5 1/3 1/4.

Bark of the mahaleb cherry: *bahār* 2 1/2 1/8.

Mahaleb cherry with its bark: *bahār* 3 3/4.

Tutty: *bahār* 3 3/4.

From the noble Bāb [al-Mandab] [and] from the eastern ports, tutty: *bahār* 5 1/4.

Cyclamen: *bahār* 7 1/6 1/48.

Cumin: *bahār* 1 1/4 1/6 1/8.

Myrtle: *bahār* 1/2 1/3 1/8 1/48.

Honey: *bahār* 3.

Wax: *bahār* 4 1/3 3/96.

Cyperus: *bahār* 1/2[736] 3/96.

Liquorice: *bahār* 1 3/4.

Sulphur: *bahār* 1 1/4 1/6 1/8 1/48.

Poor quality[737] beads: *bahār* 14 1/4 1/6.

Oak gall: *bahār* 1 1/2 1/48.

Sarcocolla: *bahār* 4 1/3 1/4 1/8 3/96.

Dahlak *durakī*:[738] *bahār* 2 3/4 1/96.

Durakī 'aqrabī:[739] *bahār* 1 1/2 1/8 1/48.

Purging cassia: *bahār* 1 1/2 1/48.

Egyptian cassia: *bahār* 1 1/8.

Lithage (which is lead oxide): *bahār* 3 1/4 1/6 1/48.

Rose oil:[740] *bahār* 8 2/3 1/8.

Raisins: *bahār* 2/3 1/8 3/96.

Dates:[741] *bahār* 1 1/8 1/48.

Vitriol from Egypt: *bahār* 1/3 1/4 1/48.

Usnea from the mountains of Egypt: *bahār* 1 1/2 1/8.

Mountain aloe from Egypt: *bahār* 1 1/2 1/8.

Ghee: *bahār* 3 1/6 1/8.

Ivory: *bahār* 5 3/4 1/48.

Round onyx: *bahār* 4 1/8 1/48.

Pale pink[742] onyx: *bahār* 1 1/8 1/48.

The Dahlak Tax[743] in the Case of Commodities Imported from Egypt

Coral:[744] box[745] and basket,[746] one special[ly made for the purpose], 1 2/3; *bahār* 2 1/2.

Basket and box 200, or as it was.

Small basket at one half; anything over a hundred, even if it were a *raṭl* [in weight], [counts as] a large basket.

Perfume:[747] 3 1/3 1/12 on it.

As for everyone else, on a hundred *raṭl* 1/8; *bahār* 2.

Animony: *bahār* 2/3 3/96.

Linen: *bahār* 1/2 3/96.

Cinnabar and calomel: hundred *mann* 2/3; *bahār* 2.

Brass, iron, lead and copper: *bahār* 2/3 1/96.

Storax, liquid and moist, Iraqi usnea and bark of storax: *bahār* 1/2 1/48.

On every 40 *raṭl* 1/24.

Mastic: *bahār* 1/2 1/8.

Mashāyikh (which is Egyptian cloth): on every 300 pieces 1/4 1/6.

To it [are added] woollen garments, [if] each piece is in fractions of a half and a third, [then] it counts as a piece.

Anything less than that has no [tax] and does not count as a piece.

[4b] Court [t]axes[748] from the Whole of Northern Tihāmah, Zabīd, Taʿizz, al-Samkar, Jiblah, al-Mafālīs, Lahej, Abyan, Ahwar, Ḥawrah, al-Shiḥr, Ẓafār, Ẓaylaʿ, Mazʿūnah and All Other Eastern Ports

As follows:

Horses: taxes on imports per head 55 1/2. The buyer is denied access to the seller when he takes the price. If the horse dies in the port of entry, the supercargo must hand over its tax: import 55 1/2, brokerage[749] 5 1/4, total 60 3/4. [This is] because he fixes this [total] with the seller according to what the price of his horse happens to be. If anyone[750] buys horses from the arsenal or from any other horse merchant, he must pay the taxes, as mentioned above.

Red mantles from Zabīd: ten 11/3 1/4.

The [type] worked with gold and mantles (i.e. commodities of Egypt): one 2 3/4 1/48.

Silk mantles, silk stockings,[751] silk pieces, striped cloths, cloaks, …,[752] silk *subāʿiyyah*s, …[753] and silk loincloths, worked with gold: one 1 1/6 1/8; ten 12 11/12.

Mantles of medium quality and *subāʿiyyah*s of medium quality and with a selvage: one 1 1/24 1/48.

Those of cotton and with a selvage a half.

Linen mantles and linen *subāʿiyyah*s: one 1/2 1/48.

Linen mantles from Egypt: ten 4 2/3.

Mantles of eastern cotton: one 1/6 1/8 1/48.

Cotton mantles: one 1/3 1/48.

Silk waistwrappers, silk loincloths and strips, plain and with a selvage: ten 5 1/4 1/8.

Waistwrappers of medium quality and with a selvage and loincloths of medium quality and of cotton with a selvage from the west:[754] ten 3 1/3 1/12.

If it is a cotton waistwrapper, with a selvage or plain, it is one 1/3 1/12. If it is linen with a selvage, there is a tax on ten: 2 1/3 1/48.

Linen waistwrappers and those with a selvage, plain linen and loincloths with a selvage: ten 2 1/3 1/48.

Cotton waistwrappers from all regions, …[755] and those with a selvage: ten 1/3 1/4 1/8 1/48.

Thulāthī waistwrappers and those of medium quality and loincloths: ten 3/4 1/48.

Linen *rubāʿī*[756] waistwrappers: ten 3/4 1/8 1/96.

Thulāthī linen waistwrappers and *thulāthī* linen loincloths: ten 1/2 1/8 1/48.

Nut-coloured cloths with a selvage and cotton ones the same: one 1/4 1/6.

Linen loincloths: ten 1 1/8 1/48.

Cotton ones, red ones and loincloths are a half.

Cotton loincloths, those with a selvage and Baalbakki cloths: ten 1 1/12 3/96.

[25a]...[757] Equal to that is the price, 100, the dues of which, 10, are estimated at 2, a fifth of the tithe.

...[758] in this way and it can be fixed from the price of this [as follows]:

Ivory: *bahār* 5 3/96 1/48.

Costus: *bahār* 2 1/6 1/48.

Memecylon: *bahār* 10.

Perfume from Abyssinia: *bahār* 3 1/4 1/6.

Honey: *bahār* 3.

Ghee and oil: *bahār* 3 1/6 1/8.

Round onyx: *bahār* 4 1/8 1/48.

Pale pink onyx: *bahār* 1 11/12 1/48.

Farsi myrtle: *bahār* 1 2/3 1/8 1/48.

Dragon's blood: *bahār* 20.

Qaqula cardamum: *bahār* 7 3/4 1/96.

Hemp: *bahār* 20.

Mountain usnea: *bahār* 1/3 1/4 1/8.[759]

Mountain aloes: *bahār* 1 1/2 1/48.

Mountain vitriol: *bahār* 1/3 1/4 1/48.

Mountain alum from Radmān: *bahār* 1/3 1/4.

Alum from all areas: *bahār* 1 1/8.

Black lead: *bahār* 1 1/2 1/48.

Batruh bismuth: *bahār* 3 1/6 1/8 1/48.

Yemeni tumeric: *bahār* 1 1/4 3/96.

Cumin: *bahār* 1 1/4 1/6 1/8.

Myrrh [coming via] the west, frankincense[760] and ...:[761] *bahār* 1 3/4 1/48.

Refined[762] sugar from the mountains: *bahār* 3 3/4 1/8.

Ṣaʿdah sugar: *bahār* 1 1/3 1/48.

Sulphur: *bahār* 1 1/4 1/6 1/8 1/48.

Hypericum: *bahār* 40 (there is [a system of] sharing out [for this item]).[763]

Wax: *bahār* 4 1/3.

Tamarind: *bahār* 1/3 1/4 1/96.

Alum: *bahār* 2 3/4.

Ripened waxy purslane:[764] *bahār* 5 1/3 1/8 1/48.

Hijri purslane: *bahār* 4 2/3 1/8.

Cyperus: *bahār* 1/2 1/3 1/8 3/96.

Perfume: *bahār* 3 1/4 1/6.

Cleaned mahaleb cherry: 5 1/3 1/4.

Sarcocolla: *bahār* 5 1/24.

Raisins from the north:[765] *bahār* 2/3 1/8 3/96.

[The Taxes placed upon] commodities arriving from eastern ports, from Qays, Hurmuz, Qalhāt, Ẓafār, al-Shiḥr, Kharj, Mogadisho, Zaylaʿ, Tajrah,[766] M.r.ʿū?ah, al-Sharjah,[767] al-Ḥādith,[768] al-Ḥirdah, al-Ahwāb and Ḥaly Ibn Yaʿqūb etc.

Saffron: one *mann* 1 11/12.

Aloes: ten *mann* 1 1/4 1/8.

Coloured veils and with a selvage: ten 5 1/8 1/12.

Veils worked with gold: one 1.

White and linen veils; ten 4 1/6 1/8 1/48.

Coloured and white fabrics: ten 1 1/6 1/8 1/48.

Those coloured fabrics worked with gold are double.

Coloured and plain veils: *bahār* 2 1/3 1/4 1/8 1/48.

The cotton [type is charged] at a half and [those] from the north: ten 1 1/3 3/96.

Tawwazi cloths: one 1/3 1/48.

Tawwazi and tabby cloths: one 1 1/6 1/8 1/48.

Cathay cloths: one 7 1/4 1/96.

Shirazi cloths: ten 5 1/8 1/48.

…[769] cloths: one 3 2/3 1/48.

Silk and cotton cloth: one 1/3 1/4 1/96.

Woven and *d.w.n.j* cloths: one 7 1/4 1/96.

[25b] Ardistan[770] and Turkestan[771] cloths: one 1/2 1/8 1/96.

…[772] silk cloths: one 1 1/3 1/96.

Bayrami[773] cloths from other parts: [one][774] 2 1/2 1/3 …[775]

Unbleached cloths from Syria:[776] corge 2 3/4 1/8.

Silk *subāʿiyyah*s, silk mantles and silk pieces: one 1 1/6 1/8.

Silk *subāʿī* c[ush]ions[777] (a tax in the name of Shams al-Dīn al-Tadmurī): one cushion 1 1/6 1/8.

Silk waistwrappers from other districts, plain and with a selvage, mercerized,[778] and strips: ten 5 1/4 1/8.

Waistwrappers of mixed material and with a selvage and linen with a selvage from Mogadisho and elsewhere (linen with a selvage is taxed in the same way): ten 3 1/12.

From other districts, Syria, by land and by sea, linen waistwrappers with a selvage and plain: ten 2 1/3 1/48.

Linen waistwrappers and waist cloths[779] with a selvage: ten 2 1/3 1/48.

High-quality red *subāʿī* waistwrappers with borders: corge (i.e. 4 waistwrappers, a set being two pieces, folded[780]) 4 3/4 1/8 1/96.

Cotton waistwrappers, Shihri, Zafari, from Jerusalem and from the east [of the Yemen]:[781] ten 1 1/6 1/48.

Cotton waistwrappers from Zabīd and northern Tihāmah: ten 1/3 1/4 1/8 1/48.

Cotton nut-coloured garments from northern Tihāmah [coming in] through the [land] gate:[782] ten 1 1/8.

Cotton nut-coloured garments with selvage from al-Shiḥr, Mogadisho, Ẓafār and Syria: one 1/4 1/8; ten 3 3/4.

Cotton towels and those with a selvage from the areas mentioned above the same, [and those from] Zabīd and northern Tihāmah: one 1/6 1/8 1/48.

Mantles and *subāʿiyyah*s: ten 3 1/8. Those with a selvage are double.

Linen *subāʿiyyah*s and linen mantles: one 1/2 3/96.

Red pillows:[783] ten 1/2 1/8 1/48.

Ta[ba]ristan[784] pillows: ten 1/4 1/6 1/8.

Red carpets: ten 1 1/3 1/4.

Ta[ba]ristan carpets: ten 1 1/8 1/48.

Turbans with a selvage: ten 2 1/3 1/8; …:[785] 1 1/2 1/3 1/8 1/48.[786]

Mantles of mixed material, *subāʿiyyah*s of mixed material, nut-coloured garments of mixed material, those with a selvage and mantles: one 1 1/24 1/96.

Cotton turbans: ten 1 1/3 1/48.

Linen pieces [coming in] by sea, and via Ẓafār and al-Shiḥr: ten 1 1/6 1/8 1/48.

Pieces of mixed material: one 1/2 1/8 1/48.

Cotton pieces from al-Shiḥr (they are [called] Shihri pieces of cloth): ten 1 1/3 1/4.

Cotton cloths and cotton cloaks:[787] ten 3/4 1/8.

Bleached cloths and plain cotton when it is mixed with them: ten 2 3/96.

Cotton turban cloths:[788] hundred 4 1/4[789] 1/8.

Linen headcloths with a selvage: ten 1 1/8.

ʿUshārī cloths (made in Abyssinia): ten 2 1/3 1/96.

Velvet pieces (made in Abyssinia): ten 6 1/6.

Khalanj-wood trays from Qays and its regions: ten 1 1/3 1/4 1/8.

Plain *khalanj*-wood trays: ten 1/3 1/4 3/96.

Worked iron has a fifth [taken] on it.

Good quality nacre: ten *mann* 3 1/24.

Nacre of mediocre quality: ten *mann* 2 1/3 1/48.

Light nacre: ten *mann* 2 1/24 1/48.

Good quality and mediocre nacre: ten *mann* 2 2/3 3/96.

Iraqi and Baghdadi paper: bundle 1 1/2 1/8 1/48.

Striped Iraqi cloaks: ten 5 1/2 1/8.

High-quality Baghdadi white silk robes: ten 7 1/6 3/96.

...[790]

[26a] ... veil,[791] aloes, ivory, wax and calomel; there is less [tax to be paid] for [each] according to the amount of time [spent] in examining it.

Cinnabar, a tenth; galingale, a tenth; local aloes, a fifth; ivory, [amount calculated] according to [the time spent] examining [it], whatever the weigher says in accordance with the demands of what is exported.

Concerning each piece: 800 700 600 500 400 300, 15 10;[792] 295, 5; 90 150, 3; 95 55, 2 *raṭl*; 50, 1 *raṭl*.

During selling and buying, when the gate is broken, foodstuffs reach two *raṭl* – one dinar.[793]

Ghee, honey, oil, curcuma, costus, tamarind, pepper, ginger, turmeric, oil-coloured myrobalan, frankincense, canella, cassumunar, beleric myrobalan, both the yellow and the Kabuli type,[794] and the other commodities – one tenth. When commodities come from Zaylaʿ, East Africa, ʿAydhāb etc. [and][795] when there is something made of leather,[796] there can be no payment[797] on them other than one tenth — nothing else. When commodities made of leather come from al-Shiḥr, Hayrīj etc., there is a tenth and a half on them. But if there is any Indian commodity, like pepper, ginger etc., and if there is a commodity other than these, there is only a tenth on them. Shaykh Kamāl al-Dīn al-Maqdashī arrived from Mogadisho in 751[798] ...[799] his ship a chest made of leather [and] {there was no payment imposed upon him}[800] other than one tenth. Also inside were some cowries covered in leather, but the only payment was one tenth, nothing else.

Exports

Pewter and lead by the piece: 700 600 500 400 300, 10.[801]
[Between] 295 [and] 200, 5 *raṭl*; 190 [and] 150, 3; 95 [and] 50, 2 *raṭl*; 5, 1 *raṭl*.
Brass: by the piece, 700 600 500 400, 15 *raṭl*; 395, 10; 300, 10; [between] 295 [and] 200, 5; 195 [and] 100, 3; 95 [and] 55, 2 *raṭl*; 50, 1 *raṭl*.
Ivory by the piece: 800 700 600 500 400, 15; 300 295 250, 10; 250 230 200, 5; 195 150 100, 3; [between] 95 [and] 50, 2 *raṭl*; 5, 1 *raṭl*.[802]
[**26b**] Leathers[803] by the piece: 1000 900 800 700, 20; 600 500 400, 10; 395 300 295, 5; 200 195 100, 3; [between] 95 [and] 55, 2 *raṭl*; 5, 1 *raṭl*.
Iron, marked[804] and unmarked, by the piece: 600 500 400 300, 10; 295 280 250, 5; 195 180 150, 3; 95 80 55, 2 *raṭl*; 50, 1 *raṭl*.
Linen: half of one tenth.
Areca nut: a third of one tenth.

Payment made by the Kārim Merchants[805]

Pepper etc., the surplus, which is 430 *raṭl* and above, the payment on that is 20 *raṭl*.
In the case of all [other] commodities, the bag[806] [which is] 425 and less, there is one tenth on it.
Stone pots[807] have no payment on them.
Brazil-wood, mahaleb cherry [and] large bed covers, there are 15 *raṭl* on them.
Sheets, parchment, a ream,[808] a thousand and …,[809] 1/2 1/4 1/8 on them; it may be 460.[810]
As for the rest, there is on them in the case of the bed covers, for the bureau 1/3 1/4 [and] for the examiner[811] 1/3 1/12.
This is the end of the regulation.

The regime employed by the governor,[812] the overseer and secretaries in the place of entry of Aden the protected

[The k]eys[813] of the port customs house and the gates are [kept] with the governor in his own residence until such time as they are required. As for [the g]ate keys, the gate-keepers and those on duty take them every morning. They open up the gates and return them [and the l]ocks to the governor's residence and they remain with him. After late afternoon prayer, they come to the governor's residence [to pi]ck up the locks and lock up.

The sealed monthly accounts[814] of the customs house are [kept] with the overseer. At the beginning of the new month, [the] governor, the overseer and the secretaries sit on the platform of Dār al-Ṭawīlah and review the troops, those posted as garrison, the officials, those in charge of the arsenal[815] and such. They write reports[816] on this and the governor and the secretaries put their written notes on them and [in them] are designated their payments[817] owed by the tax-farmers and others.

When slaves arrive from the east or from the west,[818] the officers of [the] coast bring them first to the governor and then to the overseer. The latter is the one who chooses those suitable for the felicitous government bureau **[27a]** as servants etc. The authority for this lies with the overseer. He sets free none after that except by royal order.[819]

When the supercargoes[820] arrive from east or west, the officers of the coast bring them first to the governor, then to the overseer. They write down bills of lading[821] from [the vessel] and make known what she has brought.

When Somali sheep arrive from east and west, they are put into a pen[822] just below the customs house. The deputy of the government bureau and the secretaries of the trading establishment[823] come and fix the share of the felicitous bureau, the share of the bureau being their choice. [The sheep] remain standing [there] and are brought out one by one so that they do not get injured.

The customs house opens only when the governor, the overseer and the secretaries or their deputies are present. When they come to the customs house, the authority of what enters and comes out from it rests with the overseer. It is the duty of the governor to keep watch, to scrutinize when weighing and reckoning take place, to manage the inspection and investigate it, to guard the gates and remain close to the customs house at the time of the sailing season.[824] All the secretaries are made to be present and the governor gives none of them permission to absent themselves. Everyone is present at the collection[825] of the taxes and the governor and the officials do not rise without the overseer rising, so they enter when he enters and leave when he leaves. The evaluation and purchase of cloth are in the hall which has been made for this purpose. The recording of the taxes and the takings with which the customs house comptroller deals, whatever is destined for the thriving treasury goes to the overseer.

As for the officers in the town, one of them with his company remains with the overseer; two officers with their companies remain with the governor in turn.

If there is something important and unexpected, requisitions in the hand of the governor are written with this in mind, while the overseer designates the direction this [takes].

The overseer puts his signature first on the passes[826] which are [used] at sea and at Bāb [al-Mandab], then the governor writes his.

There are two messengers[827] who bring news of the ships, one [assigned] to the overseer, one to the governor.

The transfer of the accounts from all the taxes[828] in the port of entry, like the closed accounts, what has been assigned to be paid in charges,[829] the inventories[830] of the [government] chest, the invoices,[831] the revenues, what is taken up to the flourishing treasury, the accountant and the inspector, the overseer takes all of this and passes on what is intended for the flourishing treasury and what goes on to the accountant and the inspector. He takes month by month what is due to himself.

Estates without heirs are taken into the control of[832] the government bureau and a comptroller and a supervisor are employed for them.

A fine[833] which the governor imposes is firstly dealt with[834] by the secretaries and the overseer before it is [actually] spent. As for the fines raised, the overseer spends them on vessels[835] etc. [by putting] his signature on the requisitions etc. The overseer [also] spends [income from fines] on lighters, [by putting] his signature each day [on the requisitions], with that of the governor [also] on them.

Nothing is done at the arsenal without the signature of the overseer. The latter, the governor and the officials [all] place their reliance on this [regime].

The port which has most officials[836] is this felicitous port and they are:

governor
overseer
first comptroller
second comptroller[837]
first supervisor
second supervisor
deputy [governor][838]
deputy overseer
deputy comptroller - two
deputy supervisor - two
comptroller of the chest
supervisor of the chest
customs house assayer[839]
deputy of the chest - two
first tax-collector[840]
second tax-collector
comptroller of the trading establishment
supervisor of the trading establishment
bookkeeper of the trading establishment
deputy overseer in the trading establishment
deputy governor in the trading establishment
comptroller of the shipyard
supervisor of the shipyard
deputy overseer in the shipyard
secretary of the victorious army
comptroller of the land gate[841]
supervisor of the land gate
bookkeeper of the land gate
tax-collector of the land gate
comptroller of the water containers[842]
[27b]
supervisor of the water containers
comptroller of sweet water[843]
supervisor of sweet water
inspector of sweet water
comptroller of slaves
supervisor of slaves
comptroller of the government bureau
supervisor of the government bureau
secretary of tax-farming[844]
comptroller of the [customs] bench[845]
supervisor of the [customs] bench
bookkeeper of the [customs] bench
comptroller of the coast gate
supervisor of the coast gate
comptroller of heirless estates
supervisor of heirless estates
secretary of pious endowments
comptroller of the mint
supervisor of the mint
inspector of the arsenal[846]
secretary of ship building and the arsenal[847]
secretary of the officer corps[848] at the land gate
comptroller of lighterage[849]
supervisor of lighterage
assayer of the chest
secretary of the sheep[850]
tax-collector [of the dues on] sheep
bookkeeper of the mint – four
secretary of the military officers at the port
treasurer[851] of the customs house
treasurer of the trading establishment
deputy of the commercial tax[852]
deputy of the coast gate – four
deputy …[853]
chief[854] of the coast gate – two
deputy of tax-farming at the platform
total – 67[855]

The crop tax[856] district with most officials of the government department is Zabīd the protected and they are:

governor
inspector
overseer
comptroller of the government bureau
supervisor of the government bureau
bookkeeper of the chest
comptroller of arable land[857]
supervisor of arable land
comptroller of common lands[858]
supervisor of common lands
comptroller of immovable properties[859]
supervisor of immovable property
comptroller of heirless estates
supervisor of heirless estates
secretary of ...[860]
comptroller of the customs house
supervisor of the customs house
bookkeeper of the customs house
secretary of ship-building
gate secretary - four
[comp]troller of the camel halt[861]
[super]visor of the camel halt
comptroller of the mint
supervisor of the mint
secretary of the cloth hall[862]
secretary of the fish market
tax-farmers[863] – four
secretary of the governor's office[864]
secretary of wheat store[865]
secretary of the banana store
deputy overseer
deputy inspector
deputy overseer at the four gates, four at each gate – 16
legal official – two
inspector of al-Ḥāzzatayn[866]
comptroller of al-Ḥāzzatayn
supervisor of al-Ḥāzzatayn
endowment secretary in al-Ḥāzzatayn
secretary of the coastal areas – two
assayer of the bureau
assayer of arable land
assayer of immovable properties
total – 65[867]

I know that the officials in this bureau used to be more than these. This was during the reign of al-Mujāhid[868] — God sanctify his secret in paradise, make the authority of our lord the sultan last for ever, extend the period of his rule and bless him and his descendants. There used to be twelve gate secretaries, twenty deputy overseers at the gates, five at each gate. The reductions took place immediately after the reign of al-Mujāhid.

Tithes - the port of al-Ahwāb belonging to Zabīd the protected — God render her ruler and his triumph everlasting — according to their classifications and arrivals from the districts.

Arriving from Aden the protected, royal tax collection which has been newly introduced:

Cassia bark: on the piece 7 1/2; profit[869] 1/2.

Cubeb: *haml* 3 1/2; profit 1/2.

Mixture of salt and pepper:[870] *ḥaml* 3 3/4; profit 1/2.

Pepper: *ḥaml* 3 1/2; profit 1/2.

Woven linen:[871] *ḥaml* 3 1/2; profit 1/2.[872] [catchword]**[28a]**

NOTES

1 I.e. the Rasulid sultan, al-Nāṣir Aḥmad, reg. 803–27/1401–24. [5a, line 3]

2 Al-Nāṣir's *laqab* was Ṣalāḥ al-Dīn.

3 About the end of October 1412. Text *al-ākhir*. [5a, 9]

4 Quran 2:31.

5 Text *ḥarf*. L, II, 550. Specifically 'right side of the half-nib'; G*MT*, 31. [5b, 3]

6 I.e. the government of the Rasulid sultan, al-Ashraf Ismāʿīl b. al-ʿAbbās, reg. 778–803/1377–1401. [5b, 9–10]

7 Interlinear insertion.

8 Reading '… *ma'rifat al-taghliyah wa-al-tas'īr*. The exact meaning of *taghliyah* is not apparent to me. *Tas'īr* would seem to be dealt with in detail by Ehrenkreutz in a Mesopotamian context from an eighth/tenth century source (E*T*, 46). The problem arises from a lack of uniform system of the measures of capacity in the medieval Islamic world. The resultant equation or standardization process between agricultural types is called *taṣrīf* and the apprizing of crops *tas'īr*. The latter can be made out in the text. See also SRA, 227, note 15. [5b, 10]

9 Text *li-yashula*. [5b, 12]

10 Text … *[min] al-wuṣūl*. [5b, 13]

11 Reading the interlinear *bi-rabbi-hi* instead of *qaṭṭu-hu*. [6a, 6]

12 Reading the interlinear *wa-ḥusn al-kawāghid* instead of *wa-al-rub'u min-hā*. [6a, 6]

13 Interlinear insertion *dawāwīn*. [6a, 7]

14 We are talking here of the Hajjah area in the west.

15 Ḥaql Qatāb is placed on the Aden – Ṣanʿā' route, between al-Saḥūl and Dhamār. HṢ, 189. Bīshah is in present-day Saudi Arabia about on the 20 degrees N line.

16 Illegible interlinear insertion. [6b, 4]

17 Interlinear insertion. [6b, 4]

18 Read *al-'azīz*. [6b, 5]

19 Text *wa-mi'shāru-h*.

20 Perhaps al-ʿArūsayn is meant here (see table, 15a below).

21 This is a huge mass of territory in the middle of the country, say with Wuṣāb at the northern extremity, al-Maʿāfir in the south (K*Y*, end map), the Taʿizz – Ṣanʿā' road in the east and Zabīd in the west.

22 Text *wa-mu'ānī-hā*. [6b, 8]

23 Reading *ḥusbānāt*. D, I, 285. [6b, 9]

24 Quran 96:1-2. Quoted in identical context in QṢ, II, 445.

25 Quran 68:1. QṢ, II, 445.

26 A fourth/tenth century poet from Bust. *EI*, 'al-Bustī'; QṢ, II, 445.

27 Text *li-yu'mila-hā*.

28 Text *salla dhābila-hu*.

29 Text *'alā ṭirsin anāmila-hu*.

30 Text *kuttāb al-anām*.

31 Text *riqq*.

32 Insertion from left margin, although it is not clear exactly where these verses should be placed in the text. The second hemistich of the third line is not fully legible, nor is a final line on the edge of the sheet.

33 Text *ṣufran mukhṭafātin*. [7a, 4]

34 Text *fāḍihāti al-tarā'ib*. [7a, 5]

35 Text *ṣalīl*. [7a, 9]

36 Reading *istirādah* or *istizārah*, 'asking for more'. [7a, 9]

37 Text *nuwwār*. [7a, 10]

38 A sage in Iranian tradition, a minister of the sixth century Khusrau I Anushirvan. *EI*, 'Buzurgmihr'.

39 Text *yakfulu-hum*. [7a, 12]

40 Text *yaknufu-hum*. K, II, 936. [7a, 13]

41 Reading *tarjamatan*. [7b, 7]

42 Interlinear insertion for the text's *kātibin*.

43 Or perhaps 'banners'. [7b, 7]

44 Read *fa-'aṭā-hu jazlun yuḥmadu*, the *wa-ḥālun*(?) being superfluous. [7b, 9]

45 Interlinear insertion *dawāwīn*.

46 Interlinear insertion *al-dawāwīn*.

47 Interlinear insertion *fa-arfa'u-hum*.

48 Interlinear insertion *wa-arfa'u-hum*.

49 Text *jumal*.

50 Read *'alay-himā*.

51 Text *mubāsharatu-humā*.

52 Insertion from the top of the page. I am not completely happy with the translation. I think that some sort of statistical office may be in question.

53 Text *ajwad al-kuttāb…* [8a, 2]

54 Text *al-basṭ bi-al-takhrīj*. [8a, 3]

55 D, I, 313, *dīwān al-ḥalāl*, '*la famille et les troupeaux;* en général *propriété*'; LG, I, 472, '*tout ce qui bouge*'.

56 Insertion from left margin.

57 Text *tukhla*[*t*]*u*.

58 Reading *wa-y./ṣ.l.ḥ al-ḥalāl mushiddan jāddan amīnan yajma'u-hu wa-yaḥmilu-h*.

59 Insertion from left margin.

60 Text *al-nuwwāb*. [8a, 9]

61 Text *al-ḍummān*. See L*T*, 92 ff.; R*S*, 136–7. [8a, 9]

62 Text *darak*. L, III, 874. [8a, 11]

63 Text *naẓīrah*. D, II, 687. [8a, 13]

64 Text *'ḥ d*. [8a, 13]

65 Or 'districts', *jihāt*. [8a, 13]

66 Text *tuham*. [8b, 1]

67 Text *al-manṣūr*. [8b, 1]

68 Text *'ā'idah*. D, II, 188. [8b, 3]

69 Interlinear insertion.

70 RBS, although I can find no lexicographical support. Perhaps one should associate the word with *lazīz* (K, II, 987), 'camarade inséparable'. It is clearly the practice of those who can afford to pay someone to undertake military service for them and it is not permitted by the Rasulid authorities. See SRA, 233, note 47.

71 Text *gharramū-hum*. [8b, 5]

72 Text *tawqī'*. L*T*, 152, 153, 155, 251. I am not sure what the difference between the *tawqī'* and the *manshūr* is here. The Fatimids used *manshūr*, the Ayyubids *tawqī'* and the Mamluks *manshūr* (R*S*, 33, note 1). *Tawqī'* is found in the early Rasulid archive (*Nūr*, I, 554). See note 77 below. [8b, 6]

73 Text *ahl*, interlinear insertion with cross *aṣḥāb*. [8b, 8]

74 Text *al-dawlah al-sa'īdah*. [8b, 8]

75 Text *al-khizānah al-ma'mūrah*.

76 Insertion from left margin.

77 Text *manshūr*. L*T*, 155. See note 72 above. [8b, 9]

78 Or 'inventory'. L, V, 1969; K, II, 187, *'idād*. [8b, 9]

79 Text *yukharrijū-hu*. [8b, 9]

80 Text *amlāk*, landed properties, as opposed to *ḥalāl* which is movable property. Cf. SRA, 233, note 45.

81 Text *wasāyā* pl. of *wasiy(y)ah*. RBS; D, II, 815. Cf. CCE, 265, state lands leased to tenants in Egypt. [8b, 10]

82 Interlinear insertion.

83 Text *raṣada*. L*G*, II, 1288 [8b, 12]

84 Text *ḥaṣṣala*. D, I, 295. [8b, 13]

85 Insertion from right margin.

86 Interlinear insertion.

87 Interlinear insertion.

88 Insertion from the top of the page.

89 Insertion from the left margin.

90 Reading … *ilā an yartaqiya ilā al-mudrak*? RBS *al-m.d.l.k*. L, III, 875.

91 Interlinear insertion.

92 Text *'alā rabb jāh*. [9a, 4]

93 Text … *l.s.r.bāl*? RBS *l.s.r.kāl*.

94 Text *amīr-ākhūr*. The second word is Persian; S*PD*, 26.

95 Text *mihtāriyyah*, pl. of *mihtār*. S*PD*, 1352, but cf. D, II, 628, 'chef des écuries'.

96 Text *siyāqāt*. D, I, 706–7; *Nūr*, I, 508. [9a, marginal insertion, 2]

97 Insertion from the left margin.

98 Text *mubāshir*. [9a, 5]

99 Text *sar-ākhūrī*. [9a, 5]

100 Interlinear insertion.

101 Interlinear insertion.

102 Text *al-darj al-sharīf*, the latter abbreviated. [9a, 8]

103 The word *manāshīr* has a more general meaning here and 'feudal titles' follow. [9a, 8]

104 Text *al-murabba'āt*, for *al-marāsīm al-murabba'ah*. [9a, 8]

105 Text *musāmaḥāt*. D, I, 681. [9a, 8]

106 Text *muktatabāt*, RBS. [9a, 8]

107 Text *muḥakkam*, RBS. [9a, 10]

108 Text *al-sharīfah* abbreviated. [9a, 10]

109 For *ḥawā'ij-khānāh*, D, I, 334. [9a, 11]

110 For *al-ḥawā'ij-kāsh*, D, I, 334. [9a, 12]

111 For *dīwān al-ḥalāl*, D, I, 313; L*G*, I, 472.

112 Interlinear insertion.

113 For *zimām*, D, I, 601–2. [9a, 16]

114 Text *al-makhdūm*. [9b, 1]

115 Read *wa-al-zimām yu'allimu*. D, II, 164. [9b, 1]

116 Text *wa-min sharṭi-h*. [9b, 4]

117 Interlinear insertion.

118 Interlinear insertion.

119 Text *mustamarrīn bi-qalami-h*. K, II, 1083. I.e. by the pen of the senior supervisor? [9b, 10]

120 Read *wa-adrāk*. L, III, 874; D, I, 437 [9b, 11]

121 Text *tasaḥḥaba*. RBS. [9b, 13]

122 Text *naẓā'ir al-'arā'iḍ*. The translation is tentative. [9b, 14]

123 Text *al-murattab al-kabīr*. RBS and see D, I, 508. [9b, 15]

124 Text *yuḥallī-h bi-ḥilyati-h*. L, II, 634.

125 Interlinear insertion.

126 Interlinear insertion.

127 Interlinear insertion.

128 Interlinear insertion.

129 Text *tawāqī'*. [10a, 4]

130 RBS, relying on D, II, 323. [10a, 7]

131 Text *nāẓir*. L*T*, 180; R*S*, 154–5. [10a, 7]

132 I.e. al-Malik al-Mu'ayyad Dā'ud, reg. 696–721/1296–1322. [10a,8]

133 I.e. al-Malik al-Mujāhid 'Alī, reg. 721–64/1322–63. [10a, 8]

134 Reading *markūbu-h*. [10a, 9]

135 Text *zunnār*. RBS 'saddle cloth'. [10a, 9]

136 Text *maḍāfir*. K, II, 31. [10a, 9]

137 Text *rank marāwiḥ*. D, I, 561; S*PD*, 588. [10a, 9]

138 Text *al-khāṣṣ*. D, I, 375–6; L *T*, 154, 158; R*S*, 6. [10a, 9]

139 Text *'alāmah*. D, II, 164. [10a, 12]

140 Interlinear insertion.

141 After *al-salṭanah*, interlinear *al-mamlakah* which appears superfluous. [10a, 13]

142 Interlinear insertion.

143 Text *ṣiḥḥat al-aḥkām al-ḥamīdah*. D, I, 310. See also VMS, 28 ff. [10a, 15]

144 Reading *wa-li-ikhtiyārāt* … [10b, 1]

145 Perhaps the author writes of the *dīwān al-kharāj*. [10b, 3]

146 Insertion from the right margin.

147 Text *jihāt*. D, II, 787; R*S*, 43, note 4. The word would appear to denote the 'area' or 'district' whence the tax was derived.

148 Text *muhimmāt*. RBS, 'supplies?' [10b, 4]

149 Text *bi-al-aqlām*. RBS from al-Akwaʿ: Nuwayrī (no reference) 'head of taxation' under which entries are made. [10b, 6]

150 RBS and SCC, 48, 'millet', but cf. V*MA*, 171–2, 'white sorghum'. Varisco kindly draws my attention to his V*MA*, 160–2, and writes, 'I think the reference here is to the timing of the tax assessments on these two crops… Date palms generally were assessed in mid June, but sabi'i sorghum at the end of December.' I have adjusted my translation to follow Varisco's advice. [10b, 6]

151 Text *al-murattabāt*. Or 'rations'. D, I, 508. [10b, 7]

152 Text *al-mushārakāt*. RBS. [10b, 8]

153 Text *al-mutaṣarrifīn*. D, I, 830; L*T*, 98, 181. [10b, 8]

154 Text *al-multazimīn*. Or 'the farmers', though this does not fit in well with what follows. D, II, 536. [10b, 8]

155 Text *al-jihāt*. Or 'taxes'. [10b, 8]

156 RBS reads *nidbah* and translates thus.

157 Text *mushidd*. D, I, 736–7; R*S*, 66–7; L*AT*, II, 42; S*A*, II, 124. [10b, 10]

158 Text *shāhid ṣundūq*. D, I, 794; L*T*, 180; R*S*, 159. [10b, 10]

159 Text *al-mujrā*. [10b, 10]

160 Text *al-ʿujūz*? RBS. Both this and the subject of the previous note are doubtful. [10b, 11]

161 See note 81 above. [10b, 11]

162 Text *ḥashriyyāt*. D, I, 290. [10b, 11]

163 Text *ahl al-taṣarruf*. I link this term with the financial officer, *mutaṣarrif*. D, I, 830; L*T*, 98, 181. I wonder whether this should read, 'The inspectors *and* the financial officers …', although there is clearly no *wa-* in the text. [10b, 12]

164 Text *shadd*, the office of the *shādd*, the latter synonymous with *mushidd*. D, I, 736–7. See also R*S*, 150–3. [10b, 13]

165 Reading *khidmat al-waraq*. [10b, 14]

166 Text *multazim*. Or 'farmer'; see above note 154. [10b, 15]

167 Text *yastakhrija*. RBS. [11a, 1]

168 Text *mustawfī*. D, II, 827; L*T*, 180; R*S*, 156–7; H*I*, 85. [11a, 1]

169 Text *rāja'a li-*. RBS. [11a, 2]

170 Text *yustanhaḍu*. K, II, 1356. [11a, 4]

171 Interlinear insertion.

172 Text *ḥawāṣil*. L, II, 585. [11a, 5]

173 Text *naqqādīn*. K, II, 1321. [11a, 5]

174 Text *sāqiyan*. RBS. [11a, 7]

175 Text *ḍāḥiyan*. RBS; P*D*, II, 293; SCC, 50. [11a, 7]

176 Text *'uqūm*. RBS; N*S*, VII, 4675; L*G*, III, 2315; P*D*, II, 335. [11a, 8]

177 Text *'aqāyid*. RBS. [11a, 8]

178 Text *riqāb*. RBS reveals no solution and the translation is a guess only, based on the basic meaning of the root. [11a, 8]

179 Text *shu'ūb*. Or 'terrace fields', RBS. [11a, 8]

180 Interlinear insertion.

181 Text *mubāshir*. D, I, 89. Cf. note 98 above. [11a, 11]

182 Text *rassama*. RBS. [11a, 12]

183 Text *muqaddam*. [11a, 13]

184 Reading *wa-yakūn amr al-taqaddum* … for *aw yakūn* etc. [11a, 14]

185 Text *hilālī*. I.e. that collected according to the lunar calendar. G*S*, I, 269–70; R*S*, 105–6. [11a, 15]

186 Text *muthamman*. [11a, 15]

187 Text *ahrāwāt* for *ahrā'āt*, the pl. of the pl. of *hury*. [11a, 15]

188 Text *mussāḥ*. L*T*, 179-80. [11b, 3]

189 Text *wa'd*. L*G*, III, 2938. Or 'fixed period'. [11b, 3]

190 Text *khitamāt*? RBS. R*S*, 130? [11b, 4]

191 Text *jihāt*. Or 'by districts'. RBS [11b, 4]

192 Text *muḍāf*. [11b, 5]

193 Text *siyāqāt*. See note 96 above. [11b, 5]

194 Text *naẓīr*. [11b, 7]

195 Text *'amal*. D, II, 175. [11b, 9]

196 Text *shāhid*. [11b, 10]

197 Text *musāwaqah*. RBS. [11b, 10]

198 Text *mustakhrij*. L*T*, 179. [11b, 10]

199 Interlinear insertion.

200 Text *naqqād*. This must be the meaning here; cf. note 173 above. [11b, 12]

201 Text *'ayn*. [11b, 13]

202 Text *manshūr*. [12a, 2]

203 Reading *qawā'imāt*, pl. of the pl. of *qā'imah*. D, II, 434; K, II, 840. RBS, 'written statements of accounts'. [12a, 4]

204 Text *mulakhkhaṣāt*. [12a, 6]

205 Text *al-ashghāl* for *al-ashghāl al-māliyyah/al-kharājiyyah*. D, I, 767. [12a, 6]

206 Interlinear insertion.

207 Interlinear insertion.

208 Text *rabb musāmaḥah*. See above note 105. [12a, 9]

209 Text *rabb jāh*. [12a, 9]

210 Text *dhurrā'*. [12a, 10]

211 Text *manfa'ah*. RBS. A tentative translation. [12a, 10]

212 Text *uddiba*. Or 'fined'. [12a, 11]

213 Reading *ākhar al-ḥisāb*. [12a, 12]

214 The translation of this sentence is tentative. [12a, 12]

215 Text *muhimmāt*. See above note 148. [12a, 15]

216 Text *makhāzīm*, for *al-dafātir al-makhzūmah* perhaps. D, I, 368. [12b, 1]

217 Text *qawāyimāt*. See note 203 above. [12b, 1]

218 Text *qaṭa'a*. RBS, with tenuous reference to D, II, 375, 'passer'. [12b, 4]

219 Text *wujūh al-ḍummān*. See above note 61. [12b, 5]

220 Text *hilālī*. See note 185 above. [12b, 5]

221 Text *ḥaṣṣala*. D, I, 295. [12b, 7]

222 Text *ḥamala*. RBS. [12b, 7]

223 See note 123 above.

224 Text *murattab al-istīmār* (for *isti'mār*). L, I, 96.

225 Reading *wa-in kān*, hence the perfect here.

226 Reading *murṣad*. D, I, 533.

227 Insertion from the right margin.

228 Text *multazimīn*. Cf. note 154 above.

229 Text *ummahāt*. RBS. [12b, 9]

230 Text *maqāni'*. RBS. [12b, 9]

231 Text *shu'ūb*. Cf. note 179 above. [12b, 9]

232 Text *asfalīn*. RBS. [12b, 9]

233 Text *a'līn*. RBS. [12b, 10]

234 Text *qanā'ah*. RBS. [12b, 10]

235 Text *q.nā'ah*. RBS. [12b, 10]

236 Text *aṭrāf*. RBS. [12b, 12]

237 Text *mutakhaffifīn*. RBS. [12b, 12]

238 Text *mutaḥawwilīn*. RBS. [12b, 12]

239 Text *tawaddara*. [12b, 13]

240 Text *ḍāḥī*. See note 175 above. [12b, 14]

241 Text *qiblatan*. [13a, 4]

242 Text *musayyar*. RBS.

243 Text *qāyis*. RBS.

244 Text *jallād*. RBS.

245 B. Ṣirār/Ṣirāriyyūn. H*Ṣ*, 54, 102.

246 See H*Ṣ*, 55, 80, 95, belonging to the Awdiyyūn.

247 H*Ṣ*, 180–1, under Diyār Tamīm.

248 In Wuṣāb. S*A*, 198.

249 In the Jawf. H*Ṣ*, 81; W*G*, 136.

250 H*Ṣ*, 73, 84, 136.

251 W*GC*, end map; K*Y*, end map.

252 See W*G*, Index, passim; S*A*, map I.

253 See H*Ṣ*, 48 and passim; *EI*, 'Ma<u>dh</u>ḥi<u>dj</u>'.

254 See H*Ṣ*, 54.

255 Text *murattab*. RBS.

256 Reading *aṣl al-māl min al-'ayn*.

257 Text on the same level on the left hand side of the page *jihatayn*(?), 'two districts'.

258 Text *mutaḥaṣṣil*. D, I, 296.

259 See W*GC*, end map.

260 See S*A*, 134, in the area of Kaḥlān.

261 Text Ḥaḍūr wa-al-Shihābiyyah.

262 Text *nuqabā*. 'Military officer' or 'tribal leader'. RBS.

263 Just N of Ṣan'ā'. W*GC*, end map; S*A*, 146–7.

264 Just S of Ṣan'ā'. S*A*, 172.

265 There are two. W*G*, 227.

266 Text *mashyakhah*.

267 Perhaps thus, a place in al-Jawf.

268 Text B.r.s.

269 Text *al-muḥaṣṣil*. RBS, from Yemeni informant.

270 Text *al-naẓar*.

271 Text *mikhlāf.*

272 Text *ḥāshiyah*. D, I, 293.

273 Text *khuṭṭah*. RBS.

274 Text sg. *rahīnah*. I translate as a sg., although perhaps the Arabic implies a plurality of hostages.

275 Near Kawkabān. S*A*, 144.

276 I vocalize after HṢ, 180, who has al-Shuqāq.

277 Text *khawlī*. Or 'gardener'. D, I, 413.

278 Text *dā'ilī*. RBS.

279 Text *khāṣṣah*. D, I, 375–6.

280 Text *ḥaḍāyir*, pl. of *ḥaḍīrah*. L*G*, I, 432.

281 I.e. the figure is given for one month and ten here and below.

282 Al-Faṣṣ and al-Faṣṣayn are somewhere near Ṣanʿā'. S*A*, 151.

283 The numeral is illegible.

284 Text *naqīb al-ajnād* and *nuqabā al-rajul*.

285 Text *muwāsāh*. D,II, 807; L*G*, III, 2922. Money given to heads of tribes etc. to keep them obedient and cooperative. RBS.

286 This is not clear to me. The main clause after *fa-idhā* reads *fa-fī-h* (not *fa-fī-hā*), though I am still inclined to take the masculine pronoun as referring to the *muwāsāh*.

287 SW of Ṣanʿā' in Ānis. S*A*, 135.

288 Reading *inzāl*. RBS.

289 Text *ḥāṣil tawsilah fī aḥad al-ḥuṣūn muṣawwan* whose precise meaning defeats me at present.

290 Text *kifāyah*. D, II, 479.

291 The Dhamār and Radāʿ areas. S*A*, 224.

292 The Kalāʿ area must be meant here. HṢ, 74–5.

293 In Upper ʿUzlat al-Sayf, NW of Dhū Sufāl. M*M*, 63.

294 I correct from al-Thawālī. In the Dhū Jiblah-Ibb area. Ḥ*M*, I, 169.

295 See K*Y*, 207.

296 All in the Taʿizz area.

297 A fortress in the Maʿāfir/Ḥujariyyah area, W of Dhubḥān. M*M*, 325.

298 I.e. Upper and Lower Khadīr in the Taʿizz area. RBS from a Yemeni informant.

299 I.e. on the next page of the MS.

300 Text *'imārah*. D, II, 171.

301 Reading *tazīd wa-tanquṣ*.

302 Text *ghayr muqṭa'*. These were palms controlled by the Maʿāzibah, sometimes under government authority, sometimes not. RBS.

303 Text *ijbār*. L*G*, I, 261, is helpful here; cf. L, II, 373.

304 Text *mulā'āt*. D*V*, 408–11, gives *milāyah*, *mulā'ah* and *mal'ah*. It is worn by both men and women, usually made of cotton and about eight feet by four. See also D, II, 6–7, 18 and SL*S*, 126a.

305 Text *satā'ir*, pl. of *sitārah*. D, I, 632.

306 Text *fuwaṭ*, pl. of *fūṭah*.

307 Text *mufaṣṣaṣ*. L, VI, 2402-03.

308 Text *ghāliyah*. L, VI, 2289. Perfume made of musk, ambergris, camphor and the oil of ben. The name is a pun, meaning both 'boiling' and 'expensive'!

309 Reading *jawār hunūd maghānī*.

310 Text *jawār raqqāṣāt hunūd*.

311 Text *wuṣfān*, pl. of *waṣīf*. D, II, 818.

312 Text *mā bayn 'āmayn*.

313 Text *kharj*. D, I, 359.

314 Text *biḥār* and *hujun*, pls of *baḥr and hajīnah* respectively. RBS suggests 'camels'.

315 I take this as a name. RBS 'villages'.

316 Text *ḍarāyib*.

317 Text *'ushūr*, pl. of *'ushr*. FN, *passim*.

318 Text *furḍah*. To be associated with *faraḍa 'alā*, 'imposer un paiement'. L*E*, I, 673.

319 Text *bazz*.

320 Text *kawrajah*. I use the Hobson-Jobson entry heading here and below: YB*HJ*, 255. It does not always indicate a 'score', although we can perhaps take it as a score, unless there is a specific indication otherwise. L*T*, II, 56. It is an Indian word, Portuguese *corjá*.

321 Text *tanjīl*. L*G*, III, 2748-49; P*D*, II, 479; S*P*, 194.

322 Text *thawb*.

323 CC: 'Chiffre incertain … Le calcul ne donne rien.'

324 Text *bahār*. YB*HJ*, 47-48; L*AT*, II, 24; H*MG*, 8–10.

325 Or perhaps 'the weight of the *bahār*'.

326 I take this difficult piece as one and assume that it all concerns pepper.

327 Text *marwad/mirwad*. LG, II, 1562.

328 Text *hurd*. L*E*, I, 731; L*G*, III, 2865.

329 Text *qinbār*. D, II, 416.

330 I am not sure exactly what this means, unless the implication is that the importer pays 2 1/4 dinars just to have his goods weighed and a further 3 3/4 dinars on the commodity itself.

331 Text *al-tafārīq*. SP, 209, '… the ports east of Aden are known as Bilād al-Tafārīq, a term about which I cannot be certain as yet, but from the Arabic it would seem to mean originally the ports upon which a levy of tax or contribution to a central exchequer (in Rasūlid times at Aden and Taʿizz) was apportioned out.' The word occurs in *Nūr*, I, 510, but the context throws no light on the subject. I punctuate here to suggest that the Tafārīq include Ẓafār, Hurmūz and Qalhāt.

332 Doubtful reading. CC tentatively suggests al-Ghazālī/al-Gharālī.

333 Text *qusṭ*, *Costus arabicus*. D*M*, 125–6; S*CT*, 327.

334 Text *ūqiyyah*. H*MG*, 34–5.

335 Text *jahāzāt*. D, I, 228; K*SA*, 21–2; S*PD*, 380.

336 Text *aqmishah*, pl. of *qumāsh*, in the general sense given. D, II, 413; S*T*, passim.

337 Text *ḥaml*, pl. *aḥmāl*. H*MG*, 13–14.

338 RBS reads *jābir* and translates thus with a query.

339 RBS reads 4/3 which I do not understand. I interpret after reference to Cahen's table, CS*FS*, 31.

340 Text *bukr* or *bukur*. B*A*, 4; L*G*, I, 191; M*WR*, 156; SCC, 48, 69; V*MA*, 168.

341 Text *musāmaḥīn*. See note 105 above.

342 Text *ṭa'ām*. RBS, 'millet'.

343 Reading *gharārat burr*.

344 I.e. payment is in kind, as is not unusual with metals.

345 Text *ḥinnā*, *Lawsonia inermis*. V*MS*, 198; K*S*, 203, 234.

346 Reading *qirbah*.

347 Text *ṣabir*, *Aloe vera*. K*S*, 207, 232.

348 Text *dawm*, *Hyphaene thebaica* Del. Mart. V*MS*, 136.

349 Reading *dādhī/dhādhī*, *Hypernicum perforatum* L. D*M*, 60.

350 Text *shimāl*, pl. of *shamlah*. S*T*, 122, 123.

351 Text *zubdī*. D, I, 578.

352 Text *ḥulbah*, *Trigonella foenum-graecum*. K*S*, 204, 235.

353 Text *thūm*, *Allium sativum* L. D*M*, 33.

354 Text *nathr*. RBS. Cf., however, K, II, 1196, *nathar*, 'ce qui tombe par morceaux, par miettes'.

355 I.e. exported through al-Shiḥr.

356 Text *lubān*, *Boswellia* spp. V*MA*, 230; K*S*, 205.

357 Text *ḥūt*.

358 Text *ṣayd*.

359 Text *lukham*.

360 Text *al-busr wa-hwa al-ruṭab*. The former is 'the last stage before being fully ripe', the latter 'the fresh ripe date'. V*MA*, 193.

361 Text *ḍarībah*.

362 Text *khiṭāī*. Or 'Chinese'. S*T*, 113, 150.

363 Text *nasīj*.

364 Text *d.w.n.j*. Clearly a type of fabric; Varisco suggests perhaps *duwayj* and refers me to IM*L*, *duwwāj*.

365 Text *mumazzaj*. D, II, 595; S*T*, 18.

366 Text *dhirā'*.

367 Text *sādhij*, i.e. without the gold.

368 Text *dībāj*. S*T*, passim.

369 Text *kanjī*. D, II, 500; S*T*, 150.

370 Text *'attābī*. The Umayyad ʿAttāb gave his name to a quarter of Baghdad, ʿAttābiyyah, where these striped cloth were produced. D, II, 93; S*T*, 29, 68 and passim.

371 Text *muṣmat*. S*T*, 128, 167, 202.

372 Text *durrī*. D, I, 428.

373 Text thus. Varisco draws my attention to *Nūr*, I, 65, note 520.

374 Text *mufattish*.

375 Text *amlā*. D, II, 623.

376 Text *faḍalāt*. D, II, 274.

377 Text *qirāṭ*. H*MG*, 27.

378 Text *nasaba*. I take the possible meaning from the context.

379 I think that this means that payment up to three pieces is at a twenty-fourth [of a *mithqāl*(?)] and over three at ten *qīrāṭ*. However, the sentence is an extremely difficult one and I translate with some diffidence.

380 Text *aṭlas*. *ST*, 18 and passim.

381 Text *khawāī*. RBS.

382 Text *kattān*. *ST*, 18 and passim.

383 Text *shāshāt*. *ST*, 150.

384 I.e. from Tabrīz. *ST*, 240.

385 Text *jawāzī*, pl. of *jawzī*. *ST*, 184, 197. Cf. *Nūr*, I, 422, editor's note 3155.

386 Text *subā'iyyāt*. The meaning is uncertain, 'cloth consisting of seven parts', 'seven yards in length', 'scarf' or 'waist-wrapper'. *ST*, 130.

387 Text *maṭārif*, pl. of *miṭraf*. *ST*, 16.

388 Text *shuqaq*, pl. of *shuqqah*. L, IV, 1578.

389 Text *ḥibarāt*/*ḥabarāt*. D*V*, 133–4.

390 Text *muḥashshā*. *ST*, 80.

391 Text *taqānī'*, pl. of *taqnī'*? RBS = *qinā'*?

392 Text *'aṣāyib*, pl. of *'iṣābah*. D*V*, 300–2; *ST*, 203.

393 Text *ḥawāshī*. I.e. the borders were woven separately.

394 Text *naṣāfī*. *ST*, 202; cf. A*LW*, 245–9.

395 Text *al-baqāyir al-lālis*. D*V*, 84–7. I keep the translation general. RBS suggests *lālis*=*lānis*. *ST*, 217.

396 Text *al-qawqalī*. RBS.

397 Text *shāsh*. D, I, 802; S*PD*, 723.

398 Text *'.r.tī* which I cannot identify.

399 Text *al-n.y.f.* RBS.

400 Text *qushūriyyāt*. RBS.

401 Text *mulawwasāt*. RBS.

402 Text *al-mulawwasāt al-quṭn*.

403 Text *shīl*. RBS.

404 Text *al-maqṣūr wa-al-khām*. D, II, 358; *ST*, 130.

405 Text *maḥārim*, pl. of *maḥramah*. D, I, 279. Cf. *Nūr*, I, 487, editor's note 3552.

406 Text *abdān*. D, I, 58–9; *ST*, 70.

407 Text *maqāṭi'*, pl. of *maqṭa'*. *ST*, 159.

408 Text *makhāmil*, pl. of *mukhmal*. D, I, 406.

409 Text *ḥanābil*, pl. of *ḥanbal*. D, I, 331. Cf. *ST*, 181, 'fur'.

410 Text *kanābish*, pl. of *kunbūsh*. Cf. D, II, 499, 'voile'; *ST*, 156, 'horse cloth'. RBS, 'woollen strips' in 'Awdhalī.

411 Text *maṭāriḥ*, pl. of *miṭraḥ*. *ST*, 35; *Nūr*, I, 79, note 590.

412 Text *ma'ājir*, pl. of *mi'jar*. D, II, 96; S*T*, 158.

413 It is not entirely clear to me a) the exact meaning of the entry, in particular the two *idhā* clauses and b) where the numerals fit and indeed if they are read correctly.

414 Text *maḥābis*, pl. of *maḥbas*(?). L*T*, II, 27; cf. S*T*, 130, note 64.

415 Reading *wa-al-maṣāḥifī wa-al-barūjī wa-al-banjālī*. The first has not been identified.

416 Text *nīlī*.

417 Text *'ushārī*. Presumably the ten equivalent of the seven *subā'ī*. See above note 386.

418 Text *būtalī*.

419 Text *abrād*, pl. of *burd*. D*V*, 59–64; S*T*, 49, 123.

420 'An extensive district of the mountains of al-Mahjam known as Mikhlāf Ḥajjah.' SH*Ṭ*, 24.

421 Text *'amāyim*, pl. of *'imāmah*.

422 This is an insertion running vertically after the main entry. This must refer only to cotton turbans and their permitted maximum is four.

423 Text *manādīl*, pl. of *mandīl*.

424 There are unclear numerals and the corge numerals look dubious.

425 Text *fuwaṭ*, pl. of *fūṭah*. D*V*, 339–43; S*T*, 55, 56 etc.

426 Text *kawlamī*, the Indian port. IB*T*, I, 19; S*T*, 131.

427 Maʿbar was the Arabic name for the southern Coromandel coast. IB*T*, III, 644.

428 I am not sure what to make of this expression and follow RBS. Could it mean something like 'and [this is] the practice adopted in its case', looking at D, II, 175, *mā al-'amal 'alay-h*, 'que nous suivons, que nous avons adopté'?

429 Text *rasmī*. For *rasm*, 'border', S*T*, 200.

430 I cannot be sure of the fractions.

431 I am not sure of the final fraction.

432 Text *kāghid/kāghad*. *GMT*, 121–2.

433 Text *shaddah*. D, I, 736.

434 Text *dast*. 24–5 sheets. D, I, 441, *dastah*; G*MT*, 46, *dast/dastah*.

435 Text *qaṣī*.

436 Text *al-'ūd al-raṭb*. D, I, 186. Cf. RBS, 'storax'.

437 I can make nothing of what appears to be *al-b.l.thūr*. RBS suggest *al-thalāthūn*, but this does not seem to carry any sense here.

438 Text *amnān*, pl. of *mann*. H*MG*, 16–23.

439 Text *quṭr/quṭur*. K, II, 766.

440 '5 *mann*' is clear in the text immediately before *tuḍrabu* and this is dittography.

441 Text *al-maḍrūb*. Or 'what is multiplied'.

442 All these fractions are tentative.

443 All these numbers are tentative.

444 Text *qīrāṭ*. H*MG*, 27.

445 Text *m.n.wan*, which is puzzling. RBS, 'The form *al-m n w* not known to me.' The form appears several times.

446 Text *qāqulā*, i.e. a place on the Tenasserim coast in Malaya. D, II, 304; IB*T*, III, 667, IV, 880.

447 Text *abham*. L, I, 269, = *mubham*.

448 Text *mithqāl*. SP, 193; RS, 182, 193; A*ME*, 89–90.

449 Reading *wa-laysa yataghayyar*. CC.

450 An illegible figure.

451 Text *bathth*, repeated at the end of the sentence.

452 Text *qaflah*. L*G*, III, 2518; S*P*, 182, 190.

453 Written above.

454 Written above.

455 Written above.

456 Reading with RBS *qaṭr*.

457 Text *qayṣūrī*.

458 Clearly *ḥarīr* is to be read here and RBS remarks on the strangeness of the entry in this particular position in the list.

459 Text *qurunful/qaranful*, *Syzygium aromaticum*. K*S*, 235.

460 Text *jawzā*, *Myristica fragrans*. K*S*, 234.

461 Text *basbāsah*, *Myristica frangrans*. D, I, 83; D*M*, 19-20; K*S*, 202.

462 Text *za'farān*, *Crocus sativus*. K*S*, 233.

463 Text *māmīrān*. K*S*, 205.

464 Text *rāwand*, *Rheum palmatum* sspp. D, I, 496; K*S*, 207.

465 Text *maqāsim*. This and similar expressions are the subject of some debate between Serjeant and Cahen. In a letter, S writes, 'This is said to be a reference to the practice still existing today whereby Government farms out certain taxes to tax-farmers and divides the proceeds – so that this is probably what is meant in this case.' C writes, 'Ces expressions veulent dire que certains produits, taxés

jusqu'alors ou ordinairement en monnaie à une somme fixe, sont retournés au régime originel de la dame proportionelle en nature ... Il faut donc comprendre: "il est revenu à ce qu'on a pris sur lui la taxe proportinelle ..."' The translation given reflects S's suggestion; an alternative, following C, would be: 'It reverted to proportional taxes on the instruction ...'

466 Text *khaṭṭ*.

467 Reg. 696–721/1322–63.

468 Text *al-ṣandal al-maqāṣarī/al-maqāṣirī, Santalum* spp. *KS*, 207, 235; *D*, II, 358–9; IB*T*, III, 675. Macassar is now called Celebes.

469 Text *khalanjān/khulunjān/khulinjān/khūlanjān, Alpinia galanga.* D, I, 400; K*S*, 205.

470 Text *māward*. D, II, 574; K*S*, 205.

471 Text *dhabl*.

472 Text *muqārib*. D, II, 331.

473 Text *khayzurān*. D*M*, 55.

474 Text *qanā*, pl. of *qanāh*.

475 Text *narjīl*. V*MA*, 182.

476 Text *fawfal/fūfal, Areca catechu*. D, II, 297; K*S*, 202.

477 Text *al-miyah al-alf*.

478 The numeral looks like 1/8 to me — which cannot be correct.

479 Text *'aqīq*.

480 Text *kharaz*.

481 I.e. not strung.

482 Text *halīlajī*. D, I, 43; II, 769.

483 Text *sa'arī*. L, IV, 1363.

484 Or '1/12'. RBS reads three numerals here, the first '1/4 ?'.

485 Text *safaṭ*. RBS *sifṭ*. L, IV, 1374. The word might mean 'sack' or 'basket of palm leaves'.

486 Reading *'iddah*. RBS, presumably reading *'uddah* translates in his notes 'a vessel'.

487 Reading *ṣā'irah*.

488 Text *j.mā*?

489 Begins 28 February 1351.

490 I am not sure what this means exactly; perhaps half the quantity only is reckoned for tithing purposes.

491 Text *dabbūs*.

492 Text *rikāb*.

493 Text *anājir*, pl. of *anjar*.

494 Text *būlād*. Persian *pūlād*. S*PD*, 260.

495 Reading from RBS.

496 Reading from RBS.

497 Text *muqāsam*. See note 465 above.

498 Text *sāj khām*.

499 Text *fūlādī*.

500 Perhaps *armāl*.

501 Text *m.?ā.?kāt*[?].

502 See previous note.

503 Reading *qandalah*?

504 Text *raqṣ*.

505 Text *mudd*. H*MG*, 45–7.

506 Text *mikyāl*.

507 Faknur was on the Malabar coast and survives as Barkur on the Sitanadi river. T*AN*, 456. Hili was a medieval port on the Malabar coast. IB*T*, IV, 809.

508 I vocalize tentatively as the short vowel is unknown. Serjeant suggests the word comes from an Indian word meaning trader. SP, 218. See also *Nūr*, I, 223 etc.; the references throw no further light on the word.

509 Begins 21 August 1335.

510 Text *jahāz*. K*S*, 21; G–G*G*, 110; A*W*, 96, 98, 134.

511 Text *mudallaj*(?) which gives me no meaning. With CC, I read tentatively *musannaj*. See *sanjah*, D, I, 690. RBS also suggests *al-aruzz al-mudd …*, followed by a numeral sign, i.e. 'Rice, the *mudd* being …'

512 Begins 27 November 1326.

513 Begins 21 August 1335.

514 Insertion from the left margin.

515 Interlinear insertion.

516 Text *al-musannaj al-mudd*.

517 Final fraction uncertain.

518 Text *madqūq*.

519 Text *'amālah*. D, II, 176.

520 Text *shawānī*. SMT, 131–2, 135, note 26, with full references.

521 Text Barbarah, which is not possible in the Indian context. Perhaps we should read thus.

522 These are all undoubtedly places in Gujerat, though most appear corrupt. Dunbas is near the Gulf of Surat, on the eastern side of the entrance to the Tapti river. T*AN*, 452.

523 Text *khām*.

524 Figures unclear.

525 Also note 418 above.

526 Text *ṣīnī*.

527 Text *zaytūnī*, which might of course mean olive-coloured ware, celadon.

528 Text *mathārid*, pl. of *mithrad*.

529 Text *aqdāḥ*, pl. of *qadaḥ*.

530 Text *khawāfiq*. D, I, 387, *khāfiqiyyah*, 'grand plat'.

531 Complete number unclear.

532 Fractions uncertain.

533 Text *anṣāf*.

534 Text *muṭlaq*. D, II, 57; cf. RBS 'plain'.

535 Text *athlāth*, presumably the pl. of *thulth*.

536 Text *arbā'*, presumably the pl. of *rub'*.

537 Text *sakārij*, pl. of *sukurrujah/sukurrajah*, from the Persian *sukrachah*. L, IV, 1392; D, I, 668.

538 The final fraction is doubtful and RBS appears to read 2/60!

539 The 1/2 1/3 is a doubtful reading; RBS reads only 1/48.

540 Text *kubābah/kabābah*, *Piper cubeba*. D, II, 444; S*CT*, 331; K*S*, 204.

541 The whole number is doubtful, though clearly between 10–19. RBS reads 1/17 1/8 1/12!

542 Text *nīl*.

543 There is some doubt here; RBS reads 18 1/3 1/4 1/8 1/96.

544 Text *tinkār*. S*CT*, 317. From Malay *tingkal*?

545 Text *ṭabāshīr*. SMT, 132, 136; S*CT*, 326.

546 Text *halīlaj kābūlī*. KS, 203. See note 482 above.

547 Text *sunbul*. S*CT*, 324; K*S*, 208; N*ūr*, I, 433–4, editor's note 3225.

548 Text *ḥiltīt*. *Ferula asafoetida*. S*CT*, 319; K*S*, 187.

549 Text *dār fulful/filfil*.; S*CT*, 321; K*S*, 194, 202, 231; D, II, 287, 'les premiers fruits du poivrier'.

550 Text *khuḍaḍ*, *Lycium barbarum*. *SCT*, 319; K*S*, 204.

551 Text *khawlān*, *Succus lycii*. D, I, 413.

552 Text *farāsilah*. YB*HJ*, 563–4; S*P*, 151; S*CT*, 330; SMT, 137.

553 Text *zanjabīl*, *Zingiber officinale*. S*CT*, 323; K*S*, 209.

554 Text *murabbā*.

555 Text *fāghirah*. Made either of the lotus of India, or the cubeb of China. L, VI, 2422.

556 Text *zaytī*.

557 Text *amlaḥ*. D, II, 619.

558 Text *bilīlaj*. *Myrobalana bellerica* or *Terminaria chebula*, Indian stomach medicine. L, I, 246; K*S*, 201.

559 Text *zarnubā* which I take to be *zarnab*, *Atriplex hortensis*. D*M*, 67; K*S*, 209.

560 Text *qirfah*, *Canella winterana*. K, II, 721; K*S*, 206.

561 The fractions are doubtful.

562 Text *'irq sūs*, *Glycyrrhiza glabra*. K, II, 229; D, II, 119; K*S*, 208; *Nūr*, I, 483, note 3528.

563 Text *ḥumar*, *Tamarindus indica*. D*M*, 46; YB*HJ*, 894–5; L*T*, II, 30; SMT, 137.

564 The fractions are doubtful.

565 Text *khiyār shanbar*, *Cassia fistula*. S*CT*, 320; K*S*, 204, 232.

566 Text *dādī*. D, I, 419.

567 Dā'ud, the 4th Rasulid sultan in the Yemen, reg. 696–721/1296–1322.

568 See note 465 above. I opt for Serjeant's suggestion here as it seems to make some sense, although Cahen's comments may be relevant.

569 Text *sinbād*. S*CT*, 324

570 Text *kammūn*, *Cuminum cyminum*. D, II, 498; S*CT*, 332; K*S*, 204.

571 Text *hāl*, *Elettaria cardomomum*. S*CT*, 335; K*S*, 203.

572 Text *muṣawwaf*. D, I, 853.

573 Text al-Ṣūliyān. T*AN*, 466.

574 Text Zanjibārī.

575 Text *ṣandarūs*, *Callitris quadrivalvis*. K*S*, 207.

576 Text Sīlānī. T*AN*, 462.

577 Text *kawdah* for *kawdhah*. K, II, 942.

578 Text *wada'*. K*S*, 208.

579 Numbers uncertain.

580 Text *ajribah*, pl. of *jarāb*.

581 Text *su'd, Cyperus longus/rotundus*. D, I, 654; K*S*, 208, 233.

582 Text *kuḥl*.

583 See *SCT*, 330.

584 Text *ghazl*.

585 Text *tūtiyā*. D, I, 154; *SCT*, 317, 'zinc oxide'; K*S*, 208, 237.

586 Text *wushshaq, Dorema ammoniacum*. D, II, 816; K*S*, 208.

587 Text *turbid, Operculina turpethum*. D, I, 143; K*S*, 208, 234.

588 Text *'uṣārah*. *SCT*, 326, 'absinth juice'.

589 Text *salīṭ*, i.e. either olive oil or sesame oil. L, IV, 1406.

590 Text *samn*.

591 Text *qaṣdīr*. D, II, 363.

592 Text *raṣāṣ aswad*.

593 Text *'asal*.

594 There is an epithet here which is unclear to me; RBS reads *al-b.t.r.w.h*.

595 Text *sham'*.

596 Text *maḥlab, Prunus mahaleb*. *SCT*, 328; K*S*, 205.

597 Text *munaqqā*.

598 Text *thamarah ḥamrā*. *SCT*, 317. Cf. Jāzim's note 3116 (*Nūr*, I, 417), the rose from which rose water is extracted.

599 Text *thamarah ma'ṣūr* [*sic*].

600 Text *'anzarūt, Astragalus* sarcocolla. K*S*, 201.

601 Text *kibrīt*.

602 Text *ḥashīshah*.

603 Numerals unclear.

604 Text *aẓfār*, plur. of *ẓufur*. D, II, 83.

605 Text *'afṣ, Quercus* spp. *SCT*, 328, 'gallnuts'; K*S*, 201.

606 Text *shabb*. K*S*, 207.

607 Text *zarnīkh/zirnīkh*. K*S*, 209.

608 Text *hadas*. K, II, 1400; D*M*, 8, 155; *SCT*, 336.

609 Text *zāj*. K*S*, 208.

610 Text *ābnūs/ābanūs*. *SCT*, 315.

611 Text *al-ṣandal al-Malin dī*. *SCT*, 325.

612 Text *lādhān* = *ādhān*? D, I, 15–16; *Nūr*, I, 451, note 3347.

613 Text *mā'i'ah/may'ah, Styrax* spp. D, II, 637–8; D*M*, 148; *SCT*, 332; K*S*, 205.

614 Text *murdāsanj*. D, II, 588; *SPD*, 1212, 'dross of lead'; K*S*, 206.

615 Text *martak*. D, II, 586.

616 Text *ushnah, Alectoria usneoides*. D, I, 808, *sub sh y b*; KS, 208.

617 Reading *asmaj.*

618 The *farḍ* date was considered the best in medieval times and cultivated near Aden. It is today an important variety in Oman. V*MA*, 191.

619 Text *qashsh*. K, II, 740, 'palmier d'espèce inférieure'.

620 Text *qāṭir*. K, II, 766; S*CT*, 327; *Nūr*, I, 239.

621 Text *ṣabir suquṭrī, Aloe succotrina*. KS, 207.

622 Or 1/2 1/3.

623 Text *murr, Commifora myrrha*. KS, 206.

624 I can make nothing of *al-r.w.?ā.*

625 Text *al-farfarān al-?.ṭ.r al-sham'ī*. K, II, 582, *firfir*.

626 RBS reads *al-h.j.rī*. I would prefer *al-h.j.?ī.*

627 Text *'āj*. K, II, 398; S*CT*, 333.

628 Text *wars, Memecylon tinctorium*. V*MA*, 219, 248.

629 Text *zabīb.*

630 Text *'uṭb/'uṭub, Gossypium arboreum*. V*MA*, 202.

631 Text *mūrī*. K, II, 1167, 'poil', 'laine'. This may precisely indicate the 'woolly' phase of development of the cotton, but *mubar'am* literally means 'the flower before it opens'; L, I, 189.

632 Text *lāk*. KS, 204.

633 Reading *yu'khadh 'alay-h*, rather than *ya'khudh 'alay-h* clearly in the text.

634 My oblique stroke represents a symbol in the text in the shape of a shepherd's crook which separates the two sets of numerals.

635 Text *baqqam*, species *Caesalpinia*, a red dye. L, I, 237; D*M*, 22.

636 Text *taqdimah*. D, II, 324.

637 Text *'amal*. D, II, 175.

638 The text seems to read *fa-inna-hum t.ṣ.b.*

639 Text *ḥarīr.*

640 Text *yu'ashshar hindī*. I find this puzzling. Perhaps we should read *hindī* with an understood *halīlaj*, as above, and translate 'Indian myrobolan', but this does not solve the puzzle.

641 Text *baqāyir*, pl. of *baqīr/baqīrah*. L, I, 234; D*V*, 84.

642 Read *ma'āzir*, pl. of *mi'zar.*

643 Read *ḥanābilī*, pl. of *ḥanbal*? K, I, 500; L, II, 655.

644 Text *al-'amāyim al-marqūm.*

645 Text *wujūh.* D, II, 794.

646 Read *baqyār*, a Persian word, the garment worn exclusively by qadis. D*V*, 87.

647 It is not clear exactly where this sentence fits in.

648 Text *muṭarrazah.*

649 Text *'arāḍī* which I take as the pl. of *'.r.ḍiyyah.* D, II, 113, not vocalized.

650 It is possible that this means 'skull cap' (D, II, 120, *'araqiyyah*; D*V*, 298; S*T*, 78).

651 Text *'uqadāt.* D, II, 150. Cf. *Nūr*, I, 443, Jāzim's note 3293.

652 Text *al-shiqaq al-ashkalāṭ.* S*T*, 259; D, I, 25.

653 Text *khiraq*, pl. of *khirqah.*

654 RBS '45', but the arithmetic is incorrect. The author is simply telling us that the cloth concerned is 40 cubits and, since a *qaṣabah* is 4 cubits, it is also 10 *qaṣabah* in length.

655 Text *dhirā' yad.* HMG, 61; S*P*, 160–2.

656 Text *qaṣabat ḥadīd.* HMG, 63.

657 Text *sharb.* S*T*, 259.

658 Text *taqānī'*, pl. of *taqnī'*? = *qinā'*?

659 Text *ṭaraḥāt.* D*V*, 254-62; S*T*, 261.

660 Presumably dittography.

661 Dionisius Agius kindly suggest that this may be /ṣ/ › /s/ and perhaps it is to be associated with D, I, 839, *ṣ q l*, VIII, 'être poli'.

662 Text *wiqāyah.* D*V*, 430–1, also 280–91, *ṭāqiyyah*, and 375–8, *miqna'ah*; D, II, 844; S*T*, 57 and 94, where Serjeant says it means 'belt', though with no lexicographical support.

663 Text *shāshāt.* S*T*, 150; S*A*, II, 124.

664 The fractions are unclear. RBS reads '1/3 1/12'.

665 Text *al-khiraq al-bunduqī al-rifā'.* CC. D, I, 118.

666 There would appear to be a figure here, although it is illegible.

667 Text *mutaqārib* for *muqārib.* K, II, 706; D, II, 331.

668 Text *'aṣāyib*, pl. of *'iṣābah.* D*V*, 300–3; S*T*, 248.

669 RBS reads *'.n.fah*, but the reading is uncertain.

670 Text *makhāniq*, pl. of *mikhnaqah.* K, I, 643.

671 Text *ḥawāshī.* pl. of *ḥāshiyah.* Perhaps 'ribbon'. D, I, 293; S*T*, 247.

672 Text *sha'ārī* which I take to be the pl. of *sha'riyyah.* D*V*, 226–9; D, I, 763. Or 'goat'. IM*Q*, 352, 456.

673 I accept here the figures given by RBS, although it is a sign with which I am unfamiliar.

674 The same illegible word as that is indicated in note 669 above.

675 Text clearly *b.dhalāt*. I do not think *bidhlah* in the CA meaning can be meant here (L, I, 174, 'worn, work garment'). RBS indicates that *bidhlah* is a colloquial form of *badlah*. D*V*, 396, *badlah*, 'vêtement splendide'; D, I, 58.

676 RBS '1/6'.

677 Text *al-bidhalāt al-wasaṭ*.

678 Text *alfiyyah/'.n.fah*?

679 RBS reads '1/48'.

680 Text *kāfūrī*. D, II, 477.

681 Text *tafṣīlah*, pl. *tafāṣīl*. D, II, 272.

682 Text *bi-thawb*.

683 Text *d.w.n.j*.

684 A tentative reading.

685 Reading *al-jawānī*. CC.

686 Text *ṣīdāt*. D, I, 856.

687 See above note 376.

688 Text *al-?.r.d.?ī*.

689 Text *al-b.?.d.rī*.

690 Text *al-mu'ammarah bi-al-maḥārah*. D, II, 334.

691 Cf. RBS who apparently reads '11/12'.

692 Text *mamāṭir*, pl. of *mamṭar/mimṭar*. D, II, 608; *Nūr*, I, 457.

693 There are no figures attached to this entry.

694 Text *ḥulal*, pl. of *ḥullah*. S*T*, 247; cf. D, I, 312.

695 RBS '1/3'.

696 Text *sawāsī*, pl. of *sūsī*. D, I, 701; D*V*, 317; S*T*, 130; *Nūr*, I, 434–5. This is usually a linen textile; it may be derived from Sousse in North Africa, Sūs in Khuzistan, or perhaps even Suez in Egypt.

697 There is perhaps something missing here, as this is identical with the previous item.

698 Text *rifā'*, pl. of *rafī'*. D, I, 542; D*V*, 140.

699 Text *sarīrī*.

700 This numeral is doubtful.

701 Cf. *Nūr*, 456, I, 481.

702 RBS.

703 RBS 'Qannājī', but without dots in the MS. See also *Nūr*, I, 456, 481.

704 S*T* has numerous references to *sharb* which Serjeant calls 'linen stuff' (e.g. 107, 140, 259) and I follow his vocalization here. Jāzim in the *Nūr*, I, 188, vocalizes *shurub* and defines it as *malābis ḥarīriyyah.* D, I, 740, confirms the former vocalization and mentions 'une espèce de soie', as well as 'une espèce de toile de lin très-fine et très-précieuse'. See above note 657.

705 Text *bi-jihāz jawhar al-awsī al-kibrītī* — a tentative translation.

706 August 1349.

707 See note 703 above.

708 The numerals are illegible.

709 Text *ṭarḥ*. See above note 659. Perhaps 'carpet'. D, II, 31–2.

710 Text *al-thiyāb al-'.rām.ṭ.r.bī.*

711 Text *makhāmil*, pl. of *mukhmal*. D, I, 406; S*T*, 255.

712 Text *dusūt*, pl. of *dast*. S*T*, 246.

713 Text *al-tafāṣīl al-q r/al-gh r al-m r s lī.*

714 Text *khalanj*.

715 Text *ma'āshir*, pl. of *ma'sharah*. *Nūr*, I, 24, and Jāzim's note 192 tells us this tray is usually brass.

716 In error for Qays?

717 Qaysh for Qays?

718 Text *al-m.n.q.lah*; RBS *minqalah*.

719 Text *aṭbāq*, pl. of *ṭabaq*.

720 Text *sarband*. S*PD*, 670.

721 Text *uzur*, pl. of *izār*.

722 Literally '8 and 7 cubits'.

723 Text *marjān*. S*PD*, 1210.

724 Text *māward*. D, II, 574.

725 Text *nūshādur*. S*PD*, 1434; K*S*, 206.

726 Text *rāsukht*. D, I, 496; S*PD*, 563.

727 Text *zunjafr*. D, I, 606; S*PD*, 624; K*S*, 209.

728 Text *zi'baq/zi'biq*; Persian *zībaq*. D, I, 576–7, 'mercure'; S*PD*, 632, 'quicksilver'.

729 Text *ṣufr*. D, I, 835.

730 Text *fakhr*?

731 Text *qaṣdīr*. See above note 591.

732 Text *usrub(b)*. S*PD*, 57.

733 Text *maṣṭakā*. D, II, 605; S*PD*, 1253.

734 I insert this folio, 4a, 4b, here, relying on the catchword *al-mā'i'ah* at the bottom of f. 24b and the context.

735 Text *al-mā'i'ah al-sā'ilah wa-al-raṭb*, *Styrax* spp. D, II, 637–8; K*S*, 205.

736 This fraction is not clear. It may also be '1/2 1/3'.

737 Text *'.s.m.?.j/ḥ/kh*. See above note 617. I follow RBS, *asmaj*. *Asmaḥ* is also possible, meaning 'in very large numbers'; D, I, 681. *Asmaj* also suggests *sāmij*, 'roussin', i.e. the beads are reddish in colour. *Nūr*, I, 426, has *'.s.m.s.ḥ*, and the editor admits defeat.

738 *Nūr*, I, 480, *durakī*, with no further help from the editor.

739 *Nūr*, I, 480, *al-durakī al-'abrī*.

740 Text *duhn al-ward*; K*S*, 202.

741 Text *tamr*.

742 Text *mushaqqar*, i.e. whose whiteness is greater than its redness. *Nūr*, I, 413, though the editor prefers to take *aẓfār* as perfume. In which case, what does *mudawwar* mean?

743 Text *maks*.

744 Text *marjān*. D, II, 586–7; *Nūr*, I, 166, note 1305.

745 Text *tābūt*.

746 Text *qafaṣ*.

747 Reading *shammah*.

748 There is a tear at the top right of f. 4b and the *'ayn* of *'ushūr* is missing.

749 Text *dilālah*. SMT, 134; SPP, 212–14.

750 Reading *aḥad* rather than the *aḥadan* of the text.

751 Text *ḥ.rār.b*. RBS tentatively *jawārib* (sg. *jawrab*). S*T*, 245.

752 Text *ḥ.m.rā.n/t*.

753 Text *al-b.r wāsān*. RBS *al-bazz wāsān*, with a query.

754 Text *min al-bāb*, i.e. Bāb al-Mandab.

755 Text illegible.

756 See S*T*, 258.

757 First two lines of MS torn, perhaps reading *wa-kāna* at the end of the first entry, under which is *wa-yuḍāfu 112*, the latter parallel to the first word of line two: *'.sh.r.h*. This tear means that we are unable to confirm that f. 4b with the

catchword *al-jawāzī* is directly continued on f. 25a, but it seems that there is at least one more page missing.

758 See previous note.

759 The last fraction is not entirely clear.

760 Text *rawsā*. *Nūr*, I, 430, defines it as *lubān mabṭī*, i.e. frankincense which is stripped by hand from the tree without the use of any sharp implement (Jāzim's note 3206).

761 RBS is uncertain of the reading (*al-ṭ/ẓ.r.f/q*), but suggests *ẓ.r.f.* I can throw no further light on the word which ought to indicate some kind of incense-like substance. A common meaning of *ẓarf*, if that is the correct reading, 'leather receptacle' is not likely here.

762 Text *mukarrar*. D, II, 451.

763 Reading *raja' yuqāsam*.

764 Text *al-farfarān al-sham'ī al-muraṭṭab*.

765 Text al-Shām, probably northern Tihāmah is meant.

766 This should perhaps read Tajūrah, a bay SW of Aden. T*AN*, 422.

767 On the Yemeni Red Sea coast near al-Luḥayyah. IB*T*, II, 366; T*AN*, 412.

768 See IB*T*, II, 366.

769 Text D.l.y.

770 Text *ardī*. Y*M*, I, 146, mentioning 'fine cloths'; L*L*, 208, mentioning silk in particular. S*T*, 86.

771 Text *turkī*. Another textile-producing area. S*T*, 81, 103 etc.

772 RBS reads *al-juwwāy* which I am unable to better or explain.

773 A silk cloth. S*T*, 113.

774 The verso side of the torn page. A whole entry is missing. See above note 757.

775 I think there is another fraction missing. Cf. RBS '1/96'.

776 This seems to be the meaning of al-Shām here; cf. above note 765.

777 Text *dusūt*, pl. of *dast*. I take the meaning from S*PD*, 519 and S*T*, 212, 246. Cf. the editor of the *Nūr*, I, 489, note 3564, who refers to a type of cloth. It may however mean 'a suit of clothes'; L, III, 878.

778 Text *muḥarrar*. Cf. S*T*, 255, 'silken cloth'. The Arabic form clearly implies a process of 'making like silk', hence the translation. Mercerization, named after John Mercer, a nineteenth-century English calico printer, is the process of treating cotton fabrics with an alkali solution in order to render them more

receptive to dyes. If the fabrics are stretched during the process, they assume a silk-like finish. I envisage a similar process here.

779 Text *mayāzir*, pl. of *mīzar/mi'zar*.

780 For *dast* here, see L, III, 878. The words *al-dast qiṭ'atayn malfūf'* seem to fit in this place, but I am not entirely sure.

781 Text *mashriqī*, which I understand as translated.

782 Text *ṭarīq al-bāb*. It may of course mean 'via Bāb al-Mandab' and the items may perhaps have been transported by sea from northern Tihāmah.

783 Text *makhādd*, pl. of *mikhaddah*.

784 Text *al-ṭ.r.y*.

785 Text *raja' ?.w.?.?*. The second word is illegible and may be three or four letters.

786 The last fraction is doubtful.

787 Text *malāḥif*, pl. of *milḥaf* and *milḥafah*. These could be cloaks, as translated, veils, horse cloths or shawls. D, II, 527; D*V*, 401–3.

788 Text *maṣāwin*, pl. of *maṣwan*. *Nūr*, I, 455, editor's note 3364; the word is used to this day in the Yemen.

789 This is doubtful, though I cannot see it can be anything else.

790 At this point a whole folio or more is missing. F. 25b has the catchword '*al-naṣāfī*'.

791 Text *shādar* for Persian *chādar*. D, I, 739 (*shawdhar*); D*V*, 216–9 (*chawdhar*); S*PD*, 383 (*chādar*).

792 All these figures are tentative. I take it that for each of these quantities between 10 and 15 *raṭl* are taken.

793 The 'one dinar' is placed beneath the word *raṭlayn*.

794 Reading *al-bilīlaj al-aṣfar* rather than the *al-bilīlaj wa-al-aṣfar* of the text, *Terminalia bellerica*. D*M*, 24; K*S*, 201, 235.

795 There are two *idhā* clauses and perhaps the *wāw* is missing from the second. Or perhaps this is to be taken as an after-thought and linked with the previous list of commodities.

796 Text *mujalladah*.

797 Text *ḥaṭīṭ*. D, I, 300, *ḥaṭṭa al-māl*, 'contribuer', 'payer les contributions'. Bearing in mind, however, the meaning of the root, this may mean 'reduction'.

798 Begins 11 March 1350.

799 RBS reads, seemingly accurately, *b.'.t.rār y*.

800 Insertion from the left margin.

801 I.e. the items are exported in these quantities and all between 300–700 are charged 10 *raṭl*.

802 The MS is damaged and a piece is missing. There is something illegible after this reading. The catchword is missing also.

803 Text *udum*, pl. of *adīm*.

804 Reading *al-marqūm*. RBS, 'marked with a price?', 'stamped'.

805 A group of merchants operating during Ayyubid and Mamluk times. *EI* 'Kārimī'; GNL, *passim*. This record of a special rate for the Kārimī merchants is interesting. The paucity of the material on the Kārim here can be interpreted as indicative of their decline about the beginning of the ninth/fifteenth century. CSFS, 30.

806 Text *ṣurrah*. D, I, 826.

807 Text *ḥ.r.ṣ*. RBS *ḥ r ḍ*. I read *ḥaraḍ*, pl. of *ḥarḍah*. *Nūr*, I, 528, editor's note 3849.

808 Text *rizmah*. G*MT*, 55. It may read *waraqah*, i.e. one sheet.

809 Text *wa-ilā* …, illegible.

810 This translation is extremely tentative.

811 Text *mufattish*.

812 Text *wālī*.

813 The bottom right-hand side of the page is torn and some words and letters missing.

814 Text perhaps *khitam*, pl. of *khitmah*, *khatam*, or *khutum*, pl. of *khitām*. I translate tentatively after RBS. L*T*, 153, 157; P*D*, I, 120.

815 Text *ṣinā'ah*. Perhaps 'shipyard' is meant.

816 Text *'arāyiḍ*, presumably pl. of *'arīḍah*. H*D*, 465, 'petition', 'letter'; W*D*, 604, 'petition', 'application'.

817 Text *ṭaraḥāt*.

818 Text *min al-baḥr aw min al-bāb*, i.e. from the Indian Ocean or the Bāb al-Mandab. SP, 212.

819 Reading *wa-amr dhālik ilā al-nāẓir lā yuṭliq shay'an ba'd dhālik illā bi-amr sharīf*.

820 Text *nawākhidh*.

821 Text *satāmī*. A Gujerati word. SP, 212; P*D*, I, 215.

822 Text *zarībah*.

823 Text *matjar*. The office was of Fatimid origin and administered the storage of stable goods like wood, iron, lead etc., particularly those required for military purposes. IM*Q*, 327; R*S*, 92–4; SPP, 214–15.

824 I.e. when the monsoon permits the arrival of ships in Aden.

825 Text *ta'shīr* which may also mean 'when the taxes are being calculated'. SP, 212; SPP, 218.

826 Text *fusūḥāt*, presumably the pl. of the pl. of *fasḥ*. L, VI, 2395.

827 Text *mubashshir*. SMT, 129 and SPP, 208, 211. Perhaps the Rasulid messenger carries messages to and from the overseer and the governor only, in contrast to the Ayyubid messenger who was primarily concerned with liaising with the family and/or friends of those on board ship and he was paid by those to whom he brought his message.

828 Text *jihāt*. D, II, 787; R*S*, 43, note 4. Initially the word denoted the 'district' whence the tax was derived.

829 A tentative translation of *wa-al-mujrā fī al-siyāqāt*.

830 Text *a'māl*. R*S*, 135.

831 Reading *qawā'imāt*. K, II, 840; D, II, 426.

832 Reading *tuḍbatu*. D, II, 2, 'confisquer', 'saisir'.

833 Text *ta'dīb*.

834 Reading *yunzalu 'alay-h*. K, II, 1240.

835 Reading *'amā'ir*, pl. of *'amārah* after RBS. D, II, 171.

836 The text reads *mubāshirīn*, but it is clear from the context that this translation is appropriate here. See also SRA, 237–9.

837 Cf. *Nūr*, I, 513, 'the two comptrollers in the customs house'.

838 The MS is damaged and a word missing, though this would appear to be the reading required.

839 Text *naqqād*.

840 Text *jābī*.

841 I.e. customs posts on the land side of the port.

842 Text *maṭarāt*. D, II, 608. They would appear to be made of leather or wood.

843 Text *ḥilwah*.

844 Text *iltizām*. The meaning may be 'customs dues'. D, II, 535–6.

845 Text *dukkān*. This seems to me to be the reading of the MS, although RBS has *dakkāt*. The two can be synonymous. L, III, 899–900; D, I, 454.

846 Text *ṣinā'ah*. D, I, 848; C*D*, 283, 'atelier'.

847 Text *al-'imārah wa-al-ṣinā'ah*. The latter may well mean 'shipyard' in this context.

848 Text *'irāfah*. IM*L*, IX, 154; D, II, 117.

849 Text *tanjīl*. L*G*, III, 2748; P*D*, II, 479; *Nūr*, I, 502, 512, 513, 'lighterage secretaries'.

850 Text *siyāqah*. The translation is very tentative and follows RBS; I find no lexicographical support for the word.

851 Text *khazzān*.

852 Text *rub'*. The translation is tentative. D, I, 503.

853 What follows is illegible; the MS is either stained or an attempt has been made to delete at least two words.

854 Text *muqaddam*.

855 The 6 and 7 are clear, but there may be other numerals (see above note 853). Whether I count offices, or officials, I cannot bring the total to 67! I retain the numerals in imitation of the original MS reading.

856 I think *kharāj* may simply means 'tax' here.

857 Text *jarīb*. IM*L*, II, 228; *ZT*, II, 148.

858 Text *awsiyah*, pl. of *wasiyyah*. D, II, 815. Ḥusaynī also has *wasāyā*.

859 Text *amlāk*, pl. of *milk*.

860 RBS *al-mujrā wa-al-'. jūz*, but this is far from clear.

861 Text *manākh*.

862 Text *bayt al-bazz*, part of the customs house.

863 Text *multazimīn*.

864 Text *wilāyah*.

865 Text *miḥnāṭ*.

866 A place name. See SRA, 241, note 92.

867 The numerals are clear and complete, although I cannot reconcile this total, whichever way I calculate.

868 721–64/1322–63.

869 Text *manfa'ah*.

870 Text *duqqah*. D, I, 451.

871 Text *nasīj*. S*T*, 257.

872 This is the last of the text of the *Mulakhkhaṣ* which survives. There is the catchword *al-fawfal*.

REFERENCES

Agius, Dionisius. 1984. *Arabic Literary Works as a Source of Documentation for Technical Terms of the Material Culture*. (Berlin) [A*LW*]

—— 2002. *In the Wake of the Dhow. The Arabian Gulf and Oman*. (Reading) [A*W*]

Allouche, Adel. 1994. *Mamluk Economics a Study and Translation of al-Maqrīzī's* Ighāthah. (Salt Lake City) [A*ME*]

Cahen, Claude. 1964. 'Douanes et commerce dans les ports méditerranéens de l'Egypte médiévale d'après le *Minhādj* d'al-Makhzūmī', *JESHO* 7/3, 218–314 [CD]

Cahen, Claude and R.B. Serjeant. 1957. 'A Fiscal Survey of the Medieval Yemen Notes Preparatory to a Critical Edition of the *Mulaḫḫaṣ al-fitan* [sic] of al-Ḥasan b. ʿAlī al-Šarīf al-Ḥusaynī', *Arabica* 4, 23–33 [CSFS]

al-Dimyāṭī, Maḥmūd Muṣṭafā. 1965. *Muʿjam asmāʾ al-nabātāt al-wāridah fī* Tāj al-ʿarūs *li-l-Zabīdī*. (Cairo) [D*M*]

Dozy, R.P.A. 1845. *Dictionnaire détailé des noms des vêtements chez les Arabes*, (Amsterdam) [D*V*]

Dozy, R. 1881. *Supplément aux dictionnaires arabes*. 2 vols, (Leiden) [D]

Ehrenkreutz, Andrew S. 1964. 'The *Taṣrīf* and *Taʿsīr* Calculations in Mediaeval Mesopotamian Fiscal Operations', *JESHO* 7, 46–56 [E*T*]

Forand, P.G. 1966. 'Notes on *ʿušr* and *maks*', *Arabica* 13, 137–41 [FN]

Gacek, Adam. 2001. *The Arabic Manuscript Tradition a Glossary of Technical Terms and Bibliography*. (Handbook of Oriental Studies, Section 1, the Near and Middle East, Volume 58. Leiden, Boston and Cologne) [G*MT*]

Garcin, Jean-Claude. 1976. *Un Centre musulman de la Haute-Egypte médiévale: Qūṣ*. (Textes arabes et études islamiques 6, Cairo) [G*Q*]

Goitein, S.D. 1967. *A Mediterranean Society - The Jewish Communities of the Arab World as Portrayed in the Documents of the Cairo Geniza, I, Economic Foundations*. (Berkeley, Los Angeles and London) [G*S*]

—— 1957. 'New Light on the Beginnings of the Kārim Merchants', *JESHO* 1, 175–84 [GNL]

Government of Bombay. 1909. *An Account of the Arab Tribes in the Vicinity of Aden*. (Bombay) [B*A*]

Grosset-Grange, Henri. 1993. *Glossaire nautique arabe ancien et moderne de l'Océan indien*. (Mémoires de la Section d'Histoire des Sciences et des Techniques 5, Paris) [G-G*G*] al-Hajji, Hayat Nasser. 2000. *The Internal Affairs in Egypt during the Reign of Sultan al-Nāṣir Muḥammad b. Qalāwūn, 709–741/1309–1341*. (Kuwait) [H*I*]

al-Hamdānī, al-Ḥasan b. Aḥmad. 1968. *Ṣifat Jazīrat al-'Arab*, ed. David Heinrich Müller (Leiden) [H*Ṣ*]

Hava, J.G. 1951. *Arabic-English Dictionary*. (Beirut) [H*D*]

Hinz, Walther. 1970. *Islamische Masse und Gewichte*. (Leiden) [H*MG*]

Ibn Baṭṭūṭah, Muḥammad b. ʿAbdallāh. 1958–2000. *The Travels of Ibn Baṭṭūṭa A.D. 1325–1354*, 5 vols, I–III, trans. by H.A.R. Gibb, IV, trans. by H.A.R. Gibb, finished by C.F. Beckingham, V, index to I–IV by A.D.H. Bivar. (Hakluyt Society, London) [IB*T*]

Ibn Mammātī, Asʿad. 1943. *Qawānīn al-dawāwīn*, ed. S ʿAṭiyah. (Cairo) [IM*Q*]

Ibn Manẓūr, Muḥammad b. Mukarram. 1955–6. *Lisān al-'Arab*. 15 vols, (Beirut) [IM*L*]

Ibn al-Mujāwir, Yūsuf b. Yaʿqūb. 1951–4. *Tārīkh al-Mustabṣir*, ed. Oscar Löfgren. 2 vols, (Leiden) [IM*TM*]

Kahl, Oliver. 2003. *Sābūr ibn Sahl The Small Dispensatory*. (Islamic Philosophy Theology and Science Texts and Studies, Volume 53. Leiden and Boston) [K*S*]

Kazimirski, A. de Biberstein. 1860. *Dictionnaire arabe-français*. 2 vols, (Paris) [K]

Kindermann, Hans. 1934. *Schiff im Arabischen*. (Zwickau i Sa.) [K*S*]

Landberg, Comte de. 1901. *Etudes sur les dialectes de l'Arabie méridionale, Ḥaḍramoût*. (Leiden) [L*E*]

—— 1920–42. *Glossaire daṯînois*, 3 vols. (Leiden) [L*G*]

Lane, Edward William. 1863–93. *An Arabic-English Lexicon*. 8 parts, (London and Edinburgh) [L]

Le Strange, G. 1966. *The Lands of the Eastern Caliphate*. (London) [L*L*]

Löfgren, Oscar. 1936–50. *Arabische Texte zur Kenntnis der Stadt Aden im Middelalter*. 2 vols, (Uppsala, Leipzip and Haag) [L*T*]

Løkkegaard, Frede. 1950. *Islamic Taxation in the Classical Period with Special Reference to Circumstances in Iraq*. (Copenhagen) [L*T*]

Maktari, A.M.A. 1971. *Water Rights and Irrigation Practices in Laḥj: a Study of the Application of Customary and* Sharīʿah *Law in South-West Arabia*. (Cambridge) [M*WR*]

Nashwān b. Saʿīd al-Ḥimyarī. 1999. *Shams al-'ulūm wa-dawā' kalām al-'Arab min al-kulūm*, eds Ḥusayn b. ʿAbdallāh al-ʿAmrī, Muṭahhar b. ʿAlī al-Iryānī and Yūsuf Muḥammad ʿAbdallāh. 12 vols, (Beirut and Damascus) [N*S*]

Nūr. 2003–5. *Nūr al-ma'ārif fī nuẓum wa-qawānīn wa-a'rāf al-Yaman fī al-'ahd al-muẓaffarī al-wārif, Lumière de la connaisance - Règles, lois et coutumes du Yémen sous la règne du sultan rasoulide al-Muẓaffar*, ed. Muḥammad ʿAbd al-Raḥīm Jāzim. 2 vols, (Centre Français d'Archéologie et de Sciences Sociales de Sanaa, Ṣanʿā') [*Nūr*]

Piamenta, Moshe. 1990–1. *Dictionary of Post-classical Yemeni Arabic*. 2 vols, (Leiden) [P*D*]

Qalqashandī, Aḥmad b. ʿAlī al-. 1919–22. *Ṣubḥ al-a'shā fī ṣinā'at al-inshā*. 14 vols, (Cairo) [Q*Ṣ*]

Rabie, Hassanein. 1972. *The Financial System of Egypt, A.H. 564-741/A.D. 1169–134l*. (London Oriental Series, Volume 25. London, New York and Toronto) [R*S*]

Serjeant, R.B. 1974. 'The Cultivation of Cereals in Mediaeval Yemen', *Arabian* Studies 1, 25–75 [SCC]

—— 1972. *Islamic Textiles Material for a History up to the Mongol Conquest*. (Beirut) [S*T*]

—— 1974 'The Ports of Aden and Shihr (Mediaeval Period)', *Les Grands Escales I. Recueils de la Société Jean Bodin 32 (10e Colloque d'Histoire maritime)*. (Brussels) [SP]

—— 1963. *The Portuguese off the South Arabian Coast*. (Oxford) [S*P*]

Serjeant R.B. and Ronald Lewcock. 1983. *Ṣan'ā' an Arabian Islamic City* (London) [SL*Ṣ*]

al-Shamrookh, Nayef Abdullah, *The Commerce and Trade of the Rasulids in the Yemen, 630-858/1231-1454*, Kuwait, 1996. [S*CT*]

al-Sharjī, Aḥmad b. Aḥmad. 1321[/1903]. *Ṭabaqāt al-khawāṣṣ ahl al-ṣidq wa-al-ikhlāṣ*. (Cairo, 1321[/1903]) [SI*Ṭ*]

Smith, G.R. 1978. *The Ayyubids and Early Rasulids in the Yemen*. (Gibb Memorial Series Nos 26, II. London) [S*A*]

—— 1995. 'Have You Anything to Declare? Maritime Trade and Commerce in Ayyubid Aden: Practices and Taxes', *Proceedings of the Seminar for Arabian Studies* 25, 127–40 [SMT]

—— 1996. 'More on the Port Practices and Taxes of Medieval Aden', *New Arabian Studies* 3, 208–18 [SPP]

—— 2005. 'The Rasulid Administration in Ninth/Fifteenth Century Yemen – Some Government Departments and Officials' in *Studia Semitica The Journal of*

Semitic Studies Jubilee Volume (Journal of Semitic Studies Supplement 16, Oxford). 223–47 [SRA]

Steingass, F. 1930. *A Comprehensive Persian-English Dictionary*. (London) [S*PD*]

Tibbetts, G.R. 1971. *Arab Navigation in the Indian Ocean before the Coming of the Portuguese*. (London) [T*AN*]

Varisco, Daniel Martin. 1995. 'The Magical Significance of the Lunar Stations in the 13th Century Yemeni *Kitāb al-Tabṣira fī 'ilm al-nujūm* of al-Malik al-Ashraf', *Quaderni di Studi Arabi* 13, 19–40. [VMS]

—— 1994. *Medieval Agriculture and Islamic Science The Almanac of a Yemeni Sultan*. (Publications on the Near East University of Washington 6. Seattle and London) [V*MA*]

Wehr, Hans. 1971. *A Dictionary of Modern Written Arabic*, ed. J. Milton Cowan. (Wiesbaden) [W*D*]

Yāqūt b. ʿAbdallāh al-Ḥamawī. 1979. *Mu'jam al-buldān*. 5 vols, (Beirut) [Y*M*]

Yule, Col. Henry and A.C. Burnell. 1969. *Hobson-Jobson: a Glossary of Colloquial Anglo-Indian Words and Phrases, and of Kindred Terms, Etymological, Historical, Geographical and Discursive*. (London) [YB*HJ*]

al-Zabīdī, Muḥammad Murtaḍā. 1965–. *Tāj al-'arūs min jawāhir al-qāmūs*, ed. ʿAbd al-Sattār Aḥmad Farrāj et al. (Kuwait) [Z*T*]

INDICES

All references in the indices are to the folios of the MS. NB ff. 4a and 4b follow f. 24b and precede f. 25a.

In this and the following index, only the basic commodity is listed.

1 Commodities in the translation

Agalloch 19b, 20a

Aloes 17a, 17b, 19b, 20a, 22b, 24b, 4a, 25a, 26a

Alum 22a, 25a

Ambergris 17a, 20a

Ammoniacum 22a

Anchor 21a

Anklet 17a

Antimony 22a, 24b, 4a

Apparel 23b, 24a

Arsenic 22a, 4a

Asafoetida 21b, 22a

Areca nut 20b, 26b

Bamboo 20b

Basket 17b

Beads 21a, 22b, 4a

Bed clothes 24a

Bed cover 19a, 26b

Bismuth 24b, 25a

Borax 21b

Border 24a

Bowl 21b

Bracelet 17a

Brass 22a, 4a, 26a

Brazil-wood 22b, 26b

Brocade 18a, 23b

Calico 21b

Calomel 24b, 4a, 26a

Camels 17a

Camphor 17a, 20b

Camphor water 20b

Canella 22a, 26a

Cardamom 22a, 25a

Carnelian 20b

Carpet 19a, 25b

Cassia, bark 22a, 4a, 27b

Cassumunar 26a

Celandine 20b

Chick peas 21a

Chinaware 21b

Cinnabar 24b, 4a, 26a

Civet cat 17a, 17b,

Cloak 18a, 19a, 21b 24a, 25b

Cloth 17b, 18a, 18b, 19a, 21b, 23a, 23b, 24a, 24b, 4a, 4b, 25a, 25b, 27b

Cloves 20b

Coat 23a

Coconut 20b

Coconut fibres 22a

Coir 17b

Collar 23a

Copper 4a

Coral 4a

Costus 17b, 22a, 25a, 26a

Cotton 22b

Cover 19a

Cowries 22a, 26a

Cubeb 21b, 22a, 27b

Cumin 4a, 22a, 25a

Curcuma, 26a

Cushion 24b, 25b

Cyclamen 22b, 4a

Cyperus 22a, 4a, 25a

Dates 17b, 22b, 4a

Doum palm 17b
Dragon's blood 22b, 25a
Durakī
D.w.n.j 18a, 23b
Ebony 22b
Fabric 18a, 23a, 23b, 25a
Fenugreek 17b
Fish 17b
Fleminin 22b
Frankincense 25a, 26a
Fruit 22a
Galingale 20b, 26a
Garlic 17b
Garment 18b, 22b, 23b, 4a, 25a
Ghee 17b, 22a, 4a, 25a, 26a
Ginger 22a, 26a
Girls 17a
Glass, Aleppan 21a
Grain 17b, 21b
Grapes 17b
Head rope 19a
Head-covering18a, 23a
Headcloth 23a, 25b
Headdress 18b, 24b
Hemp 22a, 25a
Henna 17b
Honey 17a, 22a, 4a, 25a, 26a
Hood 23a, 24a
Horses 17a, 4b
Hypericum 22a, 25a
Indigo 17b, 21b
Iron 17b, 21a, 4a, 25b, 26b
Ivory 22b, 4a, 25a, 26a
Juice 22a
Lac 22b
Lead 22a, 24b, 4a, 25a, 26a
Leather 26a, 26b
Linen 22b, 4a, 26b, 27b
Liquorice 22a, 4a
Lithage 22b, 4a
Loincloth 24b, 4b
Lycium 22a
Mace 20b
Mace pin 21a
Mahaleb cherry 22a, 4a, 25a, 26b
Mahaleb cherry bark 22a, 22b, 4a
Mares 17a
Mantle 17a, 18a, 24a, 24b, 4b, 25b
Mastic 24b, 4a
Material 18b
Memecylon 25a
Musk 17a, 20a
Myrobalan 21b, 22a, 22b, 26a
Myrrh 22b, 25a
Myrtle 22b, 4a, 25a
Nacre 20b, 25b
Napkin 18b, 19b, 23a, 23b
Nutmeg 20b
Oak gall 22a, 4a
Oil 17b, 22a, 25a, 26a
Olibanum 17b, 22b
Onyx 4a, 25a
Orache 22a
Paper 19b, 25b
Parchment 26b
Pearls 17a, 20a, 24b
Pepper 17b, 21b, 26a, 26b, 27b
Pepper, long 22a
Perfume 17a, 22a, 4a, 25a
Pewter 22a, 24b, 26a
Piece 18a, 23a, 24a, 24b, 4b, 25b
Pillow 19a, 25b
Pillow case 23a
Piping 23a

Plate 21b
Platter 21b
Pot 26b
Purslane 22b, 25a
Raincoat 23b
Raisins 17b, 22b, 4a, 25a
Rhubarb, Chinese 20b
Rice 21a
Ring 17a
Robe 18b, 25b
Rose oil 4a
Rose water 20b
Sack 22a
Saffron 20b, 24b, 25a
St John's wort 17b
Sal-ammoniac 24b
Salt and pepper, mixture 27b
Sandal 21a
Sandalwood 20b, 22a, 22b
Sandarac 22a
Sarcocolla 22a, 4a, 25a
Sardonyx 22a
Sesame 21a
Shark 17b
Sheep 27a
Silk 20b, 22b
Skin 21a
Skull cap 23b
Slaves, 17a, 17b, 26b
Sorghum 17b, 21a, 21b
Spear shafts 20b
Spikenard 21b
Steel 21a
Stirrups 21a
Strips 19b, 4b, 25b
Stockings 4b
Storax 22b, 4a
Stuff 18b, 23b, 24b
Subā'iyyah 18a, 18b, 22b, 4b, 25b
Sugar 25a
Sugar of bamboo 21b
Sulphur 22a, 4a, 25a
Sunbād 22a
Tabby 18a
Tamarind 22a, 4a, 25a, 26a
Teak 21a
Timber 21a
Towel 18b, 24a, 25b
Tray 24b, 25b
Turban 18b, 19a, 23a, 25b
Turmeric 17b, 22a, 25a, 26a
Turpeth 22a
Tutty 22a, 4a
Underpants 22b
Usnea 22b, 4a, 25a
Veil 17a, 19a, 23a, 25a, 26a
Velvet 18b
Vessel 21b
Vitriol 22b, 4a, 25a
Waist cloth 25b
Waistwrapper 17a, 19b, 24a, 4b, 25b
Ware 21b
Wax 22a, 4a, 25a, 26a
Wheat 17b, 21a
Yarn 22a

2 Commodities in the text

NB the entry here is the word as it is found in the text, whether singular or plural. If both singular and plural of the same commodity are found, they are listed together under the singular.

abdān 18b, 23b, 4a

'abīd 17a

ābnūs 22b

abrād 19a, 21b, 24a, 25b

ādhān 22b

'afṣ 22a, 4a

'āj 22b, 4a, 25a, 26a

ajribah 22a

aksiyah 18b, 23b

alwāḥ 21a

'amā'im 19a, 23a, 25b

amlaḥ 22a

'anbar 17a, 20a

'anzarūt 22a, 4a

aqdāḥ 21b

'aqīq 21a

'arāḍī 23a

aruzz 21a

'aṣā'ib 18b, 23a

'asal 17a, 22a, 4a, 25a, 26a

asrab 4a, 26a

aswirah 17a

aṭbāq 24b

azfār 22a, 4a, 25a

baqyār/baqāyir 18b, 22b, 23a

baqqam 22b, 26b

basbāsah 20b

bazz 17b, 4b

bidhlah 23b

biḥār 17a

bilīlaj 22a, 26a

bukr 17b

burr 17b

busr 17b

dādī 17b, 22a, 25a

dār fulful/filfil 22a

dawm 17b

dhabl 20b, 25b

dhurah 21b

dībāj 18a, 23b

duhn al-ward 4a

duqqah 27b

durakī 4a

durū' 17a

dast/dusūt 25b

d.w.n.j 18a, 25b

fāghirah 22a, 25a

farḍ 22b

farfarān 22b, 25a

fawfal/fūfal 20b

filfil/fulful 17b, 21b, 26a, 26b, 27b

fūṭah/fuwaṭ 17a, 19b, 24a, 4b, 25b

ghāliyah 17a

ghazl 22a

hadas 22b, 4a, 25a, 26a

ḥadīd 17a, 21a, 4a, 25b, 26b

hāl 22a, 25a

halīlaj 21b

ḥanābil/ḥanābilī 19a, 22b

ḥaraḍ 26b

ḥarīr 18b, 20b, 21b, 22b

ḥashīshah 22a, 25a

ḥibārāt 18a, 4b

ḥiltīt 21b, 22a, 26a

ḥimmiṣ 21a
ḥinnā' 17b
ḥinṭah 21a
ḥ.rā.n/t 4b
hujun 17a
ḥulal 24a, 24b
ḥulbah 17b
ḥumar 22a, 25a
hurd 17b, 22a, 25a
ḥūt 17b
'inab 17b
'iqālāt 19a
'irq sūs 22a, 4a
jawār[ī] 17a
jawārib 4b
jawāzī 18b, 4b, 25b
jawzā 20b
jimāl 17a
julūd 21a
kāfūr 17a, 20b
kāghid/kāghad 19b, 24a, 25b
kammūn 22a, 4a, 25a
kanābis 19a
kattān 22b, 4a, 26b, 27b
kawdah 22a, 26a
khalākhil 17a
khām 21b
kharaz 21a, 22b, 4a
khashab 21a
khawāfiq 21b
khawātim 17a
khayl 17a, 4b
khayzurān 20b
khiraq 23a
khiyār shanbar 22a, 4a
khuḍaḍ 22a
khuddām 17a
khūlinjān 20b, 26a
kibrīt 22a, 4a, 25a
kubābah 21b, 22a, 27b
kuḥl 22a, 4a
lādān 4a
lāk 22b
lubān 17b, 22b
lukham 17b
lu'lu' 17a, 20a
ma'ājir 19a, 23a, 25a
ma'āshir 24b, 25b
ma'āzir 22b
maḥbas/maḥābis 19a, 26b
maḥārim 18b, 24a, 25b
maḥlab 22a, 22b, 4a, 25a, 26b
mā'i'ah 22b, 4a
makhādd 19a, 25b
makhāmil 18b, 24b, 25b
makhāniq 23a
malā'āt/mulā'āt 17a, 18a, 24a, 4b, 25a, 25b
mamāṭir 23b
māmīrān 20b
manādīl 18b, 19b, 23a, 23b
maqāṭi' 18b, 24a, 24b
mardāsanj 4a
marjān 24b, 4a
martak 22b, 4a
maṣāwin 25b
mashāyikh 4a
masṭakā 24b, 4a
maṭārif 18a, 19a, 4b
maṭāriḥ 19a, 4b, 25b
mathārid 21b
māward 20b, 24b, 25a, 26a
mayāzir 4b, 25b

misk 17a, 20a

mulawwasāt 18b

murdāsanj 22b

murr 22b, 25a

naḥās 4a

narjīl 20b

naṣāfī 18b, 24b, 25b

nasīj 18a, 25b

n.y.f 18b

nīl 17b, 21b

nūshādur 24b

qaṣdīr 22a, 24b, 26a

qashsh 22b

qāṭir 22b, 25a

qinbār 17b

qirfah 22a, 26a

qunbār 22a

qurunful 20b

qushūriyyāt 18b

qusṭ 17b, 22a, 25a, 26a

quṭr 19b, 20a, 20b

raqīq 17b

raqṣ 21a

raṣāṣ 22a, 24b, 25a

rāsukht 24b

rawānd 20b

rawsā 25a, 26a

rimāḥ 20b

ruṭab 17b, 4a

ṣabr 17b, 22b, 4a, 25a

sāj 21a

salīṭ 17b, 22a, 25a, 26a

samn 17b, 22a, 4a, 25a, 26a

ṣandal 20b, 22a, 22b

ṣandarūs 22a

ṣandāt 18a

sarband 24b

satā'ir 17a

sawāsī 24a

ṣayd 17b

shabb 22a, 25a

shādar 26a

shakārij 21b

sham' 22a, 4a, 25a, 26a

shambar 4a

shammah 4a

shāsh/shāshāt 18a, 18b, 23a

sh.bāb (shabb?) 25a

shīl 18b

shimāl 17b, 24a, 4b, 25b

shiqaq 18a, 23a, 24b, 4b, 25b

shirāk 21a

silal 17b

simsim 21a

sinbād 22a

subā'iyyāt 18a, 18b, 22b, 4b, 25a, 25b

su'd 22a, 4a, 25a

ṣufr 22a, 24b, 4a, 25a, 26a

sukkar 25a

ṣūliyān 22a

sunbul 21b, 27b

ṭa'ām 17b

ṭabāshīr 21b

tamr 17b, 4a, 26a

taqānī' 18a, 23a

thamarah ḥamrā 22a, 4a, 25a

thamarah ma'ṣūr 4a

thawb/thiyāb 17b, 18a, 18b, 19a, 21a, 23b, 24b, 4b, 25a, 25b

thūm 17b

tinkār 21b

turbid 22a

tūtiyā 22a, 4a
'ūd 17a, 19b, 20a
udum 26b
'uqadāt 23b, 25a
'uṣārah 22a
ushnah 22b, 4a, 25a
usrub 24b
'uṭb 22b
uzur 24a, 24b, 4b
wada' 22a
waraq 26b
wars 22b, 25a, 26a
wiqāyāt 23a, 25b
wujūh 23a
wuṣfān 17a
wushshaq 22a
zabād 17a, 17b
zabīb 17b, 22b, 4a, 25a
za'farān 20b, 24b, 25a
zāj 22b, 4a, 25a
ẓarf(?) 25a
zarnīkh 22b
zarnubā 22a, 26a
zi'baq 24b, 4a, 26a
zinjibīl 22a, 26a
zirnīkh 4a
zujāj 21a
zunjafr 24b, 4a, 26a

3 Weights, measures and units of currency

bahār 17b, 18b, 19a, 19b, 20b, 21a, 21b, 22a, 22b, 23a, 24b, 4a, 25a
bundle 23b
corge 19a, 19b, 21a, 21b, 25b, 25b
cubit 18a, 18b, 23a, 23b, 24a, 24b
dast 24b
dinar 13a, 17b, 18a, 19a, 22a, 22b, 26a
dirham 17b, 19b
farāsilah 22a
ḥaml/load 17b, 27b
mann 19b, 20a, 20b, 22b, 24b, 4a, 25a
mithqāl 20a, 20b
mudd 21a
ounce 17b
qaflah 20a, 20b
qaṣabah 23a
quire 23b
qirāṭ 18a, 20a,
raṭl 15a, 17b, 20a, 24b, 4a, 26a, 26b
ream 26b
zubdī 17b

4 Place and tribal names

ʿAbīdah 13a
al-ʿAbsiyyatayn 16b
Abyan 4b
Abyssinia 18a, 25a, 25b
Aden 17a, 17b, 18a, 26b, 27b
Ahl Anʿam 13a
al-Aḥmūd 15a
al-Ahwāb 25a, 27b
Aḥwar 17b, 4b
ʿAns 13a
al-Aʿmāl al-Abyaniyyah 16b
Aʿmāl B.ṭ.ḥ.wāt 16a
Aʿmāl al-Burqah 16a
al-Aʿmāl al-Dhu'āliyyah 16b

al-Aʻmāl al-Dhubḥāniyyah 15b
al-Aʻmāl al-Dumluwiyyah 15b
al-Aʻmāl al-Ghānimiyyah 16b
al-Aʻmāl al-Ḥaṣabiyyah 15b
al-Aʻmāl al-Ḥawjiyyah 16a
al-Aʻmāl al-Ḥaysiyyah 16b
al-Aʻmāl al-Ḥuṣaybiyyah 16b
al-Aʻmāl al-Jabaʼiyyah 15b
al-Aʻmāl al-Janadiyyah 15a
Aʻmāl Khadīrayn 16a
al-Aʻmāl al-Laḥjiyyah 16b
al-Aʻmāl al-Mafālīsiyyah 15b
al-Aʻmāl al-Mawriyyah 16b
al-Aʻmāl al-Mawzaʻiyyah 16b
al-Aʻmāl al-Mikhlāfiyyah 15a
al-Aʻmāl al-Muqaṣṣiriyyah 16b
al-Aʻmāl al-Qahabiyyah 16b
al-Aʻmāl al-Qaḥriyyah 16b
al-Aʻmāl al-Raḥbāniyyah 16b
al-Aʻmāl al-Rimaʻiyyah 16b
al-Aʻmāl al-Salifiyyah 15a
al-Aʻmāl al-Samadāniyyah 15b
Aʻmāl al-Sārah 16a
al-Aʻmāl al-Sawāʼiyyah 15b
al-Aʻmāl al-Sihāmiyyah 16b
al-Aʻmāl al-Surdudiyyah 16b
al-Aʻmāl al-Yaḥṣubiyyah 6a, 15a
al-Amlūk 13a
ʻAnnah 15a
al-ʻAnsiyyīn 15b
ʻArās 13b
Ardistan 25b
al-ʻArūs 9b
al-ʻArūsayn 15a
al-Aʻrūsh 13a
Ashyaḥ 14
Aswan 24b
ʻAydhāb 22b, 26a
al-ʻAyn al-Ghurābī 17b
ʻĀzib 17a
al-ʻAẓīmah 13a, 13b, 14b
Bāb al-Mandab 24a, 24b, 27a
Balabah 21b
Balad al-Aḥmūd 6b
Balad B. ʻAlī 6b
Balad B. Murghim 6b
Balad al-Rakb 6b
Balad Ṣuhbān 6b
Balad B. Wuḥāḍah 6b
Balad Wuṣāb 6b
B. Nājī 15a
B. Sahl 13a
B. Sarḥah 15a
B. Sayf 15a
B. Shihāb 14a
B. Ṣirār 13a
Barāqish 13b, 14b
al-Bawāqir 14b
al-Bawn/al-Bawnayn 13a, 13b
Bayt Riqbān 14a
Bilād B. Nājī 6b
Bilād B. Sarḥah 6b
Bilād al-Ṭawīlah 6a, 13a
al-Bilād al-ʻUlyā 6a
Birāsh Ṣaʻdah 13b, 14b
Birāsh Ṣanʻāʼ 13b
Birpour 21b
Bīshah 6a, 13a
Broach 19b
Bukur 14a
al-Buqʻah 17a
Cambay 21a

Cathay 23b
Chaul 21b
Chitor 21b
Dahlak 17a, 22b, 4a
Damietta 24b
Dānah 13a
Darb al-Ḥazm 13b
Darwān 13b
Dathīnah 13a
Daw'ān 17b
Daybul 21b
Dehli 21b
Dhahbān 13b, 14a
Dhakhir 15b
Dhamār 13b
Dhamār As'ad 13a
Dhamarmar 13b, 14a
Dhayfān 13a
Dhū Saydam 6b
Diu 21b
al-Dumluwah 6b, 9b
Dunbas 21b
East Africa 26a
Egypt 18a, 22b, 4a, 4b
Faknur 21a
al-Faṣṣ al-Kabīr 14a
al-Faṣṣ al-Ṣaghīr 14a
Furmiyan 21b
Ghayl al-A l f 14a
Gogalah 18b
Gujerat 21b
Ḥabbān 13a
al-Habīrah 17a
al-Ḥadd 13a
Haddād 13b
al-Ḥāḍinah 13a
Ḥaḍramawt 6a, 13a, 17b
Ḥaḍūr 13a
Ḥaḍūr al-Maṣāni' 14b
Ḥaḍūr al-Shihābiyyah 13b
al-Hajarayn 13a
Haly Ibn Ya'qūb 25a
Hamdān 13a
Ḥaqīl 13b, 14b
Ḥaql Qatāb 6a, 13a
al-Ḥārith 25a
Ḥaṣī 13a
Ḥawrah 4b
Ḥayrīj 26a
al-Ḥāzzatayn 16b, 27b
Hilāl al-Kumaym 13b
Hili 21a
Ḥimlān 13a
al-Ḥirdah 25a
Hirrān 14b
Ḥiṣār 13b
al-Ḥizyaz 13a
al-Ḥubb 17a
al-Ḥujariyyah 13a
al-Ḥuqūl 13a
Hurmuz 17b, 25a
India 18a, 21b, 22b, 23a, 24a, 24b
Iraq 18a
Jabal Ba'dān 6b, 15a
Jabal B. Shihāb 13a
Jabal Dhakhir 6b
Jabal Dhubḥān 6b
Jabal Ḥajjah 13a
Jabal Ḥarīr 13a
Jabal Juḥāf 13a
Jabal al-Lawz 13a
Jabal al-Rakb 15b

Jabal al-Shawāfī 15a
Jabal Tabālah 15a
Jabal al-Ta'kar 6b
Jabal al-Ṭawr 6b, 16a
Jabal Tays 14b
al-Jabalayn 6b
al-Ja'diyyah 13a
al-Janad 6b
Janb 13a
al-Jawf 13a, 13b
Jāzān 17a
Jeddah 17a
Jerusalem 25b
Jibāl al-'Arsayn 6b
Jiblah 15a, 4b
Juban 13a
Jushmān 13a
Kathiwa 21b
Kawkabān 13b, 14b
Khadīrayn 6b
al-Khaḍrā' 6b
Khallah 13a
Khārid 13b
Kharj 25a
Khawlān 13a
Khawlān B. al-Bi'm 15b
al-Kh.ṣ.rī 14a
Khulfāt 13a
Kilwa 21a
Kubbah 13a
al-Kumaym 13b
Kutch 19b
Lahej 4b
al-Lu'lu'ah 17a
Macassar 20b
Mada' 13b
Madhḥij 13a
al-Mafālīs 4b
al-Maghrib al-Ashyam 13a
al-Maghrib al-Ayman 13a
al-Maḥālib 13a
al-Mahjam 9b
al-Maḥraqah 13a
Mahwah 21b
Malabar 21a
Malaḥ 13a
Malindi 22b
Manābir 9b
Mangalore 21a, 21b
al-Manṣūrah 13b
Maqma' 13a
Mārib 13a
Ma'saj 13a
al-Mashāqiṣah 13a
Maṣna'at al-Maḥājir 14a
Maytak 13a
Maz'ūnah 4b
Mecca 17a, 22b, 24b
Mikhlāf al-Baḥrānah 15b
Mikhlāf Ja'far 6b
Mikhlāf al-Ma'āfir 6b
Mikhlāf Raymah 6b, 15a
Mikhlāf al-Shawāfī 6b
Mikhlāf Shayyibah 15b
al-Mikhlāf al-Sulaymāniyyah 17a
Mikhlāf Yafā' 13a
al-Mīqā' 13a, 13b, 14b
al-Miqrānah 13a
Mogadishu 17b, 25a, 25b, 26a
Mosul 24b
Muda' 14b
al-Mudabbī 16b

Mudal 13a
al-Mushayriq 6b, 15a
Najrān 13a
Nakhlah 16a
al-Naʿmān 6b
al-Nijād 13a
al-Nujaymiyyah 17a
Qāf 9b
Qā'ifah 13a
Qalhāt 17b, 25a
Qaqula 20a, 22a, 25a
Qays/Qayṣ/Qaysh 24b, 25a, 25b
Qishn 13a
al-Qufāʿah 6b, 15b
Quilon 19b, 20b, 22b
al-Qurāniʿ 13b, 14b
Quseir 22b
al-Rabʿah 13b
Radāʿ al-ʿArsh 13a
Radmān 25a
al-Raḥabah 13a
al-Rāḥah 17a
al-Raydah 17b
Raymān B. Sayf 6a
al-Rikz 13b
Riqbān 14a
Saba' al-Ṣuhayb 13a
Ṣabāḥī 9b
Ṣabir 6b, 9b, 16a
Ṣaʿdah 13a, 13b
Sādhij 21b
al-Saḥūl 15a
al-Salif 6b
Sāmḥūḥ 21b
Sāmiʿ 15b
al-Samkar 4b
Ṣanʿā' 13a, 13b
Sanad 14a
al-Ṣayrāt 13a
al-Shaʿir 15a
Sharʿab 6b, 15b
Sharaf Qilḥāḥ 6a, 13a
al-Sharafayn 13a
al-Sharjah 25a
al-Shiḥr 17a, 17b, 24a, 4b, 25a, 25b, 26a
Sh.qāq 14a
Shurayb 13b, 14b
al-Ṣīf 13a
al-Sifl 13a
Sinai 22b
Sinḥān 13a, 14a
al-Sirr 13a
Suakin 22b
Ṣuhbān 15a
al-Ṣulayy 16b
Sumā'ah 13a
Sunbulah 17a
al-Sūqiyān 21b
Surat 21b
Syria 18a, 25b
Tabaristan 19a, 25b
al-Tahā'im 6b, 16a
Taʿizz 6b, 9b, 15b, 4b
Taʿizz Ṣaʿdah 13b, 14b
Tajrah 25a
al-Taʿkar 9b, 15b
al-Tanāʿim 13a
al-Tawāliq 13a
al-Ṭawīlah 14a
al-Thawābī 15b
Thawbān 13a
Thulā 13a, 14a

Tihāmah 13a, 4b, 25b
Ṭiwāl B. Juban 13a
Turkestan 25b
Uḥāẓah 15a
ʿUnnah 6b
Wadd 14a
Wādī al-Ḥār 13a
Wuṣāb 15a
Yaʿḥuj 13a
al-Yaman al-Akhḍar 6a, 14b, 15b, 16a
Yemen 22a, 25b
Zabīd 15a, 16b, 17a, 4b, 25b, 27b
Ẓafār 14a, 17b, 24a, 24b, 4b, 25a, 25b
Ẓafār al-Ḥabūẓī 13a, 17a
Ẓafār al-Wādiyayn 6a
al-Zāhir 13b, 14b
Zaylaʿ 21a, 4b, 25a
al-Z.r.tayn 15b
Ẓufur 13b, 14b
Ẓufur al-Jawf 13b

5 Government officials in the translation

accountant/*mustawfī* 7b, 8b, 9a, 9b, 10b, 11a, 11b, 12a, 12b, 27a
assayer, auditor/*naqqād* 11a, 11b, 27a, 27b
bookkeeper/*shāhid* 7b, 8b, 11b, 27a, 27b
chief/*muqaddam* 11a, 14a, 14b
comptroller/*ʿāmil* 7b, 8a, 8b, 9a, 10b, 27a, 27b
deputy/*nā'ib* 8a, 8b, 9a, 10b, 11a, 14a, 27a, 27b
examiner/*mufattish* 26b
financial officer/*mutaṣarrif* 6a, 7b, 8b, 10b
gate-keeper/*bawwāb* 26b
governor/*wālī* 10a, 10b, 13b, 14a, 26b, 27a
groom/*mihtār* 9a
head/*zimām* 9a
head of stable/*amīr-ākhūr* 9a
inspector/*mushidd* 8a, 8b, 9b, 10b, 11a, 11b, 12a, 12b, 27a, 27b
irrigation official/*dā'ilī* 14a
land-surveyor/*māsiḥ* 11b, 12a, 12b
legal official/*faqīh* 27b
measurer/*dhāriʿ* 12a
messenger/*mubashshir* 27a
minister/*wazīr* 10a
officer/*naqīb* 10a, 13b, 26b, 27a
official, secretary/*kātib* 5a, 5b, 7a, 8a, 8b, 9a, 9b, 10b, 11b, 12a, 26b, 27a, 27b
overseer/*nāẓir* 8b, 10a, 10b, 11a, 11b, 12a, 12b, 13b, 21a, 26b, 27a, 27b
provisions officer/*ḥawā'ij-kāsh* 9a
revenue collector/*mustakhrij* 11b, 12a
secretary, see official
steward/*mubāshir* 6a, 7b, 9a, 11a, 11b, 12a, 12b
supervisor/*mushārif* 7b, 8a, 8b, 9a, 9b, 10a, 10b, 11b, 13b, 14a, 27a, 27b
tax farmer/*ḍāmin, multazim* 8a, 11b, 12b, 26b, 27b
tax-collector/*jābī* 9b, 27a, 27b
tax-collector/*muḥaṣṣil* 13b
treasurer/*shāhid ṣundūq, khazzān* 10b, 27b
veterinary surgeon/*sar-ākhūrī* 9a

6 Government officials in the text

'āmil/comptroller 7b, 8a, 8b, 9a, 10b, 27a, 27b
āmīr-ākhūr/ head of stable 9a
bawwāb/gate-keeper 26b
dā'ilī/irrigation official 14a
ḍāmin/tax farmer 8a, 11b, 12b, 26b
dhāri'/measurer 12a
faqīh/legal official 27b
ḥawā'ij-kāsh/provisions officer 9a
jābī/tax-collector 9b, 27a, 27b
kātib/official, secretary 5a, 5b, 7a, 8a, 8b, 9a, 9b, 10b, 11b, 12a, 26b, 27a, 27b
khazzān/treasurer 27b
māsiḥ/land-surveyor 11b, 12a, 12b
mihtār/groom 9a
mubāshir/steward 6a, 7b, 9a, 11a, 12a, 12b
mubashshir/messenger 27a
mufattish/examiner 26b
muḥaṣṣil/tax-collector 13b
multazim, see ḍāmin
muqaddam/chief 11a, 14a, 14b
mushārif/supervisor 7b, 8a, 9a, 10a, 10b, 13b, 14a, 27a, 27b
mushidd/inspector 8a, 8b, 9b, 10b, 11a, 11b, 12a, 12b, 27a, 27b
mustakhrij/revenue collector 11b, 12a
mustawfī/accountant 7b, 8b, 9a, 9b, 10b, 11a, 11b, 12a, 12b, 27a
mutaṣarrif/financial officer 6a, 7b, 8b, 10b
nā'ib/deputy 8a, 8b, 9a, 10b, 11a, 14a, 27a, 27b
naqqād/assayer, auditor 11a, 11b, 27a
naqīb/officer 10a, 13b, 27a
nāẓir/overseer 8b, 10a, 10b, 11a, 11b, 13b, 21a, 26b, 27a
sar-ākhūrī/veterinary surgeon 9a
shāhid/bookkeeper 7b, 8b, 11b
shāhid ṣundūq/treasurer 10b, 27a
wālī/governor 10a, 10b, 13b, 14a, 26b, 27a
wazīr/minister 10a
zimām/head 9a

7 Government departments

al-amlāk 13b, 14a, 27b
al-bāb al-sharīf 9a, 9b, 11b, 12a
dār al-ḍarb 27b
al-dīwān 10b, 11a, 12b, 14a, 22a, 27b
dīwān al-ḥalāl 8a
al-dīwān al-kabīr 8a
dīwān/dawāwīn al-kharāj al-sulṭānī 5a, 5b, 6a, 7b, 8a, 8b
dīwān al-khāṣṣ 7b, 8a
al-dīwān al-sa'īd 6b, 12a, 27b
al-furḍah 18a, 26b, 27a, 27b
al-ḥawā'ij-khānāh 9a
al-ḥuṣūn 9b, 10a, 13b, 14a, 14b
al-inshā' 9a
al-iṣṭblāt 9a
al-jaysh 8b
al-khizānah 8a, 8b, 9b, 11b
al-matjar 27a
al-wuqūfāt 8

27 b

كاتب مشارف عامل مشارف عامل مثبت مشارف عامل مشارف
الالتزام الديوان الديوان الدرس الدرس الجلوه الجلوه الجلوه المطران

كاتب مشارف عامل مشارف عامل شاهد مشارف عامل
الوقف الحشريه الحشريه باب الساحل باب الساحل الدكانه الدكان البركان

نقاد مشارف عامل كاتب كاتب مشارف عامل
الصندوق البحيك السنجيات باب العوام الصاعه العار الصاعه دار الضرب دار الضرب

مقدمين نواب ناسه خزانه خزانه كاتب دار شهود عامل ثاني
باب الساحل باب الساحل الربع المسجد المرحنه السدر العوام الضرب اربعه الثانيه الثانيه
اربعه اثنان

باب الالتزام
67

واما ... مباشرين ديوان زبيد المحروس دهم

دالي مشد ... عامل مشارف شاهد الصندوق عامل مجارب عامل
الديوان الديوان تحريب الادسيم

كاتب مشارف عامل مشارف كاتب عامل مشارف عامل ... مشارف كاتب
العماره الفرضه الفرضه الفرضه المحرر المحرر محشر الحشريه باب الساحل الانتبه

كاتب كاتب الملتزمين كاتب كاتب مشارف عامل ... ثاني كاتب
المحناه الولايه اربعه سوق الصيد بيت البر دار الضرب دار الضرب ... اربعه

عاملكار بين مستند الحارس المباشرين ... نواب ... كاتب
الفرحا ... النظر المسند النظر باب اربعه
في كل باب اربعه
اثنان

16
نقادين نقاد نقاد كاتب كاتب مشارف
التحريب الاملاك الديوان الكواهل الحارس الوقف الحارس
اثنان

68

ونحن نعرف ان المباشرين في هذا الديوان اكثر من هولاي كان ذلك في الدوله المجاهديه قدس الله سره في الجنه وجعله الكل الان السلطان وفتح في مدينته دار كبه وبنديه كانوا اكثر باللابواب اثني عشر ونواب القطرين الابواب عشرون في كل ما حسنه واختصر في عقب الدوله المجاهديه

العنتور

ضرب

بندر الاهواب لرسله المحروس حط الله ذكر الكهار ونصر على حكم ما نتصل وصوله من الجهات

الواصل
من عدن المحروس حبا سلطاني حامد

التنبل الكناسه الرقه الفلفل الكان الصح
القطعه سبعه الحمل سبعه الحمل سبعه الحمل سبعه الحمل سبعه الحمل سبعه

العوذل

H 130

27 a

من خدام وغيرهم • واهم ذلك ان الناظر لا يطلق شيئاً بعد ذلك الا ام سهل واذا وصل الواصل
من البحر او من الباب تقدم بهم عرفاً انا صل الى الوالي او لا ثم بعد ذلك الى الناظر ويلبسوا الشامي سنة
ويعرفون بها وصلته • الانعام البرانية اذا وصلت من البحر او من الباب يحملها الى المرتبة
التي تحت الفرضة وحضر نايب الديوان وكتاب المتجر واقاموا منها نصيب الديوان العين ويكون
نصيب الديوان حيازها وتبقى باقيه وتصدرها ولا يأذن كلا تسلمه الفرضة لا تفتح الا بحضرة
الوالي والناظر والكتاب او نوابهم • واذا جاء الى الفرضة كان امرها يرحل الى ان يخرج منها
الى الناظر وعلى الوالي الحفظ والبحث وقت الوزن ووقت العدد وضبط الغش والكشف
عنه وحفظ الابواب وملازمة الفرضة ايام الموسم والكتاب جميعهم لا يأتون على
الحضرة ولا يرخص لهم الوالي في الغيبة ولكن التفتيش بحضرة الجميع ولا يقوم الوالي
والكتاب دون ان يقوم الناظر ويكون حولهم بحذاه وحجتهم بحروجه • وتقديم القماش
والمشترى في المجلس الذي عمل المراكب • ودرج العشور والمحصولات التي على عامل الفرضة
ما كان برسم الخزانة لعدة ويكون بيد الناظر • النقباء السادة يجري عند الناظر تقييد
جماعته وعند الوالي نقيبان جماعتهما بالدول • المحتسب الطاري يكتب التسديد عادات
وخط الوالي عليها والناظر يعين حمله ذلك • المفتوحات التي في البحر والباب يكتب الناظر عليها
خطه اولاً ثم يكتب الوالي بعده • المشتر الذي يعني المراكب اثنان واحد الى الناظر وواحد
الى الوالي • رفع الحساب في سائر الجهات في الثغر كلها تتم والمحمر على الشيا وكما الصرف
والموايمات في المحصولات وما يرفع الى الخزانة المعمورة والمشترى في المشترى الجمع تقييده الناظر
ويجهز منه ما هو برسم الخزائن المعمورة وما هو الى المشترى في المشترى ويجهز ما يعد الى كل شهر
بشهره • المواريث الحشرية يضبطه في الديوان ستمبه لها عامل الثاني الذي بيد
الوالي يتبرك علمه اولا وعند الكتاب النطع له يعرف • ويحضر الناظر فيما يحصل من الادب في العاير
وغيرها وتحظيه على الاستدعاءات وغيرها • قوارب الحطب ليعرفه الناظر حد في كل يوم وخط
الوالي عليها • الصناعة لا يتصرف شيء الا بخط الناظر على ذكر اعتماد الناظر والوالي والكتاب •

ذكر المباشرين في الثغر بعد البسملة والحمد دوهم

والي • ناظر • عامل اول • عامل ثاني • مشارف اول • مشارف ثاني • ماية

ناظر المطر • نواب الحالة الثان • نواب المتجر الثان • عامل في الصندوق • مشارف الصندوق • شاهد العرصة • نواب الصندوق الثان

جابي اول • جابي ثاني • عامل المتجر • مشارف المتجر • شاهد المتجر • نايب المتجر الثلاثة • عامل المطر الثلاثة

مستوفي • نايب • كاتب المعصور • عامل البر • مشارف البر • شاهد البر • جابي البر • عامل المطر

الأدم

القطعه [illegible]

الجديد

القطعه [illegible]

الكتان الغزل

بضع عشر ثلث عشر

حطب

العلف والشعير والحرمي البقر والجلت

العلفه هي للابل [illegible] من جميع الاضاف [illegible] المجلس الكريم [illegible]

الورق

[illegible]

ما يعتمده الوالي والناظر والكتاب في ثغر عيذاب المحروس

مفاتيح الفرضه والابواب تكون عند الوالي في بيته الى وقت الحاجه • فاما مفاتيح ابواب [illegible] البوابين اصحاب الدرك يفتحوها كل صباح ويغلقوا الابواب بعد [illegible] ويحملوها الى بيت الوالي وتبيت عنده • واذا كان بعد صلاة العصر يحملوا [illegible] الى عند الوالي ليفتحوا الاقفال ويقفلوا • وختم الفرضه يكون عند الناظر واذا استهل الشهر [illegible] الوالي والناظر والكتاب على دكة دار الطوليه واستعرضوا الاجناد والمرتبين والبوابين ارباب الصنائع [illegible] وكتبوا بذلك [illegible] ووضع الوالي والكتاب خطوطهم [illegible] على [illegible] • واذا وصل الرقيق من البحر او من الباب تقدموا بهم [illegible] الى الوالي اولا وبعد ذلك الناظر • ويكون الناظر هو الذي [illegible] الديوان [illegible]

26

والنادر والماورد والعاج والشمع والرتق يحط فيه قدر الوسط

الرجعه الحولجان السكوره
العنبر العتيق البلدي الحمسي

العسكري
على قدر الشطر ما قاله الوزان مع حطاط الصاكر

الرطعه
في ثمانية أيام ... [illegible]

في السعو والنتري اذا كان الماء مستورا يسلع المأكل رطلين

والتمن والعسل والسلط والورس والقسط والتمر والفلفل والرحل والهرد والهليلج الرومي والريبا والعرعة والبرسا والبليلج والاصبع والكابلي سائر اصناف العطر

واذا وصل الصناف من مطلع برزه وعدت بعدها اذا كانت عليه ما عليه حطط الا العشر الشوي

واذا وصل اصناف محلوه من البحر حيد وعرضها كان على عشر ونصف اذا كان صنف هندي مثل فلفل وزنجبيل وعرعها واذا كان غير هذه الاصناف كان عليه العشر فقط بعد وصل الشيخ كالدر المقدشي رحمه الله ... صندل محل الا العشر ... الا العشر الشوي

الصادر

التصدير واذا كان ...
والاشرف

الرطعه
... [illegible]

الصغير

الرطعه
... [illegible]

العسكري

الرطعه
... [illegible]

25b

25

يمان • مثال ذلك النثر عشون حمر العرب بحسب الحرف وه

على هذه الصفة ويتبين من هذه ذلك •

العاج • النشط • الورع • الشعر • العسل •
[illegible]

السمين • الانفطار • الاصحاب • المدر العاسي • القاطر •
[illegible]

الهال • الحششه • الانقنه • الصرالحلي • الدراج الكحلي •
[illegible]

الشد • السيد • الرصاص • الصبر • الجمر •
[illegible]

الكوت • [illegible] • السكر • الكريت •
[illegible]

الرادك • السمع • الجمر • الشباب • الغزوان •
[illegible]

الغرقان • السعد • الناعره • المحلب • الشمع •
[illegible]

الاصناف
الواصله من المعارف [illegible]
[illegible]

الزعفران • الماورد • المطاحن • المعاجن الذهبه •
[illegible]

المعاجين • العقد • الملاذهب • المعاجين الملون •
[illegible]

[illegible] • الشاب • البابس • البا •
[illegible]

[illegible] • الناس الشيح •
[illegible]

عشوره الباب العشرين من الشام جميعه وزيد
والسكر وجبله والفاليين ودح وابن ولحور وحوزه والشجر وطفار
وزلع دمز عونه وساير جهات التفارين جميعها مائة

الحمل عشور الوارد الداس الواحد نقطع المشتري من البايع عند نقبض الثمن واد افطس
للحصان في الثغر على المأخوذه سالم عشوره الوارد [illegible] والدلاله [illegible]

لأنه تقطعها على البايع من عرض فيه فرسه • واذا اشترا احد من الغرم الخيل
من الصاعد او غيرهم من تجار الخيل لزمه العشور كما ذكر اولا •

المطارح • المرتهن • الملاوات •
الحمير [illegible] العشره [illegible] • هو من اصناف [illegible] الواحد [illegible] • الحرير والحرار الحرير والسقو الحرير والحبرات والمطارف الحمران والسباعيات الحرير والبرداسان والازر الحرير المذهب الواحد [illegible] العشره [illegible] •

الملاوات الخلط والسباعيات الخلط [illegible] الواحد [illegible] • والقطن [illegible] السبع • الملاوات الكتان السباعيات الكتان الواحد [illegible] •

الملاوات [illegible] العشره [illegible] • الملاوات القطن المثنى الواحد [illegible] • الملاوات القطن الواحد [illegible] •

العوض الحرير والمبارد الحرير [illegible] السادج والكحلي العشره [illegible] • العوطه الخلط [illegible] والمبارد الخلط والقطن [illegible] العشره [illegible] • اذا كانت [illegible] كانت الواحد [illegible] واذا كانت [illegible] عشره العشره [illegible] •

العوض الكتان [illegible] والكتان [illegible] والمبارد [illegible] العشره [illegible] • العوطه القطن من سائر الجهات [illegible] العشره [illegible] • العوطه الملاسي الخلط والمبارد العشره [illegible] •

العوطه الكتان الطعيه العشره [illegible] • العوطه الكتان الملاسي المبارد الكتان الملاسي العشره [illegible] • الحوار [illegible] والقطن [illegible] [illegible] •

المبارد الكتان العشره [illegible] • والقطن والحمر والمبارد [illegible] • الازر القطن [illegible] العشره [illegible] •

[illegible]

4a

ووصـــــــــــــــــــــــــــــــــ

المقاطع القوصي العره	المقاطع الدمياطي للذهب العره	المقاطع الدمشقي العره	المقاطع الكتان
المقاطع الدمياطي العره	النصافي الذهب البادح	النصافي البغدادي العره	النصافي البغدادي العره
النصافي الموصلية العشره	النصافي الذهب	السا... العره	المخمل العره
المخامل العره	الدستوت	الدسوت	الشقق
المعاشير العره	دمرحكة المشرفة	درمهشت العره	المعاشير العره
الاطباق المعلية الصغار العره	السترسته العره	الازر العطر	الازار العطر
المرجان	المرجان	المرجان	المرجان
المرجان	المرجان	الزعفران	البادهنج
الموسلادر العره الامنان	الراتنج العره الامنان	الرخام العره الامنان	الزئبق العره الامنان

اصباغ
الهارم الديار المصريه

الصفر	الصفر المر وهو الماس النهار	الصبر المعروف النهار	الصبر النهار
العصفر النهار	الاسرب الرصاص الاسود النهار	المصطكي النهار	دم الاخوين النهار

24b

الأكسية • الحلل • ومن الهند بطانات • والمذهب والحرير مضاعف •
السواسي الحرير الخام • السواسي الحرير المقصور • السواسي الحرير المقصور •
السواسي [illegible] • ومن الهند العين • السواسي الوسط • السواسي العين •
الإزار • الإزار ذات [illegible] • الإزار [illegible] • [illegible] •
المحارم • [illegible] • المحارم •
الملاوات • الملاوات • الملاوات •
الملاوات • الملاوات • الملاوات • الملاوات •
الملاوات • الملاوات • [illegible] •
الفوط [illegible] • [illegible] • الفوط •
الفوط • الفوط • الفوط • الفوط •
الكاغد • [illegible] • المقاطع •

24a

البدلات الذهبية من مقطعات [illegible] • البدلات الحريري من مقطعات العمر • البدلات الوسط العمر • البدلات المعادم العمر •

البدلات المطرز [illegible] • البدلات المعادم [illegible] الواحد • العصائب [illegible] العمر • المساد[illegible] الموصلي العشر •

المساد[illegible] الباعية العمر • المساد[illegible] العالي والكافوري العمر • الثياب الاسطالي الواحد • الثياب [illegible] العمر • الثياب الاسطالي الواحد العمر •

الثياب [illegible] الاصفهاني العمر • الثياب المروي والخوارزمي والشرقي الواحد العمر • من العاصل المروري المفصلة •

الثياب الخطائي [illegible] الواحد العمر • الثياب الدمياطي والشرقي العمر الواحد • الثياب [illegible] الساده [illegible] العمر •

الثياب [illegible] الواحد العمر • الثياب [illegible] الواحد العمر • طول الثوب [illegible]

الثياب [illegible] العشرة طول الثوب [illegible] الدراع • الثياب [illegible] والسات [illegible] العمر الواحد • الثياب المروي الواحد العشر •

الثياب الحريري المعرق الواحد العشرة • الثياب الحريري الاصفهاني الواحد العمر • الثياب الحاد [illegible] الدمشقي العشرة الواحد • الثياب العطار [illegible] العمر •

الثياب العالي والحرابي [illegible] الواحد العمر • الثياب العجمي [illegible] الواحد • طول [illegible] • الثياب [illegible] المقصور [illegible] العمر • المناطير [illegible] الواحد العمر •

المناطير الصوف [illegible] العمرة الواحد • الابدان الصوف [illegible] الملونة [illegible] • الاكسية [illegible] العمر الواحد • وللمذهب مضاعف •

الاكسية

23

العمايم للاثوم والوجوه كل اثنان بعيار الواحد للعشرة الملاسه الهارية
والمذهب مضاعف

العمايم الكتان والملونه والبيض الساذج والحنا الواحد للعشرة للملاسه الهارية ● العمايم القوصي العشرة ٤ ● السواذج المطرزة العشرة

العراضي المقصورة والمناديل العشرة ● العراضي الحمام والمناديل الكتان ● المعاجر للمذهبه والملونه للذهب والحراري المذهبه الواحد

المعاجر الملونه والعراقي الحماد الكمش العشرة الواحد ● العقدات للملونه والعراقي البيض والحرير العشرة ● والمذهب مضاعف ●

الشقق الاشكلاط وهي الحرير طول الحرير ... الفضه ... الساذج ... الواحد ● العشرة ● ومن الهند الواحد ●

النقاسع الشرب المذهب ذا الطرحات المذهب الواحد ● النقاسع الحريري والشرب الساذج والحريري ... السلطاني للرقوم الواحد ●

النقاسع الكتان والوقايات الكتان الوسط الواحد ● الشاشات المذهبه وللمناديل المذهبه والحرير الواحد ●

الشاشات المرقوم والمطرزه والمناديل المطرزه والعراضي المطرزه العشرة الواحد ● الخرق السدتي السماح الواحد

العشرة طول الحرير ... ● القبضه ... ● ... لساذج

داد او صد من الهند كان الواحد

الخرق السدتي الوسط الواحد ● الخرق السدتي للسفارين الواحد ●

العصايب المذهبه والاعمر المحابس والحواشي والشعاري المذهبه والحاشيه الواحد ● العصايب الحرير الساذج والاعمر المحابس والشعاري والحواشي الساذج الواحد ● والكتان المطلق النصف ●

23a

الصندل • الابنوس • البهزاج • الهدس
المهد النهار · الهار · الهند · العاوسي النهار

المرداسنج • قشر • المحلب • اللاخوان
وهو المرتك النهار · المالعه النهار · بعشره النهار · النهار

النمر • التمر • الكرد الاشمس • الاشنه
النشر النهار · العرص النهار · النهار · العراقي النهار

العرزان • المسر • الصبر • العاطر
الطرالشعي النهار · البان الرومان النهار · السقطري النهار · النهار

الرسه • الورس • العاج • الغفار
النهار · من الهند النهار · النهار · الهجي النهار

اللاك • الكتان • العطر • العطر
عشوره الربع معلم · النهار · المري هو المبرعم النهار · المحلوج والاصفر النهار

اولمن بعشر زياده في قيمة النهار خمسه دنانير واحد عليه عاله وشواني في كل مايه دينار وما زاد
على الربع من شر النهار • ولنس الزياده خمسه دنانير الا اذا انودي عليه بباب العرضه وتقرر
شعره يراد عليه خمسه دنانير • واذا لم ينادا به ووصل بعريضه عن سادا مما عليه زياده خمسه •
مثاله اذا كان النهار ربعه يراد عاله وشواني

البقم عشوره الربع وزياده سعر النهار خمسه دنانير وزياده على الربع دينار وسبع عاله
وشواني في كل دينار في جميع البقم الكولمي والامري عين • :

عاده
مما للبجليل في الجهازات الهنديه في كل مركب • اذا كان المركب من الهند •
واذا وصل من البفاريق لم عليه شيا الا ما يحضر الشهيه الجاري رسمها العاده على ما شهد
به خط كاتب البجليل •
بلاد المعارس وصاهم علي سماعه وشواني وهو العشر وكذا ريا هنديا في الحمل على ما هو نصه •
وما هو على الاصناف
الواصله من الديار المصريه والطور والقصير وعيداب •
وسواكن ودهلك ماها •

البغاير • العدس • الكبريت •
المسر والحاسني الساعيات · من الباب يعشر هدي · من مصر ومكه للتشرفه العرم الامان

والعايم

22

الدار فلفل • الحصص وهو الحولان • الكاريسه • الكسلان •
البهار • الفراسله • الكارى البهار • البهار

الرجل • الزنجبيل المربا • الفاغره • الهليلج الزهى •
الرجل الحمر البهار • البهار • البهار

الهليلج الاصفر والاملج والبليلج البهار • الزرنباد • الهرد • الصدف الجوزى •
البهار • البهار • الزعى والجوزى البهار

العرفه • القرصعنه • العرف • الجمره •
المليبارى الكار البهار • النيلى البهار • السوس البهار • البهار

الخيار شنبر • البرادى •
البهار • البهار
رجع لحدود ايران الملك المويد حمد السلطان عليه
ختاتيم الصندد وورداهو للديوان لم يوصر على البهار
ادام نفايتم والعمل على جمع نعمات

السنباد • الكون الصدى • الهال القاقلى • الهال المصوف •
كل البهار • البهار • البهار • من الصوليان البهار

الصندروش • الصندروس • الكسوه • القصار •
البهار • السلالى البهار • وهو الودع البهار • البهار

الاحتريه • السعد • الكحل • الكحل •
البهار • البهار • الاصفهانى البهار • البهار

الغزل • الغزل • الفستق • النوتيا •
الاحمر والصولانى البهار • الاشقر البهار • البهار • البهار

الوسمه • البن • العصاره • السلط •
البهار • البهار • البهار • والثمن البهار

النصد • الرصاص • العسل • العصفر •
البهار • الاسود البهار • البهار • البهار

الشمع • فتر الحلب • المحلب المنقى • النموه •
البهار • البهار • البهار • الحمر البهار

الثمر • العنزروت • الكبريت • الحشيشه •
المقصور البهار • البهار • البهار • البهار

الاطفار • العفص • الشب • السرنيخ •
المدور البهار • البهار • البهار • البهار

ويضاف عليه عاله وشوالى الحرز فى الطعام الواصل من بلاد الهند من المزره ١
وما وصل من بربره والديو وهرمان وسريع وسند ودسر والعرش والبريول وحس
دكنو استنوك وسهوه ومجلور وصين ومشن والسوقان وساحوج وجميع بلاد الجوار
كان عليه عشر وهذه الاصناف المعينه جارى العاده ما ياتى ذكره وهى العشارى والخام
والابراد والخام الذى يبات

الثياب العشارى الكوج للبوب ● الثياب الخام الطوال الكوج للثياب ●

الابراد العطه العشره والجاعلم ● والجهر مصاعف العشره ●

الخام البلى الكوج ● الخام الدس الكوجه ●

الصبى والدنوى والابكار ●

المشارد الزنوى والادراح الكبار والخوانق ● والانصاف الكواس المطلقه الزيلع للواحد العشره للمايه العشره ●

الابلا الزنوى العشره ● للارباع الزنوى والادراح المطلقه العشره ●

السكارج الزنوى والادراج الصغار العشره ● المشارد البكار العشره ●

الانصاف البكار وخوانق البكار العشره ● السكارج البكار والادراج الكبار والصغار العشره ●

وما هو على اصناف البهار من بلاد الهند وعرها دنصاف على التعرعام شوال

الكابه الصينى البهار ● النبل البهار ● التنكار البهار ● الطباشير البهار ●

المحلب الهادون البهار ● الستنبل البهار ● الكلتهه البهار ● القلقل البهار ●

البهار

21

الزجاج الحلبي ● على المايه

الخرز [illegible] ● الصغار العشره الالاف [illegible]

الكار وهو ما كان فيه اجمر الى الالف ● العشره الالاف [illegible]

الخرز [illegible] ● الهليلجي والسعر [illegible] العشره الالف [illegible]

الحمار السعط الكبر وهو ما عليه النقش ● العشره الالف

ومن اولاد المغاربه تعشر مثل داود عشر باسم ● للسعر على فند معارب صح تعدوه [illegible] لمسك الا [illegible] للسعر

واذا كان يعشر على الصوف [illegible] ● العشر والعمال على [illegible] العليان والكسر

الحديد المعمول ● على الخمس [illegible] المسماط الدبوس والركاب والاناجر ما عليهم عشور

والبولاد [illegible] ● والنصيبي [illegible] على الخمس عشور [illegible] من جميع الجهات

الخشب ● الساج الخام مثل الالواح والعوارك والاخشاب والمساكات على الساج والمساكات العداله على العشور [illegible] من سائر الجهات [illegible] جميع الاخشاب وعن الساج [illegible] ما عليها عشور

الارز ● الخام والسلوح [illegible] العشره [illegible]

الجلود ● المحورة العشره [illegible]

الرقيق ● [illegible] اذا كانت [illegible] الكورد وفي عشره

الحنطه ● والارز والسمسم والحمص المد وهو ستين [illegible]

وفي جميع الطعام كذلك

والارز من منجلوس وما كنز وصل ولاد المنبار ● ما عليه عشور واذا وصل من الجهات [illegible]

يعشر وقد عشر ذلك في سنه ستين ثلثين [illegible] الناخذ [illegible] من منجلوس لما وصل [illegible] فما وجدوه المشايخ [illegible] المذكور [illegible] العاصي [illegible] حسب [illegible] وهو ناظر ● والارز المد [illegible] في سنه سبع [illegible] الامير [illegible] الدين [illegible] الرسولي [illegible] ذلك في [illegible] ناصر الدين [illegible] العاصي [illegible] والذره والمنبح المد وهو ستين [illegible] الا علم ● واذا كان مدفوق كان عليه [illegible]

[illegible]

والكافور الكابزه للمن الواحد المثقال مثقالا بلا مقدار والمنو بما فيه من القطر المنو القطر
وهو ما ... ادا القرد ...
وهو ما ... ومانقص من ... المنو ... هذا المقدار

الكافور والقطر في جمع الكافور في المن درهمان ومانقص من المرغ
القيصوري المنو الواحد ... المنو ... القطر ... المنو بما فيه من القطر

الكافور الصيني العشره المن الواحد • والمن بما فيه من القطر المنو القطر •

ما الكافور العشره الاثنان • العنبر العشره الاثنان للمنو ... البهار •

القرنفل المثقال العشره الاثنان للمنو ... • الكوزا للعشره الاثنان • والمنو ... علمه الثلث

البسباسه العشره الاثنان • الزعفران المن الواحد • الكمون ... العشره الاثنان للمنو •

الراوند الصيني الناجه العشره الاثنان • رجع ... عليه ... بخط المرحوم السلطان الملك المؤيد داود ... في شهر ... وسبعمايه •

الصندل المقاصري العشره الاثنان • الخولنجان العشره الاثنان •

المادرد العشره الاثنان • الزنجبيل الجيد العشره الاثنان •

الفلفل الوسط العشره الاثنان • الزنجبيل المعارس وهو الخفيف العشره الاثنان •

الدارصيني الجيد الوسط العشره الاثنان • الخيزران الصيني الالف القصب •

الرماح القنى الالف • النارجيل الالف الحبه •

العود ... الاثنان ... الالف • العقيق الاحمر والملون البهار •
... الرماح

20

كاغان القطع ● عاب البطيء لعان
[illegible]

عرع القطع لعاب ● ومراط المن في المعروس حساب للمن ●
[illegible]

واذا كان منيا واجزا الاسوى كل عشره ● العود القاقلي ●
الجيد
القمر الامان

العود الجيد الوسط ● المنوبعطره ●
القمر الامان
وما زاد من الوسط

العود الوسط ● المرتعطره ●
القمر الامان

اللولو الابيض المنظوم من تسع الحبات ● العنبر كل عمان مثاقيل ●
علم التمن في الثمن
وليس يعد الاعلى كل مثقال

واذا دخل من العرض البعارش

وزن الطال العنبر ● البيع ● وزن الرطل ●
بالعرضه

المسك ● النوافج الفارغ ●
بيع الجيد منه في الثلث وبلغ ستين
مسك يحد عليه العشر
من خطط المسك سواء كان من عرع

العنبر الي المحروم ● المسك ●
[illegible]

والعشره للنادل نقطة اذا كانت ●
على كل مائه مثقال
والقطر للعامل
على اربعه مثاقيل احد عشر نقطه

وبعد [illegible]

المناديل القطن ● المنديل الواحد اذا انفرد ● الى خمسة مناديل ●
العشرة المايه النهار الكوم [illegible] والكتان والمحشا ضاعف ●

الغوط الحرير والشال الكرزي المحشا الى الناج ● الغوط الخلط والمحشا الكتان [illegible] ●
العشرة المايه النهار والمذهب [illegible] ● العشرة المايه النهار الكوم [illegible]
[illegible] والقطن والشال [illegible]

الغوط الكتان ● الغوط الكملي الكتان [illegible] ●
العشرة للمايه النهار الكوم [illegible] الكوم منه عليه النهار [illegible]

الغوط التساعي [illegible] للنضى [illegible] ● الغوط التساعي الوسط والعمل عليه ●
الكوم اربعين [illegible] والواحد [illegible] الكوم اربعين [illegible]

الغوط الماشمي والعمل عليه ● الغوط [illegible] والعمل عليه ●
الكوم اربعين [illegible] الكوم [illegible] النهار

الغوط [illegible] والعمل عليه ● الغوط الصغار الشمي [illegible] النهار والعمل عليه ●
الكوم مايه [illegible] الكوم [illegible]

للغوط [illegible] ● الغوط [illegible] ●
الكوم [illegible] الكوم [illegible] الماء النهار

الغوط [illegible] ● والعمل عليه
الكوم [illegible] النهار

الكاغد [illegible] ● الكاغد [illegible] ●
العربي والبغدادي [illegible] المايه النهار
الشده عشرين [illegible] الشده [illegible] المايه النهار

العود الرطب ● والقطن [illegible] ●
البلنوي [illegible] النهار [illegible]
العشرة [illegible] [illegible]

[illegible] ●
[illegible] اربعة [illegible]
[illegible]

19a

العتابي الحرير والمحشا والتاج والحواشي والمذهب
والمطرز مضاعف والقطن النصف العشرة
العشرة المائة الدينار
العشرة
[illegible]

الصافي البغدادي الصافي الموصلي
الرباع العشرة المائة الدينار العشرة المائة الدينار
[illegible]

البقار [illegible] طول البقار اربعة وعشرون ذراعا وطول الثوب [illegible] ذراعا
[illegible]
العشرة المائة الدينار
[illegible]

[illegible]
العشرة المائة الدينار العشرة المائة الدينار
[illegible]

[illegible]

الملحم [illegible]
العشرة المائة الدينار
[illegible]

[illegible] العشرة المائة الدينار
[illegible]

الجواري [illegible] العشرة المائة الدينار
[illegible]

الابدان [illegible] الصوف
الواحد العشرة المائة الدينار
[illegible]

المقاطع الرباع العشرة المائة
المحامل [illegible]
العشرة المائة الدينار
[illegible]

[illegible] المائة الدينار
الاكسية
الملونة الواحد العشرة المائة الدينار
[illegible]

الحبال

18b

18

٣

العشور المبارك بفرضه تعز عدن المحروسة حماها الله ... في ذكر الاصناف الواصلة من بلاد الهند والعراق ... ومصر والغرب وسائر الاقاليم والحبشة وجميع بلاد السودان

الثياب الخطائي والنسيج والبدرنج والممزج

الثوب الواحد عليه العشر للناس ... طوله اربع اذرع ... ما الذي يكون نسيج كله الذهب بعضه ... والبدرنج ... مثل ذلك

الثياب ... والتركي الواحد العشر للناس ... الثياب الكحلي الواحد العشر للكاسة ...
طوله اربع اذرع ...

الثياب العتابي والشاهي والمصمت والبدري ... الثياب الاصفهانيات ...
طول الثوب اربع اذرع على الواحد العشر ... طول الثوب الواحد ... العشر ...

الثياب الحرير ... الثوب الواحد العشر ... اذا اصل ... من ذراع وذراع ...
على الاثنا عشر ... يكون كل ذراع ... الثوب ... من ...

الثياب ... الثوب الواحد العشر ... الثياب ... الواحد ... العشر ...

الثياب ... الثياب ... الواحد ... [illegible]

الثياب ... الواحد العشر للناس ... الثياب ... الواحد العشر ...

الملاذات الحرير ... والشاهيات الحرير والمطارف الحرير ... الحرير ... الاصناف ...
الحرير الواحد عليه دينار العشر ...

الملاذات ... الملاذات ... الواحد ... العشر ... الواحد العشر ...

النقانع الحرير والكتان ... الواحد عليه العشر ...

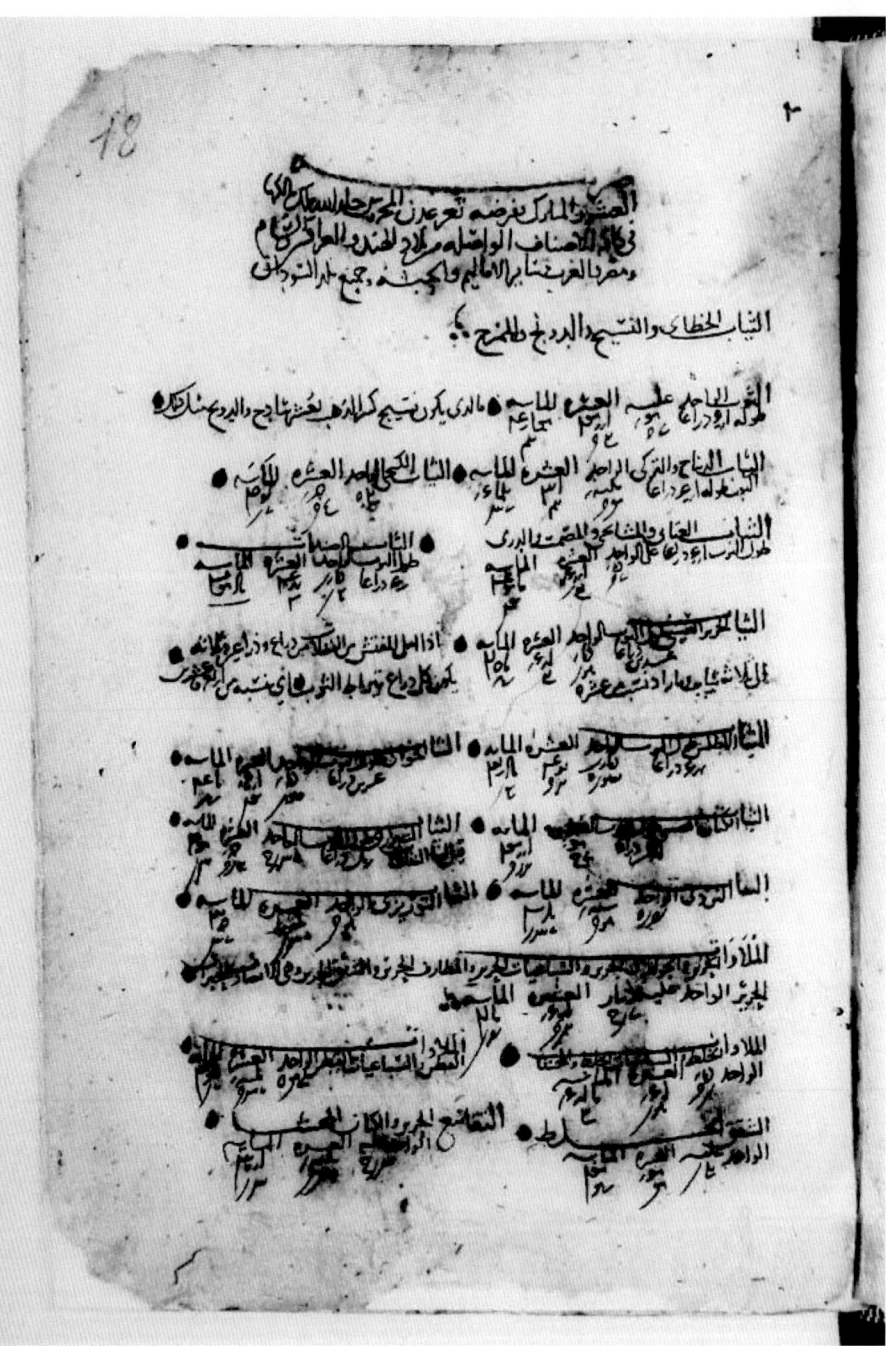

ذكر ما اشتوم ضرايب البادره الشحر اليمنية خلد الله سلطانه

ضريبة

العشور المبارك بفرضه الشحر المحروس خلد الله ملك مالكه

البسر في كل ما يشوي مائه دار عليه اللكوج السلد نحاس حق الوسق كل الحب

الفلفل والتمر ما يشوي مائة النهار ونقيبه علي كل غص

النيل التراص ما يشوي لمائة الوزد على كل عود العبد رنا في العاب كيل الطرح الغار

العارض طعاره هرمز وثلاثات صرو لحور والعيس الغزالي على كل ما يسه القطعه والزباد على الاد

والرس عرب دما والاها الرانج عليه • جهارات عيدتمه الراس للوش والتمر المليه واتى الافته

والواصل من البسر

على مرما دال الاحمال التمر الحاس الكر واذا كان للعوامل الماعين يوزن على التحص

وركل الطعام • البر على الحمل وعليه • الزبيب على الحمل • الحديد على النهار • الحنا على

الصبر الحمل • الدوم على الخمس • البادي عليه الخمس • العنب عليه • الشمال على

الحلبه الحمل ودرس • النوم الحمل • التمر النقي • اللبان الشحري • الصهباء الحمل

على النخر • واذا وصل من طرس الزيله طعام كان على الحمل واذا وصل حضر

والبسر وهو الرطب على الحمل دينار

حرسه

17b

17

والمحلات السليماني جازان والنخميه والجب والراحه والحبيره واللولوه

مع الاشراف بني الحسن علم الاخبار والانطاع وعليهم في كل سنه قود خيل ودرسا

ودروع ثلثون درع حسنه واذا طلبوا للحرب حضروا للغزو الى حيث طلبوا له

المقالة الثالثة في ذكر سواحل البنادر والثغور ومعانيها

وضر لبيانها فاول البنادر بندر ظفار الحبوظي واخرها بندر جده ساحل مكه المشرفه كما في
الجدول

مقصد المقالة الثالثة في [illegible] البنادر		
اصناف / جهات	من الذهب للتي لا الماعار	انواع الهدايا
بندر ظفار الحبوظي	لا عار	[illegible] سيار [illegible] حرير [illegible] واسوده وجواهر ذهب [illegible] ومسك وعنبر [illegible] وجوار هنود [illegible]
بندر الشحر المحروس	لا الفا	عنبر كافور ولولو وجوار رقاصات هنود وحبش الزباد
بندر [illegible] ثغر عدن المحروس	لا الا لا عار	عود وعنبر وكافور ومسك وزباد ومن جميع تحف الهند والعراق وحرامي القماش
بندر المقعه الزبيدي	[illegible] الفا	عبيد وجوار ووصفان وحرير ومما خرج من البحر من تحف الهند
البنادر الشاميه	[illegible] الفا	[illegible] اللولو [illegible] ومن تحف الكرك [illegible] وخرج مكه المشرفه [illegible]
بندر دهلك	[illegible] الفا	من البحار [illegible] وسائر التحف والوحوش والعبيد النوبه
عامر بندر حلي	[illegible] عار [illegible]	من الوصفان المولدات وكمال للسعوديه الحلويه والعبيد [illegible]
جده بندر مكه المشرفه	[illegible] الفا	من التحف والحور [illegible] النسيبات والرواحل

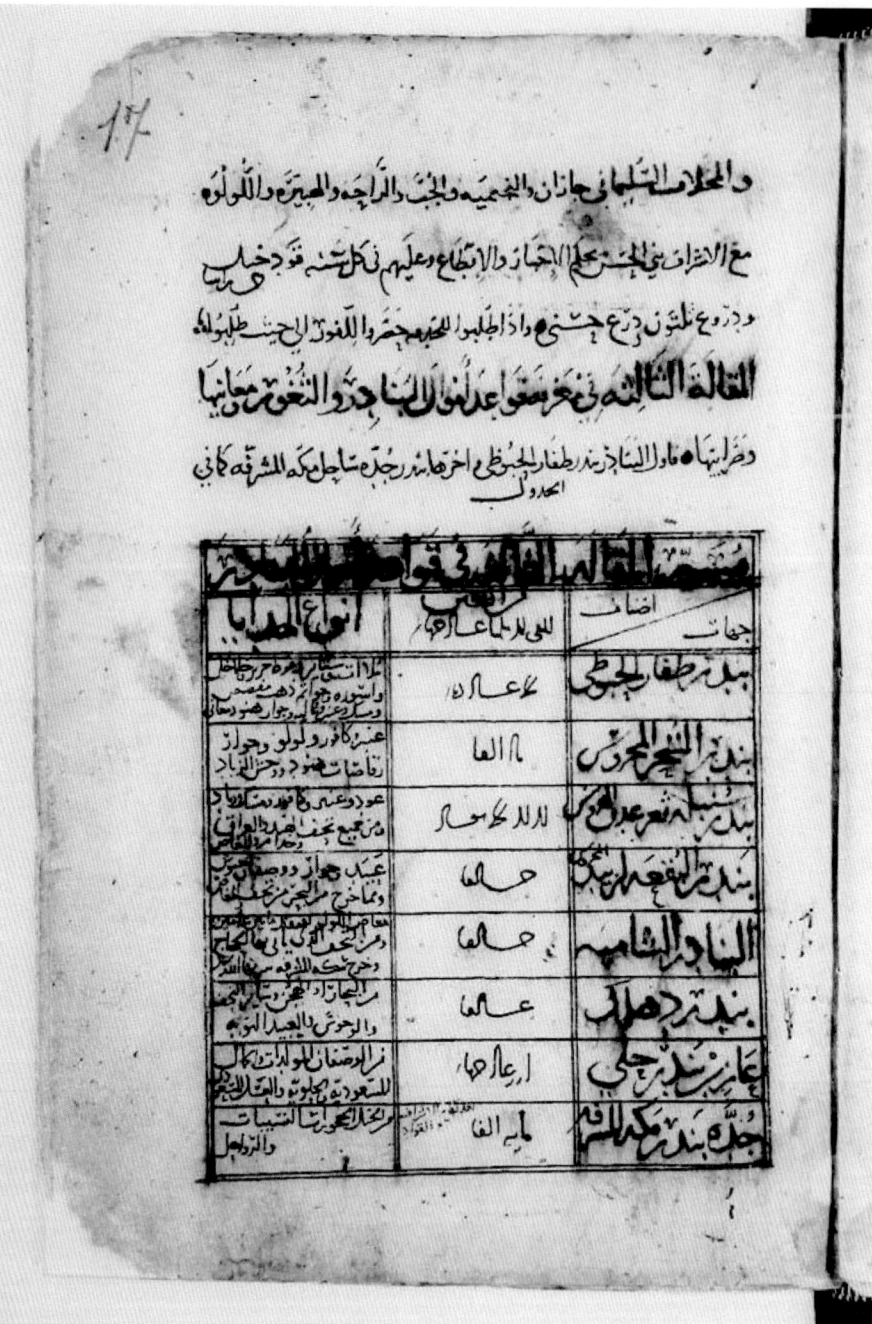

و و هـ —— لله سبحانه

مشجّر المقالة الثانية في قواعد أقوال التهايم				
جهات / أصناف	مراعٍ	هلالي	خراجي	مختلف
الأعمال اللجّية	[illegible]	[illegible]	[illegible]	[illegible]
الأعمال الأبنية	[illegible]	[illegible]	[illegible]	//
الأعمال الموزعية	[illegible]	[illegible]	[illegible]	[illegible]
الأعمال الحطبية والسلم العيشين والطلى	[illegible]	[illegible]	[illegible]	[illegible]
الأعمال الخضيبة ... والكازرين	[illegible]	[illegible]	[illegible]	[illegible]
الأعمال الزمعية	[illegible]	[illegible]	[illegible]	//
الأعمال الدوالية بحكم الأقطاع والبه المبدى عن مقطع	[illegible]	[illegible]	[illegible]	[illegible]
الأعمال السهامية والبه العائمية	[illegible]	[illegible]	[illegible]	//
الأعمال النعجرية بحكم الأقطاع	[illegible]	[illegible]	[illegible]	//
الأعمال المستردية والمقصرية	[illegible]	[illegible]	[illegible]	//
الأعمال الموتية والقهبية	[illegible]	[illegible]	[illegible]	//
الأعمال الرحبانية بحكم الاقطاع	[illegible]	[illegible]	[illegible]	//

الخلاف

تتمة قسمة الجهة الثانية من المقالة الأولى بالبر الأخضر					
أعمال الجوجبه	عاكه	〃	〃	〃	ماكل
أعمال البرقه	ماهام	〃	〃	〃	ماكسا
أعمال التارة ومحله	عاكا	〃	〃	حايط	〃
أعمال بطحوات	ماله	〃	〃	〃	ماود
أعمال حبدرين	عاكا	〃	حاطا	〃	ماكيا
جبل الطور وهو صبر المجرد ك	اعاله	〃	〃	〃	〃

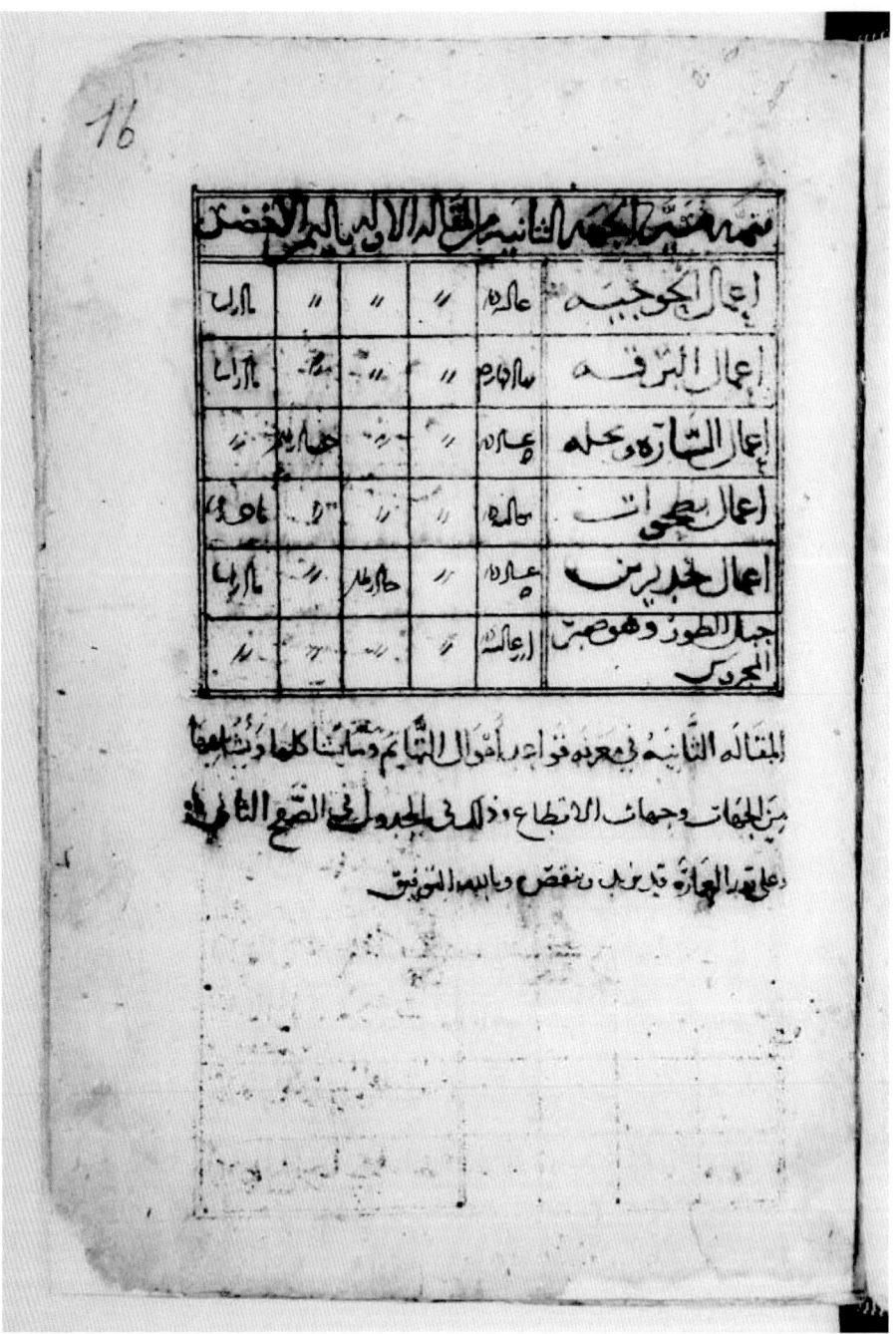

المقالة الثانية في معرفة قواعد أموال التهايم وما بينا كلما ونشاعها
من الجهات وجهات الاقطاع وذلك في الجدول في الصفح الثاني
على قدر العمارة قد يزيد وينقص وبالله التوفيق

تمام [illegible] الجهة الثانية من المقالة الأولى [illegible] الأخضر

أصناف / جهات	عين	غلة	عشر	سكر احمر	كباش
بلد العنسيين ومغار المعلا [illegible]	[illegible]	//	//	//	//
القفاعه من رعنب	[illegible]	//	//	//	//
مخلاف حراز والتوب والرز [illegible]	[illegible]	//	//	//	//
مخلاف [illegible]	[illegible]	//	//	//	//
الاعمال النعرية	[illegible]	[illegible]	//	//	//
بلد خولان [illegible]	[illegible]	[illegible]	//	//	//
الاعمال [illegible] والحقيه [illegible]	[illegible]	[illegible]	//	//	[illegible]
الاعمال الشمرانية	[illegible]	//	//	//	//
الاعمال [illegible]	[illegible]	[illegible]	[illegible]	//	[illegible]
جبل [illegible]	[illegible]	//	//	//	[illegible]
الاعمال [illegible] وتابع	[illegible]	//	//	//	
الاعمال [illegible]	[illegible]	//	//	//	//

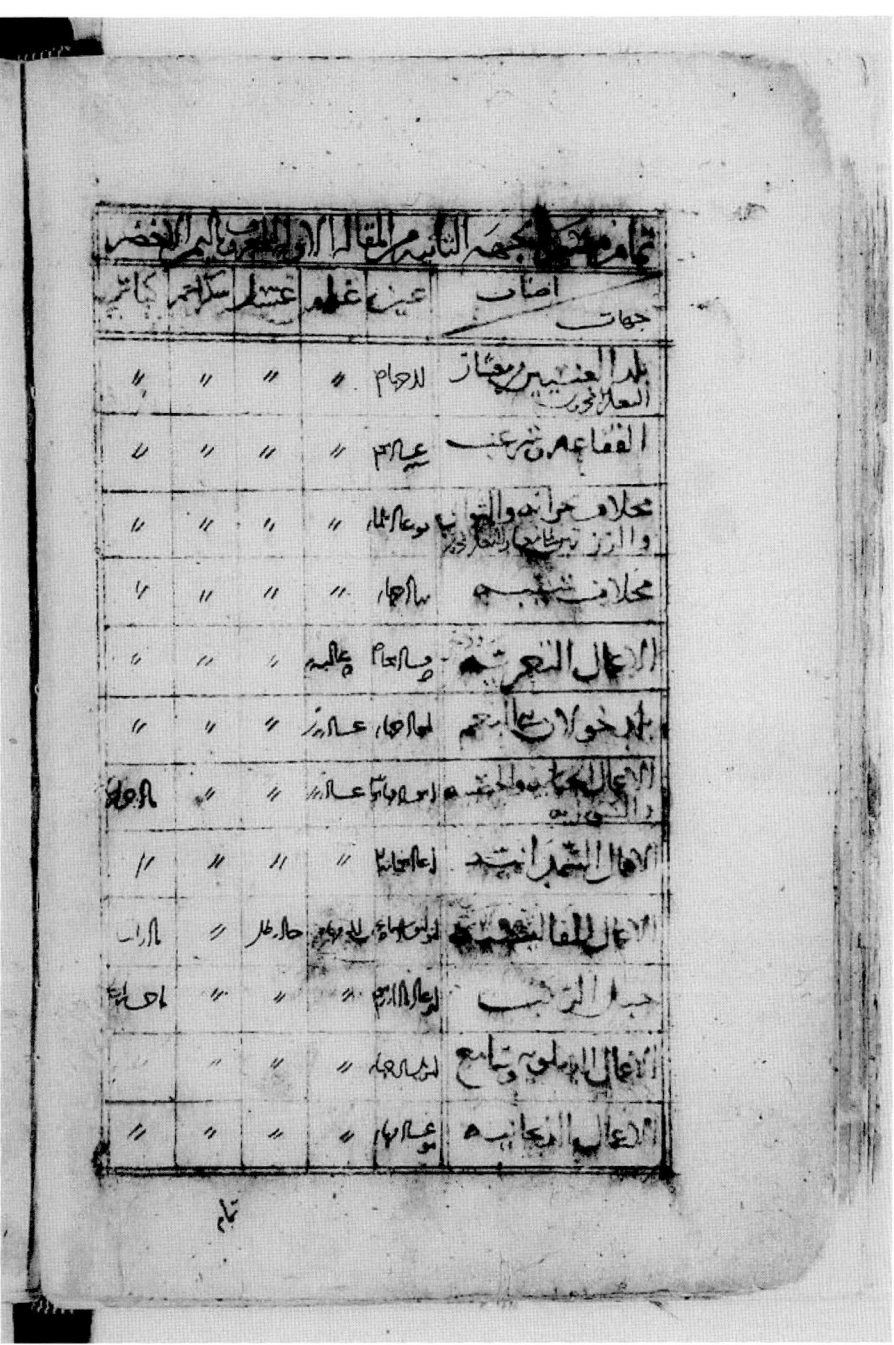

تم

ويجعهم على يونس النفس والرفق ما كان في شيء إلا زانه وكانت الخيرات إخوانه ٥
والأعمال الصالحات إخوانه وملائكة الخير أعوانه والسعد أخيرانه ٥

أصناف / جهات	[illegible]	[illegible]	عشر [illegible]	[illegible]	كاشف [illegible]
الأعمال البحيرية ادي [illegible] سيف [illegible]	عالهام	عالحما	//	//	//
الثغور [illegible] كفاية الحصون	ماحالا	ماحما	لعالطلا	//	//
[illegible] وما الأهالي [illegible]	عسالا	ما الا	//	//	//
بلد [illegible] [illegible] والنخول	عسالا	فسا	//	//	//
بلد المشرق وما الأهالي	عسالا	//	//	//	//
جبل الشوامي وما [illegible]	عسالا	//	//	//	//
الأعمال الجلالية [illegible] جبله و[illegible]	وسالطلا	//	//	عسالطلا	//
[illegible]	مسالطا	وسالحما	//	//	//
بلد [illegible] و[illegible]	بسالا	//	//	[illegible]	ماحما
[illegible] الشلفية	العالمام	بسالا	//	//	[illegible]
مخلاف [illegible]	هوالسالحا	//	//	//	//

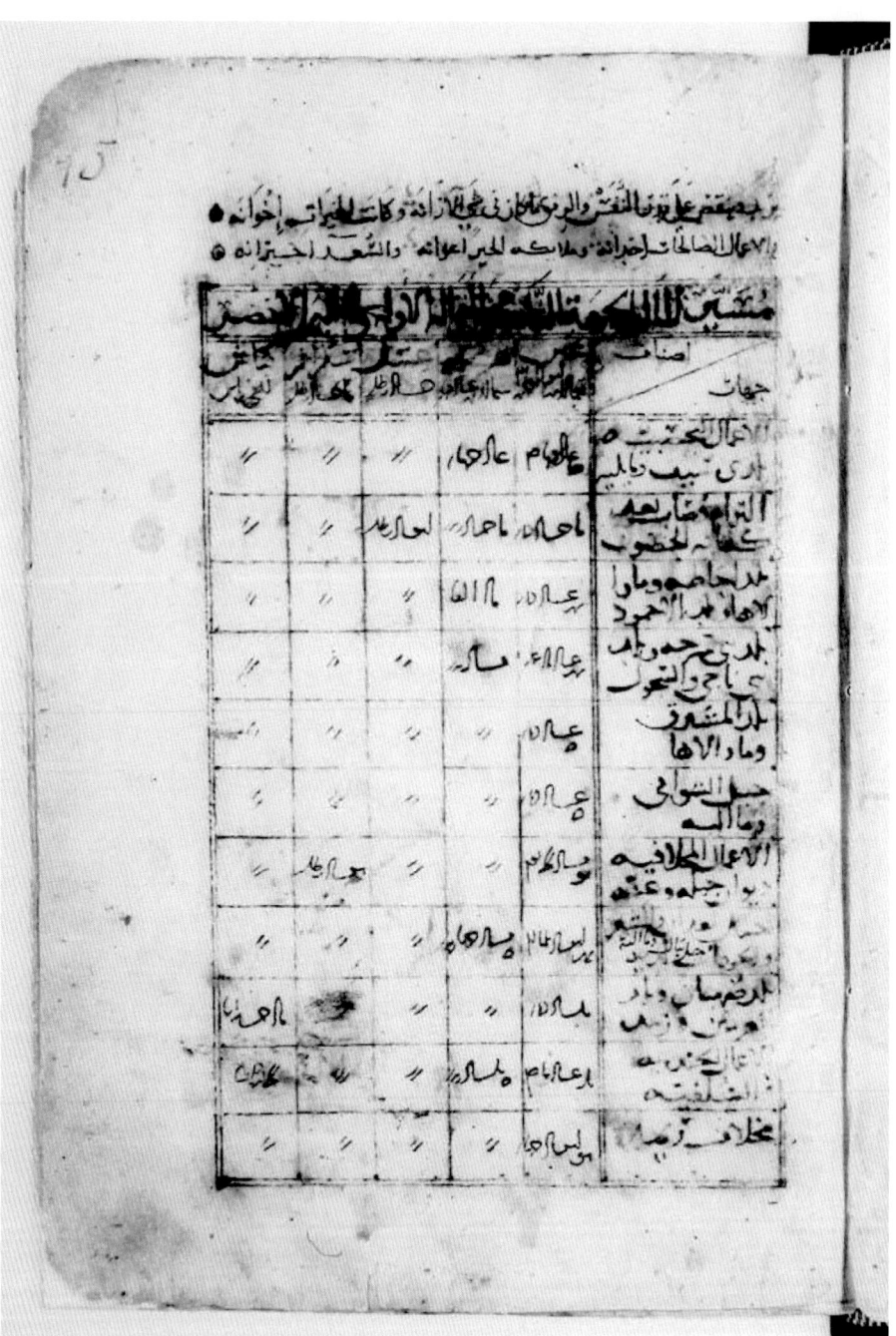

حصني العش والناصين ‌ه حصني [illegible]

عاداته ‌م

حصن غضر ‌ه حصن مدع حصن [illegible]

مواساه على البلاد

حصن كوكبان ‌ه حصن [illegible] ‌ه حصن [illegible]

حصن حضور المصانع ‌ه حصني العطمه والمينزع ‌ه

زياده على بلاده

مواساه زياده على بلدها

حصني ‌ه

تراش وتعرضعه عادته

حصن [illegible] ‌ه حصن تعرضغله ‌ه

[illegible]

... من الحساب على المعروف باليمن الاخضر ومبلغ التمام ...

يرتبل

14b

[illegible]

[illegible] بالعا[illegible] [illegible]

المعروف [illegible]

[illegible] الحاشية والعمارة [illegible]

[illegible]

خاصة جامكية الرهاين [illegible]

[illegible] صاحب سند [illegible] صاحب [illegible] صاحب الحصن [illegible] صاحب [illegible]

[illegible] جامكية حاشية الاملاك [illegible]

[illegible]

[illegible] عمارة الحصن [illegible]

[illegible]

المعروف بجامكية [illegible] الحصون [illegible]

حصون ذمر وما اليه [illegible]

عشرة شهور [illegible]

[illegible]

[illegible]

14a

وأضفت الى ذلك الحصون السلطانية

المذكورة

الحصون على الأملاك

المبذول من الولاة والنقباء والمتأزفين

مبذول الولاة والنقباء

مبذول المتأزفين

13b

واضفت الى ذلك الحصون السلطانية وبلغ مجموعها بما في جهات الملك جاعلا ...
المذكورة والاداد الكلية العدة زيادة على الجهات مرتبها اصل الحال من العربي على الالف [illegible]
ما يو عالا الى ... بجماعة
... الحصون على الاف [illegible] وذمار ه
عليها [illegible]
بجماعة
اجمالا
من تحصيل بلاد الحصون ه
عليها ... اجمالا ...
تحصيل
بلاد ذمار ... ي الحصون ... بلاد حضور والشعابية ... ي [illegible]
[illegible]
بلاد الجارد ● المبذول من الولاة والنقباء والمشارفين ه
للغد [illegible]
تحصيل
مبذول الولاة والنقباء ه
صاحب ... يا صاحب ... يا صاحب الكيم يا صاحب الدكر يا صاحب حصارة يا صاحب ... يا نقيب ...
نقيب حصن ... نقيب حصن ... صاحب حصن ... نقيب حصن ... صاحب ...
مبذول المشارفين ه
مشارف حصن ... مشارف ... مشارف ... مشارف ... مشارف ... مشارف ...
مشارف ... مشارف ... مشارف ... مشارف ... مشارف ... مشارف ...
غير ...
الاعمال الصعدية ... يا ... [illegible]
المدينة

في معرفة قواعد اموال الجهات اليمنية بكمالها وهذا الفصل يحتوي على [illegible] مقالة

المقالة الاولة في قواعد اموال الجبال وهي تحتوي على جهتين الجهة تسمى البلاد

العليا وهي [illegible] من شرقي حضرموت الى البلاد الطويلة وشرقا [illegible] غربا [illegible] على تهامة والجبال

[illegible] جنوبا والى بيشة قبلة [illegible] الآن

جهات / اصناف	عين [illegible]	[illegible]	[illegible]	[illegible]	[illegible]
بلد صنعاء [illegible] وبلد [illegible]	ما [illegible]	//	[illegible]	//	//
بلد ذراع [illegible] وبلد [illegible]	[illegible]	//	//	ما مار[illegible]	//
[illegible] وبلد عبيدة	[illegible]	//	//	//	//
[illegible]	ماية الفا	//	//	//	//
[illegible] ودواد [illegible] الحارث [illegible]	[illegible]	//	[illegible]	//	//
[illegible] جبل اللوز	[illegible]	//	//	ما مار[illegible]	[illegible]
جبل بني شهاب [illegible] خولان وبلد [illegible]	ماية الفا	//	//	//	[illegible]
جبل [illegible]	[illegible]	//	//	//	//
بلد [illegible] دخان [illegible]	[illegible]	[illegible]	//	//	[illegible]
[illegible] الاعلى والاسفل	//	//	//	ما مار[illegible]	[illegible]
بلاد [illegible]	[illegible]	//	//	ما مار[illegible]	//
[illegible] الاقطاع [illegible]	//	//	//	[illegible]	[illegible]
[illegible]	[illegible]	[illegible]	[illegible]	[illegible]	[illegible]

المشقة ونوبته • وما طالبه الناظر من المتحصل من الحصاد في الأمر اشتغل زيادة في آنها كان ثم
بنوبه والجناة كل شهر بشهره على ما اشهد به المذكره للمستدركين المقيد ان يكسو له • ولا
يمنعه المستدين التصرف في مصالح الديوان ووضعه للمرء في موضعه بحكم الزراعة • وما عجز
الناظر عن استخراجه بطبعه للمستدين يستخرجه في هو الحدها الى استخراجه لزم منه غرامته
بعد ان يتضح له ذلك • ووجوه ضمان الحلال اليه وتدبيره شهود المساح اليه • واذا اشكل اليه
المتولي ان يلبد المساح عرعرهم تعالى وتدبير النقد الامين الخبير • ومهما ورد الامر به من حكم
مهمات او حوائج سلطانه • او درك مرزمان يحتاج اليه يحمله بحكم في اقرب مدة • وادركه حسنا كذمة
تصحيحه من كانه المباشرين من الجهة وما يجب على الأمر الذي يعين على الملزم
شون الكال الى النهاية من منافع الرعية في الحبوب والوادي ولا يبقي احد من الاسفلب
دون ان يجمع الاعلين بحسن كل قناعه بقناعتهما من خالف المنكر عليه وادبه على ذنب
عوضه وعليه حبس الرعية من النقمة والمحلف بعرض المشتد بجميعه التي ترك كل شعوبها
وعليه ان يكون اول الغلة يعرض المشتد بالاطراف والمتحققين والمتجوز لبر المحوج منهم قبل ان يحلوا
ويتودد زواله • واذا امكن الملتزم ان لا يزرعوا ولا يعزبوا الوادي • ولا اتى الملتزم من اول
العمل بالفعل • ولا يأت ان يزرعوا في النواحي ولا يقطعهم عن الحرث بالعمل •

الفصل الثالث

في معرفة

[illegible]

الجريده التي يكون على المغال • ولا يقوم المستدعي باحد ورقته مكمله العلايم المفوض •
ويجري للرعيه على ما شهد به المنشور السلطاني الذي يكرمهم بكل سنه لتستقر خواطرهم •
وهو الذي ينتدب المساح اذا وصله كتاب المستوفي بالندب بعد من اشار اليه المستوفي ولحاضر
ناظره يزيد وينقص بحسب ما راى فيه المصلحه وديته فمع ما بيان كل تاريخ بتاريخه ليكمل تكرر
وعدد ويعطي كتاب الجهه لتختم عدد موها ويرسل الى المستوفي الطاير كالجري العادة في
كل ثمانيه ايام • وعند كمال التواريخ وحضور المحاسبات على الاسفال تكون المقابله يرفع المستوفي
الى المقام الشريف في كتب ويبعثها اليه في وقت تحتاج الى اعتقادها • وعند تجرد ا
للمساح والمباشرين للمباشره ويكتبوا في كل جهه ملخص بالكاين والمزال فلا يكتب
اسم زرع في اسم زرع مسامحه ولا ارتفاعه من جدي ولا كان ولا سبح والامداد •
ويلزم المساح والذراع عند المباشره لا يحدو امر الرعيه الا المعتاد من المنفعه ومن
علم به انه اخذ زياده على العاده انكر عليه وادب ويستعاد منه للرعوى حقه • ومتى
اطلع شي من الجاني في الجهه اخر الحساب لزم للشد بالجهه استخراجه • النظار
الجهات • وما يجب عليهم في جهات الخراج خاصه يجب على الناظر تعيين الاموال
التي للمخزون بعد المستخرج والمخزن عند المستخرج الى الديوان العمده لا يصرف درهم الا من حيث
يعينه الناظر • لا يصرف المصرف في المهمات الا برقاع مكمله العلايم من الناظر والكاتب

12a

وإما من هلالي ويمنع عنهم التعسفات كلها ● وإذا طلب الناظر احدا من رعية الخراج السلطاني

فلا يمنعه الا ما كان باطلا امنع عنه ● ويسترفع حسبانات الجمعة من المباشرين ومن

المساح التواريخ كل عشرة ايام ويرسلها الى الباب الشريف الى مشيد الاستيفا العمد

وكل شهر شهره من اعمال الجزا واعمال الصندوق والختمات مفصل بجهات الاصل في الاصل

والمضاف في المضاف واعمال المثمر مفصل بجهاته وكذا اسباب الاهرا بجملها الى مشيد الاستيفا الكبير

والمشيد يسلمها الى المستوفي وهو حينئذ يعطي المباشرين كلا نسخته ويعطي المشيد نسخة والمشيد

يعطيها نايبه يجعلها كان المشيد كاتبا او عاميا ما يدرك على المستوفين ويرفع بطرح الخزانه

الى المقام الشريف السلطاني ● ومشارف الاستيفا مثل العامل الجنة والمعرفة والامانة

خشية حوادث الزمان وعوارض الامتحان فاذا حدث على احدهما حادث نجد العوض

الاخر وعند الشاهد ● ويكون المشاورة على المستخرج كل يوم بيومه ● واذا استخرج

المباشرين تاريخ

مال فلا يغير قواصي بعض المشيد رفقة الحاصل مكملة العلامة ● ويعتبر الحاصل تاريخ

كما ذكر في الورقه والا الزم النقاد العجز في ساعته تلك ● والمثمر والمسع لا يكون

الا بحضر كتاب العين وكتاب الاهرا ليكون المباشرة مرتبط بعضها بعضا ● حتى الحسن لحد

المباشرين لا خذ من مال الديوان درهم الا بعلم جميع المباشرين ومتى ظهر علم ذلك الى النايب افتقار

ذاع السر وافتضحوا ● ويحضر المشيد مقبوض الاهرا الان انسطلم الرعيث ويكون القبض ببينة

الجديدة

11

عليه أن يستخرج ما عينه له المستوفي فان ورد عليه امر المخدوم بالتقدم لاستخراج

الاموال الراجحة عليه المستوفي من ان يتقدم معه فقد يرد امر الملك على ان يتقدم معه تقرير

من كل ديوان نفرا وقد يرد الامر بواحد مخصوص ويستخرج ما عينه له المستوفيين

[illegible]

فالبدركة دركهم ويستنهض الاموال ويطلع • وقد يرد عليه الامر ان يسير الى مشدين

الجهات يستخرجوا ويرسلوا بالحواصل دفعه او دفعات ويطلعوا النقاد بصحبة

الحواصل المعتبر من حاصل كل جهة كثير او يسير على العادة ويعودوا الى جهاتهم ••

والذي يجب على مشد بين الجهات القيام بعمارة الوادي شاقيا وضاحيا واصلاح الردم

والعقوم والعقايد والرقاب والشعوب والشد في استخراج الاموال جميعها الا ترك

باقيا ويستخرجها من وجوهها • والجهات التي يجب المبادرة الى مباشرتها واستخراج اموالها

[illegible]

يبادر اليها • وان المستخرج لا يكون الا في الديوان الذي قد اصطلح عليه والمستخرج

درهم الا بحضر المباشرين كلهم ومن اعتذر منهم عن الحضور بعذر واضح ظاهر مثل مرض

او عرض النوبه المشد ان يرسل نايبه يحضر المستخرج • ومن ابطا منهم استعجله ورسم عليه

في تسبب تعوقه • وعليه ضبط الجسور وقمع اهل الفساد في جهته ومقدم الجهه

نجيده او يكون امر التقدمة اليه وامر العسكر والرتبة اليه • ويعضد الناظر على

مصالح الديوان المعمور واستخراج الاموال الخراج والهلالي والمثمن وغلة الاهراء والمظالم عوض

القديمة والجديدة ۞ ولا يفارقوا الباب المرتب بلواح الحديد ولا رصاد المواليد على اختيار ذات
الحركات ۞ وان كانوا اثنين او ثلاثة او اربعة فاستغنى منهم عما هو
الديوان فان الديوان هو المستوفي عامل الاستيفاء الكبير فاذا غاب لعذر اما مرض

(في الهامش: ... المستوفي في الديوان)

واما عرض فالمشارف هو مقامه يتصدر بما يجري من الجهات والمهمات ۞ فالمستوفي هو
الذي عليه المدار والعمل وتحصيل الاموال وعلم ما يستقر في كل جهة من الجهات الى الارتفاع
بالاقلام التي تستخرج ما بين قلم النخل وقلم السابع ۞ لان المستوفي نايب الملك امين
على سوق الاموال شحيح على تفريقها عند المرتبات ۞ لا ينقطع عنه مكاتبات العمال في
الجهات كلها والمشارفات من المتصرفين والملتزمين بامر الجهات ۞ وما وصله من علم انهاه
في ساعته الى مخدومه ۞ ويرتبه كتاب الجهات الذي يضع الكاتب الظريف حسن تعرف
نفعه ويرتب في كل جهة مشد وناظر وعامل ومشارف وشاهد ضبط وتقويم وكاتب الخراج
والعجز ۞ وكاتب الاملاك وكاتبين على قدر ما في الجهة واركانها وسايا جشريات
بدل كل عمل كاتبين ۞ واما المشد من اهل التصرف في الجهات قد يكون من عوام
الناس او من احد الاجناد يرتب لاجل هيبته وما عليه الا الشد فيما عينه له الكتاب
فالمدار على الكاتب في ضبط الورق وتقويم التوارخ وتفسير الاموال ۞ ولي كل جهة
من طنترم ومدكى ما يجب له وعليه ۞ ونبدأ بالمشد الكبير شد الاستيفاء المتوجه
عليه

10

باقي شهور السنه كل شهر بشهره ويكتبوا صفات الرجال عندهم في دفاترهم حتى لا يقع لهم

الخيانات على جهة الصفه فلان بن فلان صفته [كذا او كذا بحليه تحليته] • وذلك قد يعرض

واحد على اسم اخر وهذا [نايب] يفعلوه الخائنين من النقباء • ثم يكتب المشارف الكبير بعد عراضة [بكلم] اول

السنه تواقيع الحصون بعد ان يراجع لهم الوزير ويعرضوا على النظر الشريف لاجل علامه العلامه

والاطلاق • فاذا ابرزت التواقيع الى الوزير طلب مشارف الحصون وسلم اليه التواقيع

فيقبضهم ويقدم الى بيته ويطالب المخاطبين ويدخل كل اصحاب حصن على قدر مراتبهم

ويحضر المشارفين ويعقدها كما جرت العاده • والمشارف الكبير ناظر الحصون وكان

له شان في الدوله الموحديه وما قبلها الى نحو سنين من الدوله المجاهديه واختصر •

وكان [illegible] يتعلمه [illegible] وله مضافين ويذكر مراد مثل مشد الاستيفاء وناظر الخاص •

[خص] وامر الحصون الى الوزير لا يتكلم عليها احد غيره والحسن ان يكون امر الحصون الا الى

النقيب فان الحصون كالطيور يخشى عليها النفور • ومع هذا ما كان يستمر والي ولا نقيب

[تسليم] في الحصون في غيرها الا بمنشور ممنوح بالعلامه الشريفه وما يكتب الحد [illegible] الا ورقه

[المعهود] العهده وما اشبه ذلك • ولا باس اذا وقعت الحصون للحفظ والحذر فالتزم ان السلطنه

ما تساعدها النظر • ثم حسابا يعلمون خبرا فلا يشغله قد قرا الكتب المفيده [وذكر]

[عالهم] عنهم صحه الاحكام الجيده وان اختياراتهم الحركات السعيده وصحت [illegible]

10a

الى المخدوم كتب الكتاب والزمام بعلمه ثم اتفاق حاكمها الامرا الخدام يتعهدها بنيابة

عن كتاب الخزانة المعمورة وان احتاجوا الى حضور واحد منهم او هو من جهة ... الملازمة

على مرتب حاكميهم في طول السنة ويكون من قصد ما وصل الى الزمام حتى يستوفوا المرتب

ان كونه

وقد سدوا الجواري ما يتعهدها الا كاتب الباب الشريف ومن شرطه كبيرا كهلا مسلما

امينا على المال والمرج صينا صاينا اديبا لبيبا عاملا خطاطا كامل الخصال الحسنة

والمعاني المستحسنة ان شا الله تعالى ثم كاتب الحصون البحرية يسمى منار الحصون

هو المنار الكبير ومن دونه منارين كثيرة وليس منار من الصغار حاكم الا في

حصون دون حصون وذلك في حصن نعل البحر منار وفي حصن صبر المسمى العربان

حصون البحر

منار وفي حصن النعكر منار وفي حصن الرملوه البحرين كاسن وفي الحصون العجابية

حصن مان المعر بحصن مان منار وباقي المنارين مستمرين بقلعه ولهم حاكميه

من التما المهمين وهم من نفات الكاتب والنائم وافارسهم وعليهم عهدوا ادراك ذلك

ان المنار الكبير يتعرض كافة الحصون في اول الاشهر واذا كان احد المرتبين مات

او تنحى استحضر عوضه وما يحصل من حاكميه من الاعيب فاعرف الجباه بخطه

وكتب سطاير العرايض في اخر ذلك وذكر ما يحصل من الغيبات وملكت منه جزا الى المستوفي

والمشد واسجل الجداول كالذي بحضرة المرتب الكبير والمنارين الصغار منار الحصون

باقي

ويتبع ما شرطه الواقف لا يحول عنه

ومن ادرك البلوغ من الايتام رتب عوضه • ومن اكمل من المدرسة ثلثة اعوام رتب

مكانه من قابلته زكاه الى ان رفع منه وابقاه الى ان يرتع الى المدارك

بوضعه خاصة المرتبة والايتام • واما المدرسين من عرف منهم بالعلم والمعرفة والصبر

على التدريس وظهور الفايدة فلا يغير عليه • والنايب لا يوجر الوقف اكثر من ثلاث سنين

ولا يوجر على من يتجاه • ثم كاتب الاصطبلات السعيدة يكون في كل اصطبل كاتبين

عامل ومشارف ويكون معهم مباشر ويسمى شر اخوري يكون ظريف عارف باوجاع الدواب

وهو اخوري

وما ينفعهم وما يضرهم ويكون له مطالعة في كتاب البيطرة ومداوات الدواب من دون اخيره •

ثم كاتب الانشا السعيد وهو كاتب الدرج للمهم لكتب المناشير والمربعات والمثالات ويحمل المكتبات

الى ساير الجهات الى حيث يحد امر الملك ومناشير الاقطاعات التي تشتمل على اللفظ المقوم •

المعنى المحكم والمحكم • والشعر العذب المجود على المعنى الموجود • وكل ذلك على

لسان الملك بكليم وطبع عن منشلك • ثم كاتب الحوايجخاناه للمهم يكتبوا ما يصرفه

الحوايج كاش من المرتب والطاري في كل يوم جاري • ويرفعه الى الديوان وهو المتولي

وكيف به استدعا ويصرف من مال الحلال للعمر ما كان من الملك وجملة لجاري العادة • وما

كان من مرتب المطبخ الكبير والحوايج خاناه للمهم الكبير فمرتبه الى الحد وداوم تمامه لجاري

العادة • ثم كاتب الباب الشريف السلطاني كاتبا ولحد الاعيرهم علم من وصل الى

الباب الشريف من الاشراف واقبال العز على الجهات وما اراد مقام الباب الشريف ان يشارك به

وقف ... سبحانه

علم الملك ذلك فيكون اما من عدم معرفته او [illegible] كاتب الجيش المتقدم لا شيء عامل مباشر

وشاهد والشاهد من دون المتصدرين الحاكم والمشارف ولم ان [illegible] اكل الرتب

الجهات ولهم عليهم عوايد من العيد من الكبير من علي كل جندي عشره دنانير في العيدين

وعلي الرجال دنانير وهذا اي عمل نسبه من سائر الجهات واذا وجد انهم لم ابق عند الغرامة

غير هم الحاكم وتطعوهم من الخدمه الا في جهات الاقطاع ليس لهم كلام علي الا رابق

واما العراصه والمنفعه فلهم ذلك وعليهم ان يكتبوا التواقيع المتضمنه لعسكر الباب الشريف

في كل شهر وتقبضوها كاتب الخزانة المعمورة منهم ويعرضوها علي النظر الشريف ليطلع عليها اعلا

الشريفه فاستواهل الكتاب المعمورة الا التواقيع كما جرت العاده من اول الدوله المعمورة

وان يكتبوا علي المناشير الاقطاعات الاشتراطات من العسكر بالمال والعداد وما يخرجوه عن

اقطاع المقطعين كالاملاك والجتريات والوصايا دعوز الابل وحسابات الغلال

ويكتبوا علي مربعات المستوحم وكاتبه كتاب المستبقا ثم كاتب المرقومات هو كالمستوفي

بجانب كل نائب وتقدمه لديه علي تحصيل وقفها ويصرف النفقات ويرصد للعماره ما يراه

علي قدر الحاصل فان توفر بعد ذلك شي يحصله في دفتره وعلي مشد الوقف ان يباشر

العماره اذا احتاجت بنفسها ويندب من صحت عدالته ودينه ويكون له اعيان

وثقات يحضروا النفقات ويقيم حسبته ودهنه مع المعلمين والايام في استيفا النفقات تعم

ومن

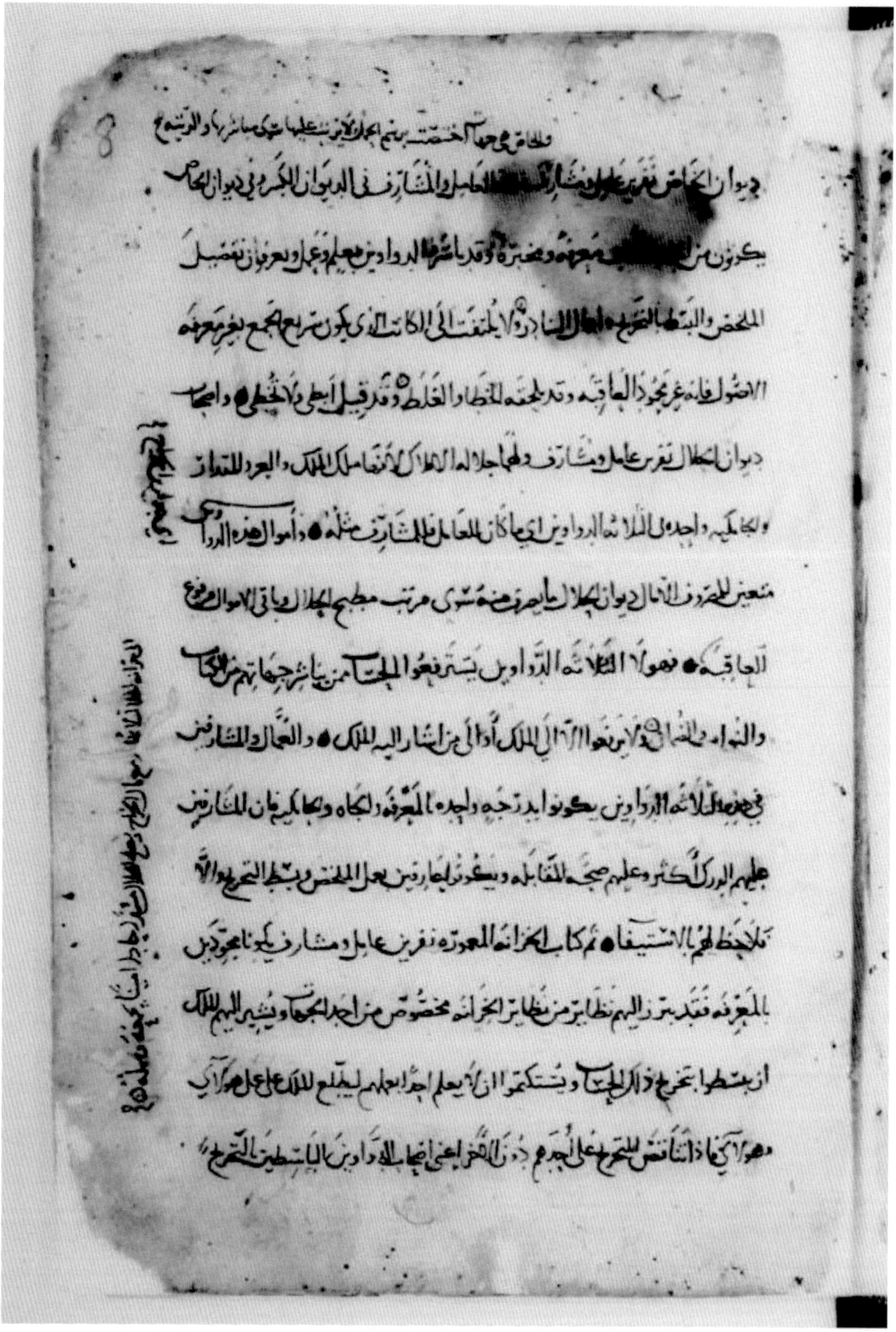

والخاص مع جهات اختصت [illegible] عليها [illegible] والتوقيع

ديوان الخاص نفرين عامل ومشارف [illegible] العامل والمشارف في الديوان الكبير في ديوان الخاص

يكونون من [illegible] معرفة وخبرة وقد باشروا الدواوين فعلموا وعملوا وعرفوا تفصيل

الملخص والبسط والتوجيه وأحوال النادرة ولا يلتفت إلى الكاتب الذي يكون سريع الجمع بغير معرفة

الأصول فإنه غير محمود العاقبة وقد يحمله ذلك على الخطأ والغلط وقد قيل أبطئ ولا تخطئ [illegible]

ديوان الحلال نفرين عامل ومشارف [illegible] لأنها أملاك الملك [illegible]

والحاكمية واحدى الثلاثة الدواوين أي ما كان للعامل فللمشارف مثله وأموال هذه الدواوين

متعين للصرف في أعمال ديوان الحلال ما يصرف منه سوى مرتب مطبخ الحلال وباقي الأموال مرفوع

العاقبة فهو لا الثلاثة الدواوين يسترفعوا الحساب من باشر جهاتهم من الكتاب

والنواب والضمان ولا يرفعوا [illegible] إلى الملك أو إلى من أشار إليه الملك والعمال والمشارفين

في هذه الثلاثة الدواوين يكونوا [illegible] واحده المعرفة والجاه والحاكمية فإن المشارفين

عليهم الدرك الكثير وعليهم صحة المقابلة ويكونوا عارفين بعمل الملخص وبسط التوجيه ولا

يلاحظ لهم بالاستيفاء ثم كتاب الخزانة المعمورة نفرين عامل ومشارف يكونا محمودين

بالمعرفة فتقدير إليهم نظاير من نظاير الخزانة مخصوص من أحد الجهات ويشير إليهم الملك

أن يبسطوا بتخريج ذلك الحساب ويستكتموا أن لا يعلم أحد بعملهم ليطلع الملك على [illegible]

[illegible] للتخريج على الجرم [illegible] على إحاطة الدواوين بالبسط والتخريج

8a

ووزير العقل وامين الذات وامينه القلم وكاتم سره وثقة الملك ومعيشه

من قبضة يمينه ◦ ما القلم جامع الملك ومقيم الجال [illegible]

لما رايت لساني غير منطلق اليك في حاجتي رجعت بالقلم ◦

ترجمانه وجانبك ممتنعي يا اخير الناس من عرب ومن عجم ◦ وقال بعض الحكما

القلم قايد الملك والسيف ناصره ◦ وقال في وصف القلم والكاتب ◦

ما راينا ضاربه من بطل بحسام تطيعه الف قلم ◦

بل راينا موجه من كاتب بمراد تكتسب الف علم ◦ وقال في وصف كاتب

وكانما القلم اليراع بكفه رمح به الاعدا اذا ما تطرد ◦

وكانما في كفه بحر نحو لموجه فعطاه جزل وحال محمد ◦

الفصل الثاني

في معرفة قواعد ديوان الخراج السلطاني ◦ وما هو الذي وقع عليه اسم الديوان ◦

وما يجب لهم وعليه وعلى المتصرفين والمباشرين لجهاتهم التي هم عليها حاكم بحكم الملك وما الذي

يجب لهم وعليهم اما قواعد الديوان فهم المباشرين بالقلم وهم الكتاب فاعلاهم منزله

كتاب الملك ◦ ولهم درجات فاعلاهم درجة المشايخ المستوفيون واعلاهم اصحاب

الديوان الكبير وهم عامل ومشارف ومن دونهما شاهد والمعرف من تبعهم واصحاب

ديوان

مدح القلم وأهله • هذين البيتين للبستي رحمه الله

إذا أقسم الأبطال يوماً بسيفهم وعدّوه مما يكسب المجد والكرم •

كفى قلم الكتّاب عزاً ورفعة مدى الدهر أن الله أقسم بالقلم • وقال آخر

بقوم ويصغرا مخطفات كأنها أنامل ربات الخدود الكواعب •

إذا أرعفوها زينت عن عارفها قراطيس تحكي ناضحات الترائب • وقال آخر

إن التشاغل بالدفاتر والمحابر والدراسة •

أشكل التعبد والتزهد والرياسة والسياسة • وقال بعض الحكما

الخط صنعة روحانية والعلم ترجمان الصدور وهو الكلام • صرير الأقلام

أفصح من صليل الحسام • والعلم مجموع الجيش الإرادة • وينظم الكلام ولا يصل الا بتمام •

يقول لسلطان او يفتح نوار بستان وقال حكيم جمع العالم

بستان سياجه الدولة • الدولة سلطان تحميه السنة • السنة سياسة يسوسها

الملك • الملك راع يعضده الجيش • الجيش أعوان يكفلهم المال • المال رزق تجمع

من الرعية • الرعية عبيد يكنفهم العدل • العدل مألوف وبه قوام العالم •

وقال بعض الحكما العلم معنا طيش المال كالجديد • وقال الملك

لا رجال إلا بالمال ولا مال إلا من رعية ولا رعية إلا بعدل هذا العدل قوام الخلق

7a

على الادني ترجمه على الادنى ناحي على المشيرق و[illegible] وجماعته [illegible] من عم على ابر

وحاضنه وادي بهاوذي سدم و[illegible] جبل المر وصاب و[illegible] الخضرا

ونعمان وجبل المعكر وجبل بعدان بافيه واليه وبلد شبان [illegible] بلاد ريمه الحليلين

ومابينهم وادعه

وعند العقاعه وشرعب وجبل الطور وهو صبر ومابينهم من حصون امصار وانهار

وحصن تعز الغر المحروسة كرسي اليمن وحماته وجبل ذخر ومخلاف المعافر وجبل ذبحان

وحصن الدمالوه المحروسة ومعشاره وبلد الركب وخدير بن الحبشي والسلف وجبال العرين

وزبيد ونها والاعم المقالة الثانية في معرفة قواعد اموال البهايم وما يشاكلها من الحيوان

وجهات الاقطاع المقالة الثالثة في قواعد اموال البنادر والثغور ومعاينها ظرايها

الفصل الرابع في معرفة ما يترفع من الاشغال والحساب الى الديوان السعيد على

حكم ما يأتي ذكره من قواعد جاجر مستغلات الاموال وعلى تعلي النمو والزيادة • ثم نذكر منه

مما يفتقر الى مطالعته وهي ان ختمت الكتاب بذكر القلم وذكر ما قاله

اهل العلم •

الفصل الاول

في معرفة فضل القلم واهله الذي عليهم قواعد الملك قال الله تعالى اقرا باسم

ربك الذي خلق خلق الانسان من علق اقرا وربك الاكرم الذي علم بالقلم علم الانسان

ما لم يعلم وقال عز من قائل كريم نون والقلم وما يسطرون وقال بعضهم في

مدح

ضناعة الخط فى أوضاعها حكم وهم أربابها فيهم لها قسم •

مثل الطبايع فى الإنسان أربعة اليد والحبر والقرطاس والقلم • وقال آخر

الخط أربعة لونه ليل على فوق النهار الواضح •

ويحتف يجري على خرطومه بأنامل وأنامل الخط غير فواضح • وقال آخر

ربع الكتابة فى سواد مدادها والربع منها فى يد الكتاب •

والربع فى قلم مليح قطه والربع منها رابع الأسباب •

دواوين

الفصل الأول فى فضل القلم وأهله الفصل الثانى فى معرفة قواعد ديوان

الخراج السلطانى وما هو الذى وقع عليه اسم الديوان وما يجب له وعليه وعلى الحكام

والمباشرين فى الجهات التى قلمه عليهم جار بحكم الملك وما يجب لهم وعليهم الفصل الثالث

فى معرفة قواعد أموال الجهات اليمنية بكمالها • وهذا الفصل يحتوى على ثلاث مقالات

المقالة الأولى فى قواعد أموال الجبال وهو يحتوى على جهتين الجهة الأولى وهى

الجبل الأعلى وتسمى البلاد العليا • وهى طولاً من شرقى حضرموت إلى بلاد الطور المشرق

تلجاح غرباً • وعرضاً من جهة قنا إلى بلد بيشة قبلة وشمالاً • ومبلغ خراجها •

والجهة الثانية وهى المعروف بالبر الأخضر وهى مدورة الشكل طولاً وعرضاً •

وجنوباً وشمالاً • أولها من الأعمال اليحصبية من زبيد من بنى سيف على ظفار الوادين

6a

وبه نستعين سبحانه وتعالى

بسم الله الرحمن الرحيم وصلى الله على [illegible] وآله وسلم

الحمد لله الموصوف بالجود وال[illegible] المتفرد بالأحدية [illegible] الذي أوجد

كل شيء من عدم ● علم آدم الأسماء قبل أن يتكلم ● وأشار [illegible] إلى معرفة الجرب — الأسماء

بالقلم ● وأشهد أن لا إله إلا الله وحده لا شريك له شهادة أختم بها تحلى العمل أول

الختم ● وأشهد أن محمدا عبده ورسوله أفضل من نبع على قلبه ● المبعوث

إلى سائر الأمم ● صلى الله عليه وعلى آله معادن العلم والكرم ● وأصحابه وخلفائه

ما تعاقبت الأنوار والظلم ● أما بعد فإن العبد الفقير إلى عفو الله تعالى ورضاه

أضعف

الحسن بن علي الشريف الحسيني نسبا الطباطبائي [illegible] المسلمين أحببت أن أصنف

كتابا في معرفة قواعد دواوين الخراج السلطاني في الجهات اليمنية ● لخدمة الدولة

أعزها الله [illegible]

السعيدة الأشرفية بكتاب بغية الديوان الجامع المتيسر في معرفة التفصيل و

وسألني الله لها السعيدة الناظرة بهذا الكتاب ● وسميته ملخص الفطن والألباب

ومصباح المبتدي بالكتاب وجعلته مرتبا أبوابا وفصولا ● ليسهل إلى معرفته وصولا ●

فامتنع كثير من الناس الوصول إلا بتضييعهم لمعرفة الأصول ● فمن فصل من طلب معرفة

النهاية بعد البداية [illegible] ● ومن طلب معرفة النهاية قبل البداية تعب تعبا محالا ●

وجعلته فصولا أربعة كطبائع الإنسان التي فيه مجتمعة ● وقال بعضهم

صناعة

5b

وقف [illegible] وحبس وتصدق العبد الفقير الى كرم الله تعالى وعفوه [illegible]
[illegible] في هذا الكتاب المبارك على اولاده واولاد اولاده [illegible]
[illegible] على [illegible] من عصبته [illegible] من طلبة العلم الشريف
[illegible] بشرط ان رجعه الى الموقف المذكور ثم اولاده وحمل النظر في ذلك [illegible]
[illegible] من ذريته [illegible] الى عصبته [illegible] وقفا

كتاب ملخص الفطن والالباب ومصباح الهدى للكتاب

كتاب ملخص الفطن والالباب ومصباح الهدى للكتاب

في معرفة قواعد اموال دواوين الخراج السلطاني المالكي الملكي
الناصري الصلاحي الجهات اليمنية خلد الله ملكه الكريم ونصره تاليف
العبد الفقير الى مغفرة الله تعالى ورضاه الحسن بن علي الشريف
الحسيني نسبا الى ذروة المصطفى صلى الله عليه واله وسلم
خدمت به الدولة السعيدة طالبا لبث شفقاتها واضافني
صفا احسانها وصدقاتها وحظ كريم هباتها وطويل طول
صلاتها ادام الله سبحانه بقاها وجعل النصر حولها وامامها ووراها
كان ذلك ابتدايه ونهايته بتاريخ شهر جمادى الاخرة من شهور سنة [illegible]
هجرية على صاحبها افضل الصلاة والسلام والحمد لله وحده
وصلى الله على سيدنا محمد النبي الامي واله وصحبه وسلم

في اليمن [illegible] الجهات جميعها [illegible] في الاثر الصحيح [illegible]
بها [illegible] يحي بن حمزة لنا [illegible] النبي شفيعها

[illegible]

[illegible]

كتاب
ملخّص الفطن والألباب
ومصباح الهدى للكتاب
للحسن بن علي
الحسيني